GREATEST GAMES
CELTIC
DAVID POTTER

Published by **Know the Score Books** 2010
Reprinted by Pitch Publishing 2018

Pitch Publishing Ltd
A2 Yeoman Gate
Yeoman Way
Worthing
Sussex
BN13 3QZ

www.pitchpublishing.co.uk
www.knowthescorebooks.com

A CIP catalogue record for this book is available from the British Library.

ISBN: 978-1-84818-203-5

Printed and bound in India by Replika Press Pvt. Ltd.

CONTENTS

INTRODUCTION

I T HAS of course been no easy task to choose 50 of Celtic's Greatest Games. No doubt the reader will disagree with quite a few of my choices and will wonder why others have not been included, but my choice had been based on several criteria. One is that you always remember the first time, it is said, and for this reason the first times that Celtic won the Glasgow Cup, the Scottish Cup, the Scottish League Cup and of course the European Cup have all been included. Another factor has been the desire to spread the choice over all ages – there is at least one game from every decade of the club's 120 years. This is because the love of Celtic is a continuum, and those who rose to acclaim the goal scored by Neil McCallum in 1888 did so with the same love of the club and the passionate commitment to its welfare as those who became hysterical when Aiden McGeady's penalty kick finally killed off Rangers in the 2009 Scottish League Cup Final.

Three times Celtic have won all-British tournaments and in 1902, 1938 and 1953 our supporters might have felt entitled to call themselves the Champions of Britain. The finals of these tournaments have been included. The Scottish Cup has always had a special relationship with Celtic and many of the cup finals in that tournament have been included, notably the games in 1904, 1925, 1931, 1965, 1985 and 1988 when the team came back from the dead to claim their deserved place in Celtic history. Four times have Celtic won a Scottish clean sweep; in 1908, 1967, 1969 and 2001. Such seasons are also well represented in this book.

The word 'Rangers' inevitably must occur a great deal, but a deliberate effort in this book has been made to limit the amount of games against our Glasgow rivals. This is because the author has a firm conviction that sometimes too much emphasis is laid on clashes with Rangers, and that supporters can have an understandable tendency to forget the much stated mantra of Jock Stein that the points one gets for beating St Johnstone and Partick Thistle are just as valuable as those for beating Rangers. Nevertheless, many games against our oldest rivals from the very first friendly game in 1888 to the League Cup Final of 2009 are all included, with a special place for the great and famous triumphs of 1904, 1957, 1969 and a few others.

The importance of beating teams other than Rangers was never shown more starkly than in 1968. Rangers had beaten and drawn with Celtic in their two encounters in the Scottish League. Rangers were ahead in the league race and on the face of it there was nothing that Celtic could do about it, for they had no other opportunity to play them. Yet football being played in the head as much as it is on the field, Celtic knew that if they played brilliantly and won games well, there was some invisible and intangible rule that would compel Rangers to crack. This is the reason for the inclusion of a brilliant Celtic performance at Tannadice Park in 1968. Rangers saw this performance from afar, and did indeed crack.

Some games are included as a special tribute for great Celtic players. Jimmy McGrory's hat-trick in three minutes in 1936 sums up his contribution to the club; Dixie Deans emulated Jimmy Quinn in 1972 in scoring a goal in the Scottish Cup Final and Bertie Auld's singular contribution to the club is the reason for the inclusion of an otherwise fairly insignificant game at Dens Park, Dundee in 1971.

Europe began for Celtic in the early 1960s, and although one would never minimise the effect that Lisbon in 1967 had on many people's lives, it is probably fair to say that Celtic's successes in Europe have not been as widespread or as sustained as the vast support would like. The 2003 UEFA Cup Final has not been included because it was, after all, a disappointment, but the great occasions when Celtic beat Leeds United and Liverpool are here, as is the heroic game against Vojvodina en route to Lisbon.

Other games owe their inclusion for no other reason than they showed Celtic at their best. After over half a century of watching Celtic – and what a gut-wrenching, bowel-churning, delightful, deflating, exhilarating, orgasmic, life-threatening 50 years that has been! – it has long been the author's contention that Celtic at their best in their green and white jerseys (never mind this bumblebee or yellow nonsense that is sometimes inflicted on us!) in full flow in attack with the Celtic crowd in their thousands at the game and their millions following it by some other medium is the greatest sight that sport can offer.

It is my earnest hope and prayer that this compendium of great games can make Patsy Gallacher, Jimmy Quinn, Jimmy McGrory, Jimmy Johnstone, Bertie Auld and Dixie Deans – not to mention Henrik Larsson, Aiden McGeady and others of a more recent vintage – appear before one's eyes once more. That would be a great achievement if I could do it for one simple second!

It is also salutary to remember that the story of this club will run and run. We whose privilege it is to support the team in the early years of the 21st century will some day be looked upon as the 'early Celts', as this story is definitely not going to go away. As long as the game of football is to be played there will be a 'Celtic' in some shape or form. Those whom you will read about in this book have ensured that this is the case.

As for those 'other sheep who are not of this fold' (as the New Testament would put it), by which I mean those for whom the name Celtic does not take on the all-conquering, overwhelming, totalitarian, plenipotentiary and autocratic command of lives that it does for us, I trust that you will enjoy this book as well, and will come to appreciate just how much the name Celtic means to so many millions. These 50 Greatest Games are an attempt to do just that.

David Potter

ACKNOWLEDGEMENTS

THIS BOOK owes absolutely everything to Celtic supporters, living and dead. Of those who are still with us, Tom Campbell, Craig McAughtrie, Andrew Milne, Pat Woods, George Sheridan, Dan Leslie, Marie Rowan, John Fallon, Kathleen Murdoch, Bertie Auld and Charlie Gallagher deserve a special mention, but there are others with whom I have perhaps exchanged a casual word at a game and who have indirectly and unconsciously contributed to this book.

Of those who will be reading this book in another Paradise, Frank Black, Eugene McBride and Angus Potter deserve a special mention.

Tribute must also be paid to the staff at various libraries, in particular the Wellgate Library in Dundee and the National Library of Scotland, who have always shown solid professionalism in helping me to dig out all sorts of obscure information. My publisher Simon Lowe of Know The Score Books and his excellent staff have also been very supportive and encouraging, as indeed have non-Celtic lovers but genuine football enthusiasts in Richard Grant, John McCue and Phil H. Jones.

But the main debt lies with the players and backroom staffs at Celtic Park over the past 120 years who are the ones who have produced so many great games.

David Potter

v Rangers 5-2
Friendly, Old Celtic Park
May 28 1888

CELTIC	RANGERS	REFEREE
Dolan	Nicol	Mr McFadden, Hibernian
Pearson	McIntyre	
McLaughlin	Muir	
W. Maley	McPherson	
Kelly	McIntyre	
Murray	Meikle	
McCallum	Robb	
T. Maley	McLaren	
Madden	McKenzie	
Dunbar	Souter	
Gorevin	Wilson	

THERE WAS excitement in the air in the east end of Glasgow on the slightly cold but dry early summer evening of 28 May, 1888, as 2,000 spectators gathered to see what had been advertised as a great football match, involving the much talked about Rangers and this new team called the Keltic, or as they should be more properly called, the Celtic with a soft 'c'. A great deal had been heard of this new club formed by the Glasgow Irish community with the avowed intention of providing soup kitchens for poor children. Cynics of course stated that the Catholic community felt that they had to do that, lest their flock defected to the soup kitchens run by the Church of Scotland and other well-meaning, benevolent institutions which were so much a part of the Victorian age.

But there was more to Celtic than that. Certainly there had been a great investment, not only of money from a subscription list but of effort and hard work. They had rented some ground on the outskirts of the city near London Road and their followers had worked hard to get it ready for football. Already there had been a game played on the ground some three weeks previously when local side Cowlairs had played the Edinburgh Hibernians. For this first game for the Glasgow club, Mr McFadden of the Edinburgh club had agreed to act as referee.

The Edinburgh Hibernians had shown them the way. They had won the Scottish Cup in 1887, a prodigious achievement (apart from anything else, they were the first team from the east of Scotland to do this) and had offered advice to their Glasgow equivalents. There was, however, to be one vital difference. Hibernians (or Hibs as they called themselves) had been founded as an exclusive Catholics-only side in 1875 and had deliberately chosen to call themselves after the land of their birth (Hibernia being the Latin name for Ireland). This Glasgow team on the other hand had chosen to call themselves the Keltic or the Celtic, a name which seemed to combine the land from which they had sprung and the land into which they had settled. Even though the founding members were undeniably Irish and Catholic, there was nothing to suggest that Scottish Protestants would not be welcome to join the club. Similarly there was no suggestion that Protestant children would not have been welcome at their soup kitchens.

Ambition had been the key word for this new club. Feeding poor children had been laudable, but there was now, even at this early stage, a desire to widen the parameters of ambition for the new club. Hibs had done well, but suffered from a kind of parochial exclusiveness. In Glasgow and the surrounding area there were far more Irish people than in Edinburgh and they kept flooding in. They were driven out of their native country by the continuing and almost endemic poverty, the lack of opportunity to improve themselves, the unsympathetic attitude of landlords and their own Church to their plight, and of course the ever-present threat of another famine. They were attracted not by Scotland being a land of milk and honey (it was anything but!) but because it was reasonably close to home, and there was already an Irish community there. The founders of the club realised that in this huge catchment area there was scope for tremendous support and indeed the ability to make money. In return, the club could give them something to be happy about, as they would play the game of football at which the Scots excelled and were increasingly becoming obsessed by.

Football! It had been started in England, officially at least, but had been played in Scotland for centuries. Now Scotland had at last found something at which they were at least the equal and possibly the superior of the English. An annual game was played between the two nations and Scotland had won 10 out of the 17 already played. In the early 1880s they had beaten England five years in a row, and football seemed to Brother Walfrid and his devoted followers to be the way forward. It was a fast, exciting game, could rouse passions and was very healthy for young men to take part in; it could also keep them away from the demon drink! At the historic meeting at St Mary's in the Calton on 6 November, 1887, the decision to form a football club was taken – and football in Scotland would never be the same again! One wonders what would have happened, incidentally, if someone had said 'And what about a cricket team for the summer as well?'

The winter of 1887/88 had seen a tremendous amount of hard work from an enthusiastic group of men to form this club. A patch of land near to the Eastern Necropolis was hired for £50 per annum. The first job after the preparation of the pitch was to gather together a team to represent the 'Celtic' on their first outing. Football was a totally amateur game at that time, and there was no real commitment to a club in terms of registration or anything like that. Thus the Celtic committee men could approach whoever they wanted. The best team in Scotland (and as they claimed, the world) were Renton, in Dunbartonshire. Not only had they won the Scottish Cup that year of 1888, but they had also beaten West Bromwich Albion, the English Cup winners, in a match they had entitled, not without cause, as the Championship of the World.

Celtic approached James Kelly to be the centre-half and Neil McCallum to play on the right wing. Tom Maley who had turned out for Third Lanark and Hibs was approached, but was not in on the night that the men called at his house in Cathcart. However his younger brother Willie was quite keen to pass on the message and was himself invited to come along as well, on the grounds that he looked to be an athletic fellow who had indeed played football as well as being a keen cyclist and runner.

The new club's opponents that night were to be the famous Rangers team. They came from the other side of the city, and had been in existence from 1873. They had been good enough, but had not yet challenged teams like Dumbarton, Vale of Leven or Queen's Park on any regular basis. But based near the shipyards in the very industrial part of Glasgow, they had a big support and were much talked about. That night for the game against the new Celtic team, they sent a side which contained quite a few first-team men, but also some young up-and-coming reserves. They called themselves the Rangers Swifts – the word 'Swifts' being used to describe youngsters who were supposed to be very quick.

Rangers would appear in their light blue, as usual, but, in a primitive form of sponsorship the new Celtic team had been given a set of strips from Penman and Company, Drapers at Bridgeton Cross. They were wearing a white jersey with a green collar and a Celtic Cross of red and green on the breast. They were a fine sight as they trotted out to a warm welcome from the crowd which seemed to be about 2,000. This was a very encouraging attendance for the new club, and was an eloquent tribute to the work that had been put in over the winter. And how nice the ground looked!

The game was played in a good spirit throughout and Celtic won the game 5-2. Taking advantage of having the wind behind them in the first half, they reached half-time 2-1 up and but for some good Rangers defending and goalkeeping, they would have been further ahead. The first goal came from a corner kick well taken by Mick Dunbar and Neil McCALLUM rose to head home. After Rangers equalised, Celtic went ahead and this time it was scored by James KELLY, playing the attacking centre-half role, forcing a corner and then being on the right spot to head home.

At this point, the supporters of the new club were in good heart as their team had scored two lovely headed goals, and everyone was happy. Rangers however, not without their supporters in the crowd, fought back, but kept foundering on the rocks of James Kelly and Willie Maley. It was however Tom MALEY whose night it was. He scored a third, and after Rangers had pulled one back through SOUTER (or Suter as he is sometimes called), Tom MALEY added a fourth and a fifth, the latter added by 'the instrumentality of McCallum'. Indeed McCallum scored yet another, but it was chalked off through 'the intricacies of the offside rule' – something that the spectators were none too happy about – for the law was complex, difficult to understand and not always applied consistently – and an 'outburst of booing' was heard.

That however was the only discordant note of the whole night, for Celtic won 5-2 and both teams were given their 'three cheers' by the 2,000 crowd in the traditional Victorian fashion. Also in the traditional Victorian fashion, both teams, the triumphant Celts and the 'disappointed but not despondent' Rangers adjourned in the same horse-driven charabanc to St Mary's Hall for a supper and soiree in which various members of each team entertained the others with renditions of songs and poetry, with the hero of the hour Tom Maley in particular, rounding off a great evening for himself by proving his versatility as a reciter and artiste.

The supporters returned homewards happy and enthusiastic, talking about the Maley brothers, James Kelly and Neil McCallum, and already looking forward to the next game against Dundee Harp, a team which represented the Irish community in

Dundee. Some of the Rangers fans too said that they might come back and see the Celts again, and the hope was expressed that they would see a good deal more of one another.

v Third Lanark 4-0
Glasgow Cup Final, Hampden
14 February 1891

CELTIC	THIRD LANARK	REFEREE
Bell	Downie	Mr Watson, Dundee
Reynolds	A. Thomson	
McKeown	Smith	
Gallagher	Scott	
Kelly	Love	
W. Maley	Lochead	
Madden	Lapsley	
Boyle	W. Thomson	
Dowds	Johnstone	
Dunbar	McInnes	
Campbell	Burke	

THERE WAS little doubt that this new Irish team in the east end of Glasgow was here to stay. The immediately noticeable thing about them was the sheer size and commitment of their support, far more than that of any other team, and far more passionate. In football of the 1880s and 1890s the tendency was for a supporter to go to a match, watch it for a few minutes and then decide a certain preference for one team or another.

Even at international matches where everyone in Glasgow supported Scotland, one presumes, we find sentences in newspaper reports like: 'England came out to a cheer as well, and some fine play was applauded by the Tartans [sic].'

Not so with 'the Celtic'. The use of the definite article was significant, for their massive support was entirely committed to their team. They did very definitely represent one section of Scottish society, the ethnic Irish. There were of course other Irish teams around, notably the Edinburgh Hibernians, but in Glasgow and West Central Scotland, there were so many people of Irish extraction (and immigration from Ireland was still ongoing in 1891) that this team was immediately successful, possibly more so than the founding fathers of the club had realised they would be. There were already plans to move from their ground – adequate for most things, including the Scotland v Ireland international already scheduled for 28 March of this year (1891) – to a larger one. Clearly this club had ambitions.

Their supporters were loyal, occasionally excessively so. On 22 November 1890 for example, on the day of the Glasgow Cup semi-final at Celtic Park, a day of excessive and constant rain (not unusually for Glasgow in November!), the *Glasgow Herald* is moved to remark, 'The Irish have a reputation for pluck, but the way that some of the poorer classes stood out the storm on Saturday with absolutely nothing to protect them but their ordinary clothes was more foolhardy than brave'. They were well rewarded for their fortitude, for their team beat Partick Thistle 5-1.

This result put Celtic into the Glasgow Cup Final, in which they had already beaten Battlefield, Northern and Clyde. It would be their second final in this competition, as they had been beaten in the previous season's final by Queen's Park. They had met their opponents, Third Lanark, before in the 1889 Scottish Cup Final, but had lost. It had actually been a double Scottish Cup Final that year in 1889, for the first game was played in a snowstorm and declared a 'friendly', then replayed the following week. Celtic and their huge support had yet to win a major cup. It was much craved by those who loved the Celtic, and it was certainly felt that once one cup was won, many others would follow.

The winter of 1890/91 was hard with a great deal of frost. It was also a tough, unpleasant time for Celtic, being involved in a number of incidents which reflected little credit on the club. There was, for example, a prolonged and nasty struggle in the Scottish Cup to beat Larkhall Royal Albert, a team known even then for its anti-Catholic sympathies. The first game was played in unsuitable conditions and declared a friendly, but not before the spectators had been conned out of their admission money. Then the following week, 6 December, with the conditions only marginally better, things got out of hand.

In these days, each side provided an umpire (the equivalent of a linesman). Each umpire was duty bound to be honest, and indeed most of them were, even being accused on occasion of bending over backwards to give 'flings' (as throw-ins were then called) to the other side. On this occasion, however, Celtic's umpire Tom Maley was less than totally impartial, for after a Larkhall player called Frame tripped up Celtic's Johnny Madden, Tom Maley punched Mr Frame! Only two policemen were on duty, and after a struggle they managed to deal with the subsequent pitch invasion, but following subsequent thuggery on and off the field, the referee was compelled to abandon the game which Celtic were comfortably winning 4-0.

Celtic might have hoped that they would be awarded the tie, but the SFA ordered a third game at Ibrox the following week. This time things passed reasonably peacefully and Celtic won 2-0 with goals from Barney Crossan and Johnny Campbell. But the success was short lived because the following week on 20 December at Boghead, Dumbarton, Celtic lost 0-3 in the next round of the Scottish Cup. Once again there was controversy about whether the pitch was playable or not, and again there was violence (this time involving the ever pugnacious Barney Crossan) and threats of crowd invasion; but the bottom line was that Celtic were out of the Scottish Cup.

They would not win the Scottish League (in its first year of existence) either. A few early lapses and the loss of points for fielding an illegal player would see to that, so the only chance of a much-craved major trophy lay in the Glasgow Cup. Their opponents were Third Lanark, a team remarkable for the amount of nicknames they had. Because of their military connections, they were named 'the volunteers', 'the sodgers' or 'the warriors', and in later days they would be known as 'the hi-hi-his' or simply 'the thirds'.

The game was scheduled for 14 February 1891 and the weather by now had taken a turn for the better following the frost and ice of December. The game was played at Hampden Park, but this was of course Second Hampden, the ground that would eventually become Cathkin Park, the home of Third Lanark. In 1891 it was a neutral venue, the home of Queen's Park. The same venue had played host the previous week to the Scottish Cup Final when Hearts had won the Cup for the first time, beating Dumbarton 1-0. Clearly concerned about the possibility of trouble, the Glasgow FA appointed a referee from Dundee, a Mr Watson, and even appointed two neutral umpires, neither of them from the city of Glasgow itself – a Mr Bishop from Falkirk and Mr Mackay from Campsie.

A large crowd attended, possibly around 10,000, although no exact figure was given. This was of course large for the standards of the time and owed a great deal to the presence of 'the Irish, who were very voluble' as the green and white vertical stripes appeared. Celtic's star men included centre-half James Kelly and left-half Willie Maley, brother of Tom who had been involved in the Larkhall fisticuffs. Willie Maley would of course go on to be the manager of the club. Up front there was Johnny Madden, Peter Dowds and the new star Johnny Campbell on the left wing. Full-backs were Jerry Reynolds and Mick McKeown, both of them loose cannons off the field, but generally considered to be as good as any on it. (McKeown in particular would not find much stability in his life after Celtic. He joined the Army but was dismissed as 'incorrigible' and 'worthless' before being found dead one day in 1903, monstrously asphyxiated in a lime kiln in Camlachie!) In goal was Jamie Bell, a fine goalkeeper but the unwitting cause of Celtic losing four points at the start of the league season, for he had not been registered in time and had not allowed 14 days to lapse since he had played for Dumbarton.

Arguably Celtic's best player was left-winger Johnny Campbell, a great dribbler. When Sandy McMahon was given the inside-left position, the left wing of McMahon and Campbell would become the most feared in all football. Campbell would have a brief spell with Aston Villa (winning the English League with them in 1896 and then a league and cup double in 1897) before returning to Celtic, then finishing his illustrious career with Third Lanark and helping them to their one and only triumph in the Scottish League in 1904.

The game started well with chances at both ends. Third Lanark's goalkeeper saved well from Maley, and at the other end as Thirds pressed, 'Jerry Reynolds' head came in useful several times' as Maley himself put it in his own account of the game. It was Celtic who went ahead through an OWN GOAL. A cross from Campbell hit the post and the luckless LOCHEAD in trying to head clear, put the ball pass his own goalkeeper, the wet ball slicing off his head into the goal. Lochead's head (like that of Jerry Reynolds) had also come in useful for the Celts!

Half-time was reached with the score still at 1-0 for Celtic, and then came Third Lanark's big moment. They scored and their supporters cheered, but Lapsley was offside. That might have made a difference to the eventual outcome, but after that Celtic simply took charge with some excellent half-back and forward play. Peter DOWDS scored from a corner, and then Johnny CAMPBELL scored a third, and towards the end of the game CAMPBELL added a fourth, as Celtic ran out 4-0 winners.

To say that the crowd were delighted was an understatement. Banners were waved, hats were thrown in the air, and there was an 'outburst of singing' as the teams left the field. 'Celtic have won a cup at last,' was the cry. Celtic fans revelling in their first major trophy now talked excitedly about what the future could bring as they celebrated long and hard throughout that night. There was now the feeling that their team had arrived, and that the Irish in Glasgow now had a standard around which they could rally. The poverty and the discrimination against the Irish in Scotland would continue for many decades, but there was now a football team which could make them feel good about themselves. Perhaps next year they could even win the Scottish Cup as well!

As this was 1891, the Glasgow Cup was presented not to the players in front of their supporters, but to the committee men of the club behind closed doors. But in the tradition of sporting events in Victorian Britain, both teams went to have a meal together, in this case in the Alexandra Hotel in Bath Street. Glasgow being the gossipy place that it always would be, this could not be kept secret and hundreds gathered in the centre of Glasgow hoping to catch a glimpse of their heroes with the Glasgow Cup draped in green and white ribbons. Cheers and songs rent the air almost all night to celebrate this very important triumph for their side.

v Queen's Park 5-1
Scottish Cup Final, Ibrox
9 April 1892

CELTIC	QUEEN'S PARK	REFEREE
Cullen	Baird	Mr G. Sneddon
Reynolds	Sillars	
Doyle	Sellar	
W. Maley	Gillespie	
Kelly	Robertson	
Gallacher	Stewart	
McCallum	Gulliland	
Brady	Waddell	
Dowds	J. Hamilton	
McMahon	W. Lambie	
Campbell	J. Lambie	

BIG THINGS were happening in the east end of Glasgow in the early months of 1892. Celtic, for all sorts of reasons, were on the crest of a wave following their 7-1 defeat of Clyde in the Glasgow Cup Final in December 1891 – the second season in a row that they had lifted that prestigious trophy – and hopes were high that they could now build on that success and win the most important trophy of all – the Scottish Cup, commonly regarded as the blue riband of the game, the one that everyone wanted to win. That trophy would indeed show the world that this Celtic team had come to stay.

But there was another indication of the ambition of this Irish club. They were moving. Problems with the landlord (nothing new for the Irish in the 19th century!) meant that they decided that they would no longer pay rent to anyone but that they would buy and forever own their new ground. A piece of land became available slightly to the south of where their rented ground was, and it was decided to buy this and develop it into the best ground in the world.

This meant it being big, but the attraction there was the chance to stage the greatest football game on earth – the biennial Scotland v England international match. This would of course bring in a huge amount of money, but more important was the prestige that it would attract to the club – the team of the Glasgow Irish hosting Scotland in their biggest game of all. There was of course no problem about staging Scotland v Ireland – already in fact Old Celtic Park had done just that – but the idea of the pride of English football appearing at Celtic Park was just too good to miss and worth spending money on.

Rumour had it that other teams like Rangers, Queen's Park, Third Lanark and possibly even Hearts were contemplating building a huge stadium as well with the express purpose of hosting 'The International' as the Scotland v England game was called.

While all the work was going on in the winter of 1891/92, Celtic continued to make progress towards collecting their first ever Scottish Cup, and indeed (less successfully this year) their first ever Scottish League championship. There were some fine players at Celtic Park, notably centre-half James Kelly, wing-half Willie Maley, the indomitable and controversial left-back Dan Doyle, often referred to in Scottish footballing circles as simply 'Dan', a magnificent inside-right in Alec Brady and on the left wing a tremendous pairing of Sandy McMahon ('The Duke') and Johnny Campbell, who combined pace, artistry and the ability to score goals.

The cup final was reached by defeats of St Mirren, Kilmarnock, Cowlairs and then Rangers in the semi-final at Old Celtic Park when Celtic delighted their followers by going into a five-goal lead before conceding three in the rain and the mud to the hardworking but not particularly inspired Rangers team. This was in early February, and the Scottish Cup Final against Queen's Park was scheduled for 12 March, 1892 at Ibrox Park.

It was somehow appropriate for 1892 that it was Queen's Park who were the opponents. Each team represented diametrically opposed factions; Queen's Park were rich, snobby and had, for example, resolutely refused to join the Scottish League which was now in the second year of its existence; The Queens, strictly amateur, feared (correctly, as it turned out) that this league might lead to the introduction of professionalism as had happened in England. They wished football to be played strictly on an amateur basis, as their motto – *ludere causa ludendi* – 'to play for the sake of playing', would indicate. If they had played cricket they would have been the Gentlemen as distinct from the Players.

This is all very well if one already had loads of money as Queen's Park and their minions tended to do. For Celtic and their supporters in the 1890s, the life of a football dilettante was not an option. For young men of their background to be attracted into the game, they would have to be paid. Celtic's followers were of course the Glasgow Irish, mired in poverty and despair, but determined, through their football team, to do better for themselves. There was thus a tremendous cultural clash when the two met in the Scottish Cup Final of 1892. In addition, there was the sheer weight of history, for Celtic, the up-and-coming side who had played their first game less than four years ago in 1888 and had never won the Scottish Cup, were pitted against Queen's Park, founded in 1867 and who out of the previous 18 Scottish Cup competitions, had won 9, exactly half the times the cup had been on offer.

It had been Celtic's intention to have the Scottish Cup won on 12 March, so that both it and the Glasgow Cup would be on display on their sideboard at Old Celtic Park for their very important guest who was due to arrive on the 19th. This was to be Michael Davitt, one-time Fenian with a history of terrorism, but now associated with the far more respectable Irish Land League which rejected violence but still strongly espoused the cause of Irish Nationalism. The idea was that Davitt would plant a few shamrocks on the centre spot of the new and still uncompleted ground at New Celtic Park to symbolise the link between the new successful football club and the 'ould country' as it was frequently referred to, then return to Old Celtic Park to watch the game against Clyde.

The one-armed Davitt (he had lost his right arm in an accident in a Lancashire cotton mill when he was only 12) did indeed do the needful on 19 March, but there was no Scottish Cup on view after the unfortunate events of the previous week. The cup final had indeed been played and Celtic had won 1-0, but the game had been declared a friendly in view of the encroachment of the huge crowd onto the field of play who caused suspension of the action several times. Celtic's supporters had every right to feel cheated of their victory, and the decision to play the game again on 9 April does indeed look, well over 100 years down the line, to be an effort to make even more money (of course this had happened before, as Celtic well remembered, in the 1889 Scottish Cup Final). In the 1890s there was also the perception that Queen's Park and the SFA were virtually synonymous, and that those in power would do whatever they could to ensure that Queen's would win the trophy!

For whatever reason, the game was played again at Ibrox, a week after Scotland had suffered a severe blow to its pride at the same ground when it lost comprehensively to England. Doyle, Kelly and McMahon had all been involved, and they may well have felt that they had a point to make in the Scottish Cup Final. Celtic fans who felt aggrieved at the nullification of the first Scottish Cup Final in March were even more appalled to hear that the price of admission had been doubled from one shilling (bad enough, in all conscience) to two shillings (out of the question to most working-class families). This was ostensibly to deter too many people from turning up.

Celtic, to their shame, did not object to this even though it clearly discriminated against their own supporters who would be a lot less likely to be able to afford two shillings than the better-heeled Queen's Park fans. But then things took a mystifying turn when the SFA changed its mind – but did not tell anyone, other than by putting, without any fuss, in the newspapers an advertisement about the game with the price for admission at one shilling after all! Women would be admitted free, but it would cost more for any of the stands or pavilions. One presumes that this newspaper advertisement was a device to avoid charges of greed and avarice but, given the standard of literacy in Glasgow in 1892 (especially among the immigrant Irish community), an advertisement in the newspapers on the day of the game would not necessarily make any huge difference!

Be that as it may, 23,000 attended – still an enormous crowd for 1892 – and they saw Celtic win at a canter after an early setback. The weather was fine, and Queen's Park, with the benefit of the wind, scored through WADDELL halfway through the first half – but the general opinion was the Celtic had been unlucky.

In the second half Celtic turned on the fine football that they had shown on many occasions that season, and Willie Maley in particular was immense. His 'blocking and feeding were simply perfect', the *Glasgow Observer* tells us, and he contributed a lot of 'checking, returning and general engineering'. Maley is much more modest about his own achievements in his own account of the game in *The Story of The Celtic*, but he does give us a flavour of how good some of the Celtic goals were in the 5-1 rout. Maley recalled that 'McMahon and Campbell served up delightful football' and the 'crowd often found themselves compelled to applaud, although their sympathies clearly lay elsewhere'. CAMPBELL equalised early in the second half, then put Celtic ahead, before McMAHON 'indulging in one of those mazy runs – head down arms outstretched – simply walked through the Amateurs' defence to register the third goal'. There followed an OWN GOAL, then a brilliant header from a corner kick by Sandy McMAHON once again. Some sources (notably the *Scotsman*) attribute one of the earlier goals to McMahon as well, which would have given him a hat-trick, but the balance of evidence is in favour of Campbell.

The writer of the *Scotsman* is clearly overwhelmed by the size and volume of the Celtic support who cheered and 'sang ditties' all through the second half, but that was only the start of it.

The two teams went to a meal (as was the custom) in the Alexandra Hotel in Bath Street, but then the charabanc took the Celtic team and the cup to St Mary's Hall, Calton, the spiritual home of the Celtic team where the impoverished urchins, the lonely widows and downtrodden men of Glasgow's east end got a chance to see the Scottish Cup. The smiles on the faces of those whose moments of glory seldom came made a huge impact on Willie Maley who then vowed that he would dedicate his life to make this happen more often. Committee man John Glass said unequivocally that this was the happiest moment of his life.

The celebrations went on in the east end for several days, as Irish bands with bugles, drums and even flutes appeared and men and women danced with joy, hugging and kissing each other indiscriminately and with abandon. For once there was a smile on the faces of the underprivileged ethnic minority. 'Our Bhoys have won the Cup!' was the cry, and when, on 1 June of that year, Celtic lifted the Glasgow Charity Cup as well, committee man Ned McGinn sent a telegram to the Vatican asking for candles to be lit in honour of the three trophies won by Celtic in 1892! Whether his Holiness acceded to that request, history does not record...

v Queen's Park 4-3
Scottish Cup Final, Ibrox
14 April 1900

CELTIC	QUEEN'S PARK	REFEREE
McArthur	Gourley	Mr J. Walker,
Storrier	D. Stewart	Kilmarnock
Battles	Swan	
Russell	Irons	
Marshall	Christie	
Orr	Templeton	
Hodge	W. Stewart	
Campbell	Wilson	
Divers	McColl	
McMahon	Kennedy	
Bell	Hay	

THE NEW century was bringing changes. There were improvements in communication, transport and (to a certain limited extent) health and hygiene, but there still remained the appalling social problems that befouled British society, and makes us wonder, more than a hundred years later, how a nation that could build a huge Empire (and was in 1900 engaged in a bloody war in South Africa 'to protect the nation's interests' as some put it while others more cynically said 'to steal the diamonds from the Boers') could not address its major and pressing internal problems.

It was not that Britain did not have wealth. It was simply that it was badly divided. The 'haves' had a great deal; the 'have-nots' lived in appalling conditions. The Labour Party had not yet risen, and the Liberals had been unable to achieve effective office since Gladstone had stumbled repeatedly over Ireland. Thus life remained grim for the urban working class, while the middle classes were comfortable.

Nowhere was this contrast more obvious than in Glasgow, and nowhere the contrast more apparent than in the lifestyles of the supporters of the two football teams – Celtic and Queen's Park. Queen's Park remained snobby, stuffy and would not even deign to join the Scottish League, so redolent was it of professionalism and the associated evils. Yet it would be a mistake to assume that all Queen's Park supporters were 'gentlemen', if we may believe contemporary accounts in the press. The *Glasgow Observer* is quite vitriolic from time to time about the 'well-bred roughs in the Hampden stands ... the most ill-mannered, uncouth, unsportsman-like of all football crowds ... Queen's Park supporters carry it off for downright unreasoning and frenzied hooliganism ... the motley gang of freaks, lunatics, roughs and maniacs ... they should be fenced in with bars ... the public could be charged to see this wild beast show ... ignorant, bestial, howling ... give me the moulders of Cathkin, the riveters of Ibrox, the navvies of Parkhead any day. Their linen is neither as immaculate nor extensive as that of the Crosshill dudes, but they are sportsmen.'

Celtic, on the other hand, supported by the 'navvies of Parkhead' as the *Glasgow Observer* would say, had been one of the leading lights in the struggle to bring professionalism to the country and frequently bought and sold players to English teams, so determined were they to give their fans, the Glasgow Irish – a downtrodden minority if ever there was one – something to be happy about.

In recent years a third team had risen in Glasgow on the west side of the city, and this was the Rangers team. They had been an ordinary outfit for a long time, but now under the energetic William Wilton, had won the Scottish Cup in 1894, 1897 and 1898 and the Scottish League in 1899 (undefeated all season), and even before the turn of the century had won the Scottish League for 1900. In addition to this, in December 1899 they had opened their magnificent new stadium at Ibrox, and it was at this venue that the 1900 Scottish Cup Final would be played.

Rangers would of course have hoped to be playing in this final, but they had lost in a semi-final replay to Celtic. Celtic had been a funny team that season. Too many draws had cost them the chance of winning the league – yet on New Century's Day after Rangers had won the league, Celtic beat them 3-2 at Celtic Park. This had avenged their defeat in the Glasgow Cup Final in November of 1899 when the fog had been so bad that only 6,000 had appeared, with everyone else convinced that the game would be off. Rangers had won 1-0, and Celtic had threatened to appeal against this result on the grounds that the game should never have been played, but apparently had decided against it.

The Scottish Cup was of course the trophy which mattered in 1900. Celtic, who had won the trophy in 1899, had done well against Bo'ness, Port Glasgow and Kilmarnock, and then on their first visit to the new Ibrox scored a late goal to earn them what they thought was a winner only for Rangers to come up with an even later goal. A fortnight later the teams appeared at Parkhead, and Celtic 'staggered humanity' (as Sandy McMahon somewhat hyperbolically said) by beating Rangers 4-0. It was indeed a fine performance, with Sandy McMahon himself scoring twice, Jack Bell once and Johnny Hodge the other one as 'spectators were spellbound by the brilliance of Celtic's forward play', as the manifestly pro-Celtic *Glasgow Observer* put it.

A week before the Scottish Cup Final, there had been a great event at Celtic Park when Scotland beat England in what was known as the 'Rosebery International' in the presence of the said Lord Rosebery, one-time Prime Minister of Great Britain and then patron of the Scotland team. Scotland's hat-trick hero in the 4-1 win had been 'Toffee Bob' otherwise known as R.S. McColl, a name not unfamiliar to those who have walked Scotland's high streets over the following century and a bit, for it was he who was the founder of that confectionery dynasty. He would be the man that the Celtic defence would want to keep an eye on in the cup final.

April 14 was a bright day but dominated by the wind. Maley describes it as being 'rather gusty'; other accounts use words like 'storm' or 'hurricane' and it certainly had a large effect on the game itself. It may also have been responsible for keeping the crowd down to a slightly disappointing 18,000, but the low attendance may also have had a little to do with the high prices for admission and the fact that too many supporters had 'spent all their loose change at the International last week.'

Harry 'Beef' Marshall, Celtic's centre-half and captain won the toss and decided to play with the wind in the first half. He presumably hoped that the wind would die down in the second or that playing against it would tire Queen's Park out. Harry was an interesting man who had the nickname of the 'Portobello boatman' as that was what he did when he wasn't playing football – hiring out boats to families and trippers at Portobello. He was however a tough character, somewhat undervalued in Celtic history, but this was to be his day.

Celtic's decision to play with the wind may not have met with a great deal of favour with the supporters. The wind was sweeping across the field from where the Broomloan Road end is now, and there was, at that end, little to act as a windbreak. It was therefore all the more of a shock when Queen's Park took the lead when a long-range shot from CHRISTIE was hit in a lull in the wind and deceived Dan McArthur in the Celtic goal. Dan had a few critics among the Celtic support; this in no way lessened their numbers.

But Celtic now buckled to the task, and before half-time scored three goals. One was a surprise shot from the wing by Sandy McMAHON, the second a header from John DIVERS after fine work from Sandy McMahon and Jack Bell, and then shortly before half-time BELL himself was on hand to prod home a loose ball after a goal-mouth scrimmage, or according to the *Glasgow Herald* 'after much hustle and bustle'. Goalkeeper Gourley who had had a good game hitherto was at fault here for he should have caught Bell's prod, but opted to try and punch it out. This was foolish against the wind, and the ball went in the wrong direction, hit the post and rebounded into the net. Thus it was that the teams turned round with Celtic 3-1 up, but with the knowledge that it would be a long second half against that 'breeze'.

Just as Queen's Park scored against the wind in the first half, Celtic did likewise in the second, DIVERS scoring 'in a quick dash' in the 55th minute to put Celtic 4-1 up. It was Queen's Park's turn to rally, but McColl was getting nowhere against the hard tackling and determination of Marshall, and they had to look elsewhere for their goals. They pulled one back through D. STEWART (some reports say HAY) as the Celtic forwards who had done a great deal of running, visibly wilted in the face of the wind. Celtic's defence were guilty of timewasting, but it was often the constructive timewasting of passing the ball to each other; the conditions did not allow the players to boot it up the field.

'The wind would not have got past them' is a phrase much used of full-backs; it may well have owed its genesis to Celtic's two full-backs that day. Davie Storrier, the cricket-playing stalwart of Arbroath and Forfarshire was immense, as indeed was Barney Battles, that 'prodigal son' of Celtic on occasion – but what a game he had that day! Battles was ironically known as 'Gentle Barney' – he took no prisoners, himself risking a broken leg time and time again as he went in for tackles. It was all the more painful for BATTLES as he miscued a header and the wind carried the ball into Celtic's goal. Other reports describe it as the ball 'cannoning' off Battles. It mattered little; Queen's were now back in the game. McArthur shouted at Barney and Barney shouted back, but the more important thing was to survive the last ten minutes as Queen's renewed their efforts to get the draw that they might have deserved.

The *Scotsman* reported that 'these happenings were to the liking of most of the spectators' – an indication, as in 1892, that the admission charge of two shillings was so high that Celtic supporters couldn't afford it – and the Queen's Park fans cheered on their team for the last ten minutes. McColl came very close near the end 'by a foot or so' after a brilliant effort, but Celtic's defence was superb.

Thus the green and white vertical stripes of Celtic retained the Scottish Cup. Once again their supporters, in the minority at Ibrox, but a very vocal one, were delighted, and the new century beckoned with the promise of more glory. Queen's Park were very sporting in their defeat – Maley talks about their 'vigour and pluck' but 1900, the turn of the century, was a significant year for the amateurs of Queen's Park. With ten victories they captured the Scottish Cup more often than anyone else, but they would never again appear in a Scottish Cup Final, for professionalism had defeated them. They had already decided, reluctantly, to join the Scottish League the following season, but to this day remain proudly amateur. This is laudable and quaint, but anyone who despises Queen's Park does so at their peril. On four occasions in 1965, 1967, 1986 and 2009, Queen's Park, now irretrievably one fears, in the lower divisions, nevertheless gave Celtic a good run for their money in the Scottish Cup.

v **Rangers** 3-2 <small>after extra time</small>
British League Cup Final, Cathkin
17 June 1902

CELTIC	RANGERS	REFEREE
McPherson	Dickie	Mr J. Hay, Greenock
Davidson	N. Smith	
Battles	Crawford	
Loney	Gibson	
Marshall	Stark	
Orr	Robertson	
Crawford	Lennie	
Campbell	Walker	
Quinn	Hamilton	
McDermott	Speedie	
Hamilton	A. Smith	

THIS WAS a curious tournament. Rangers had won the Glasgow Exhibition Trophy in 1901, but had put the trophy up for competition again to raise funds for the Ibrox Disaster Fund after 26 people had lost their lives at the Scotland v England international at Ibrox on 5 April, 1902. They invited Celtic, Sunderland and Everton to compete in what became known as the British League Cup or the Inter-League Cup or, because of the events of 1902 which involved the Royal Family, the Coronation Cup. (This latter title is not used so much because it might be confused with the Coronation Cup of 1953.) Most still called it the Glasgow Exhibition Trophy, but whatever the title, it was a prestigious tournament as the four teams competing were the winners and the runners-up of the Scottish and English leagues of 1902.

1902 had not been a great year for Celtic. Rangers had now won the league four years in a row, and Celtic lost the Scottish Cup to Hibs in a poor final. The Scottish Cup Final defeat hurt all the more because they had been given home advantage, the game being played at Celtic Park because Ibrox was still damaged after the disaster, new Hampden Park was not yet built and Old Hampden Park was not big enough. Celtic's Glasgow Charity Cup Final loss to Hibs followed. Hibs had been invited to compete that year in what was normally an exclusively Glasgow affair to swell the coffers for the Ibrox Disaster Fund.

But Celtic had defeated Sunderland in the semi-final of this all-British cup on the Wednesday after their Scottish Cup Final defeat at Parkhead before a small crowd of 4,000. The game had seen Celtic play one of their few games of really good football that season and they had run out comfortable winners, putting five goals past Scotland's goalkeeper Ned Doig. The only sad point had been the low attendance, but it was reckoned that Celtic supporters were so disgusted with their team's performance against Hibs in the Scottish Cup Final that they had given up for the season.

The following night Rangers and Everton drew 1-1 at Goodison and a replay was scheduled for Celtic Park, because Ibrox was still out of commission. Indeed on that very day (3 May 1902) Scotland were playing England at Villa Park, the 'disaster game' having been declared null and void. Rangers won the replay 3-2 – an excellent result for them considering that they were without four men who were playing for Scotland.

It would be a long time before the final was to be played, as late as the lovely evening of Tuesday 17 June. The idea was to have the game played as near as possible to the coronation of King Edward VII with the idea of attracting a large crowd to Cathkin Park at Govanhill. (This was the first Cathkin Park, not the one that is otherwise known as 'Second Hampden' to which Third Lanark moved when Queen's Park opened the magnificent 'Third Hampden' in October 1903.) It was for this reason that a few newspapers began to talk about this being the Coronation Cup, but as it happened, any chance of this tournament becoming known by posterity as the Coronation Cup was overtaken by events a few days after Celtic won the trophy.

King Edward, already well over 60 (he had been the Prince of Wales for a very long time and even the Victorian press had been unable to hush up all his indiscretions) was taken ill with severe abdominal pains only two days before the planned coronation on 26 June, and the coronation had to be postponed to allow the King to undergo an extremely complicated and highly dangerous operation to remove his appendix. It was commonly believed that he was the first person to undergo an appendicectomy. This was not quite true, but he was certainly one of the first, and the success of this operation (so successful that the coronation was able to go ahead on 9 August 1902) encouraged the development of this kind of surgery. In fact a few years later Celtic captain James Hay would be successfully operated on for this complaint.

The crowd was given as 12,000, although some put it as low as 7,000. It was indeed well out of season, for in 1902 the season would finish at the end of April with only trophies like the Glasgow Charity Cup, tour games and friendlies being played in May, and football in June and July was virtually unheard of. By 17 June 1902 the main topic for sporting conversation (even in Scotland) was the Ashes battle between Archie MacLaren's England and Joe Darling's Australia. Already two Test Matches had been played, both of them ruined by rain and were drawn, but not without Australia falling foul of Wilfred Rhodes at Edgbaston where they were dismissed for 36 as the great Yorkshireman took 7 for 17.

Back in football, Rangers, the league champions, were of course the favourites. Celtic were a team in transition. They still had Johnny Campbell, 'Beef' Marshall and Barney Battles, but they were also introducing a few younger players like Alec Crawford, Willie Loney, Davie Hamilton – and the man over whom all the arguments centred – the miner boy from Croy, Jimmy Quinn. Gauche and shy off the field, and very unpredictable on it, this left-winger was beginning to look as if he was one of the many players who came to Celtic Park, but did not quite make it. Already he had played in two losing Scottish Cup finals in 1901 and 1902, and it was hard to see why Maley retained such faith in him. He was a little better when he played in the centre, but so often he was clumsy, awkward and clearly upset when his own fans turned on him. He did have strength and courage – but he simply wasn't scoring goals regularly enough.

Thankfully for Celtic he decided to turn it on this particular night. He was playing in the centre, allowing Davie Hamilton to occupy the left wing. Celtic pressed from the start and QUINN scored 'after a prolonged siege' as Willie Maley put it in *The Story Of The Celtic*. This was in the 7th minute, and then halfway through the first half, QUINN scored again, this time being in the right place at the right moment when a shot from Campbell hit the bar and rebounded to him.

Celtic were now two goals up, but defensive frailties let them down as Rangers scored twice before half-time, once when HAMILTON took advantage of a goalkeeping error by Andy McPherson, and they doubled following some good play by Finlay SPEEDIE. The second half then was somewhat of an anti-climax as both teams were clearly tired after the pace of the first half on such a warm evening, and no further scoring occurred before Mr Hay blew for full time.

At this point, the press went home, thinking that there would be a replay and clearly in a hurry to file their copy before deadline time. Some of the crowd did so as well, not realising that there would be extra time. It is not clear whether extra time had been scheduled in advance or whether it was agreed on the spot, but ten minutes each way was played. Certainly no-one wanted a replay and it was assumed that if the game was still tied, Rangers would quite simply take the trophy home with them on the grounds that they had won it as the Glasgow Exhibition Trophy the previous year and had put it up only to raise funds for the disaster that had happened at their stadium.

But Celtic slowly gained the ascendancy during the extra 20 minutes, with Willie Loney and Willie Orr in particular getting the better of their exhausted counterparts. Just as time was running out, Celtic won a corner after some good work by Willie Loney. Alec Crawford took it with Quinn loitering just at the edge of the penalty box, hoping for a high ball that he could run on to and head home. But the minute Quinn saw it, he realised that this ball was just too high and would probably sail out of play on the far side, effectively losing the cup for Celtic, as the referee was clearly looking at his watch. But then an idea struck Quinn. Standing just in front of him was his team-mate Tommy McDermott. A stentorian voice was heard: "Stey whaur you are, Tommy!" Tommy did was he was told, as Jimmy ran forward, placed his hands on McDermott's shoulders and rose like a bird to connect and head the ball downwards into the net.

QUINN was immediately engulfed by his colleagues as hundreds of fans also ran onto the field to give him their congratulations. Indeed the game was over, for there was no time to restart the game and Celtic had won this trophy, by whatever name it was to be called. Curiously, Willie Maley himself has a memory that plays tricks on him as far as this tournament was concerned. For one thing, in his book *The Story of The Celtic*, written almost 40 years after the event, he seems to believe that the goalkeeper was Rab MacFarlane rather than Andy McPherson, and he also states that the game finished at 2-2, then went to a replay a few days later, which also finished 2-2 before they had the extra time!

This tournament might seem to be of no great importance, and has been eschewed by many historians, but it is significant in that it was the start of the Celtic tradition (carried on in 1938 and 1953) of winning all-British tournaments. It also heralded the arrival of Jimmy Quinn as a centre-forward rather than a left-winger (although that particular penny would not drop for a long time!) and it was Celtic's first trophy since the Scottish Cup of 1900. And once again, it gave the impoverished Glasgow Irish something to be happy about, evidenced by a song they made up about the win:

> Some say that the Rangers are guid at fitba',
> That Gibson and Lennie and Speedie are braw,
> But Jimmy Quinn, he diddled them a'
> At the Glasgow Exhibition oh!

v Rangers 3-2

Scottish Cup Final, Hampden
16 April 1904

CELTIC	RANGERS	REFEREE
Adams	Watson	Mr T. Robertson,
McLeod	N. Smith	Queen's Park
Orr	Drummond	
Young	Henderson	
Loney	Stark	
Hay	Robertson	
Muir	Walker	
McMenemy	Speedie	
Quinn	Mackie	
Somers	Donnachie	
Hamilton	A. Smith	

HAMPDEN PARK was a sight to behold that pleasant spring day of 16 April 1904. It was a new stadium, opened in October 1903, clearly built by Queen's Park with the express intention of it becoming the home of Scotland as well. It was not yet complete, for the East Terracing was not yet opened and for this reason the Scotland v England game was still held at Celtic Park the previous week (that, at least, was the ostensible reason – the reality was that Celtic had 'knocked on a few doors'!), but it was clear that Queen's Park had great ambitions for the ground. Indeed from 1906 onwards, no other ground would be contemplated for 'The International' (as the clashes with the Auld Enemy were entitled).

The writer of the *Scotsman* is impressed with the great view that is afforded for all spectators – some 64,323, by some distance a world record for a club game and the sort of crowd that 'normally only appears for games against England'. But it had been apparent for some years that the pulling power of Celtic was something special, as indeed, increasingly, was that of Rangers. It was finely balanced – East of Glasgow v West of Glasgow, Irish potato famine immigrants v Highland clearance immigrants, flair football v solid, conservative stuff. Indeed the day before the final, *The Scottish Referee*, in a comment on their ability to make money, had made a joke about 'The Old Firm of Rangers, Celtic Ltd', and thus the phrase entered the language.

In a welcome recognition that football was now the 'people's game', the SFA decided to reduce the admission charge to six pence. It was normally double that at one shilling, and had on occasion been as high as a florin (two shillings) for international matches and cup finals in the past, but the SFA had reckoned correctly that with a shilling charge, the attendance might have been 30,000 whereas at half the charge, they could double that. And, of course, the SFA and Queen's Park now had the stadium to hold such a crowd with a degree of comfort.

From early in the morning the crowd began to assemble with clear evidence at railway stations of fans arriving from well beyond the immediate area of Glasgow, for Celtic in particular had a broad fan base throughout the country – and they were not all Irish either. Stalls were set up outside Hampden Park for the sale of rosettes and favours in the colours of both teams, and it was noticeable that some fans arrived at the game without any great predisposition for either team but deciding, almost on the spur of the moment, that they would buy a green rosette and support Celtic – because they wanted to see this man that everyone talked about but whose ability to produce the goods was limited. This was Jimmy Quinn.

Indeed, Jimmy Quinn was the man of the moment. But also that year there had developed a great half-back line of Young, Loney and Hay which effectively gave Celtic a stranglehold over the middle of the park. There was also a wily inside-forward called Jimmy McMenemy, balanced on the other side by Peter Somers. At the back, Celtic had Donny McLeod who would in later years earn the nickname of 'Slasher' for his ruthless tackling. He was partnered by Willie Orr, a similarly deter-mined character. Yet the talking point among the Celtic fans was the right-winger Alec Bennett. Would he play?

Bennett was unhappy at Celtic Park. He had played in the centre, and on the right wing – with a certain amount of success – but he, and his family, were fans of Rangers, who had, it was rumoured, approached him with offers. Yet Bennett was a decent man and felt that he owed Celtic something as well. He discussed the matter with Maley, and Maley felt that it would be better in the circumstances to omit the honest Alec Bennett. Bobby Muir could play on the right wing, Quinn could go in the centre (which Maley now more and more believed was his best position) and Davie Hamilton could come in on the left wing. Maley's recommendation won the day with the Celtic directors (who still had the final say in team selection in 1904) and Celtic were never the same again!

1903/04 had not been the greatest of seasons for Celtic whose young team were developing but were not there yet. The team of the season were in fact Third Lanark. With ex-Celt Johnny Campbell on board and with a manager with the unlikely name of Frank Heaven, they had beaten Celtic in the final of the Glasgow Cup, and were on the brink of winning the Scottish League. Thirds had however lost out to Celtic in the semi-final of the Scottish Cup on 19 March. It had been a tough game but Celtic, after being 0-1 behind for a long time in the game and seeing Willie Orr miss a penalty, showed their character by coming back with two late goals from Muir and Quinn, and then goalkeeper Davie Adams saved the day in the last minute with a fine save.

Celtic had not won the Scottish Cup since 1900 and had lost two desperately unlucky finals in 1901 and 1902 to the Edinburgh duo of Hearts and Hibs. The league had not been won for even longer than that because 1898 was the last year of Celtic being champions, and the Glasgow Charity Cup of 1903 was the only trophy Celtic had won since 1900. But supporters now felt that with this developing team, the trophy drought might well be coming to an end.

Yet, disaster seemed to be looming after only ten minutes were played. Against the run of play, Rangers were two ahead, both goals scored by their excellent inside-forward Finlay SPEEDIE. The first was a header which goalkeeper Davie Adams gathered but not cleanly, and as he collided with a post, the ball trickled into the net. It was an extraordinary goalkeeping error, and things became a lot worse a minute later when SPEEDIE took a snap shot at goal from the edge of the penalty box which missed everyone and entered the net past a bewildered Davie Adams.

The Rangers players and their fans could hardly believe their luck. Celtic supporters were despondent, but told themselves that there was still a long time to go and this young team of theirs was resilient and could yet fight back. Indeed the key thing about them was their youth. They were also determined that they could yet do it, and knew that a goal would bring them back into it. Poor Davie Adams, jeered by the crowd, reckoned that things could not get any worse and wondered what people would think of him for his dreadful mistake in New Hampden's first Scottish Cup Final. Fortunately for the amiable Angus man, someone else would appear as the eponymous hero of the 1904 final.

Celtic now concentrated on their two triangles. On the right were Young, Muir and McMenemy who could interchange passes, and on the left were Hay, Somers and Hamilton who could do similarly, while in the middle Quinn and Loney (an attacking centre-half) were beginning to alarm the Rangers defence with their 'strength in the barging' as the *Glasgow Observer* put it.

Half-time was approaching when Celtic's hard work paid off. But it was really all due to one man – Jimmy QUINN. He picked up a ball in the middle of the Rangers half and charged at goal using his speed to swerve and avoid some challenges and his sheer brute strength to brush others out of the way before he arrived inside the penalty box and lashed a shot past Watson. It was a great solo goal, much applauded by the large crowd, and the writer of the *Scotsman* even saw some supporters with blue rosettes 'applauding vigorously and sportingly'. That would be an unlikely scenario in 2010.

And then just before Mr Robertson 'called for half-time', Celtic and QUINN scored again. This time credit must be given to right-winger Bobby Muir, who in what would become known as a trademark Scottish goal, 'skinned' the Rangers defence at full speed, hit the line, crossed low and hard, and there was Jimmy to bang the ball first time into the net. There was seldom anything complicated about Quinn. He would never dribble in the penalty area, but believed that the ball was there to be hit once – hard and accurately.

Thus half-time saw Celtic in better spirits than Rangers, for they were the team who had come back and were now on level terms. It would be a prolonged interval for a collection was being taken for the families of the victims of a crowd disaster at a cricket match. This was the Perthshire v Forfarshire game at the North Inch, Perth last summer when a temporary stand had collapsed, injuring many people, some of whom were permanently maimed and therefore unable, in those pre-welfare state days, to support their families. The huge crowd contributed generously, throwing coins into sheets which volunteers walked round the running track with.

The second half opened with Rangers on top, but that was only a temporary phenomenon as the Celtic midfield once again rallied and took control. Playing towards the as yet unbuilt East Terracing (which in years to come would house huge Celtic crowds), Celtic charged forward. Yet the Rangers defence held out, and a replay looked the most likely outcome, until Jimmy QUINN, already a hero, became immortal and ensured that his name would be mentioned whenever anyone talks about Celtic and football.

The winning goal had some similarities to his first, but this time it came from a visionary pass from captain James 'Dun' Hay. Quinn was on his way to goal when he was tackled fiercely by the fair-haired Nick Smith. It was brutal and might have floored lesser men, but this was Jimmy Quinn! He stumbled, but picked himself up, gathered the ball and slid it past the advancing goalkeeper. As Hampden erupted in applause, Jimmy merely turned round and walked back to the centre circle looking as 'cool as Hell' in the unlikely simile of the *Glasgow Observer*, as his team-mates went berserk all around him. 'The game's no finished yet,' he muttered grimly.

Indeed there were ten minutes to go, but Rangers were a beaten team. As full time approached, so too did the volume of applause and cheering rise around Hampden, with green and white favours now prominent. Full time came and Celtic had won their fourth Scottish Cup, now level with Rangers and Hearts, although still some way behind the ten of Queen's Park.

The significance of this game, however, lay in what happened next. It was the springboard for the team that would go on to dominate Edwardian Scotland and become, without any great doubt, the greatest team on earth, winning six league titles in a row. Jimmy Quinn, the hat-trick hero, would go on to become the most talked-about man in Great Britain, and his mining village of Croy, to which he would return and live a private life 'just like an ordinary man', would become forever associated with the name of Jimmy Quinn.

v Hearts 3-0
Scottish Cup Final, Hampden
20 April 1907

CELTIC	HEARTS	REFEREE
Adams	Allan	Mr D. Philip,
McLeod	Reid	Dunfermline
Orr	Collins	
Young	Philip	
McNair	McLaren	
Hay	Henderson	
Bennett	Bauchop	
McMenemy	Walker	
Quinn	Axford	
Somers	Yates	
Templeton	Wombwell	

1907 WAS the first of the really great Celtic seasons. The team, reared more or less in their entirety from the junior ranks, swept away all before them, winning the Glasgow Cup in the autumn of 1906, being so far ahead in the Scottish League by spring 1907 that it looked like a formality that they would win it, and now the intriguing question was being posed: could they become the first Scottish team to do a double and win the Scottish League and the Scottish Cup in the same season? The 'double' had been achieved in England twice – by Preston North End in 1889 and by Aston Villa in 1897, but no-one had ever done so in Scotland. Rangers had come close in 1899, but as yet the double had not been achieved in Scotland.

Celtic's success in 1907 had been achieved without the services of two of their star men. Centre-half Willie Loney had broken his arm in September in a game against Hearts, and Jimmy Quinn had been involved in a rather unfortunate incident on New Year's Day 1907 against Rangers and had been suspended for two months. The punishment had looked not a little draconian (and not only to Celtic sympathisers), but now Jimmy was back playing (in his first game on his return) a vital part in the defeat of Rangers at Ibrox in the Scottish Cup quarter-final. Loney, however, was still out, but his place was filled more than adequately by Alec McNair, the quiet man from Stenhousemuir who would in later years be called 'the icicle' for his cool, calm and collected play at right-back.

It was the 'capitalists' as the press called them who stood between Celtic and the Scottish Cup, following Celtic's defeat of Rangers; not 'capitalists' in the sense of Henry Ford and Andrew Carnegie, rather the football people of Edinburgh. Hibs put up a fine performance on two occasions in the semi-final, earning goalless draws on both occasions at Celtic Park and Easter Road, but on the third occasion (Celtic having won the toss for venue), Celtic simply devastated Hibs who were lucky to get off with a 3-0 defeat. Bobby Templeton, the charismatic left-winger, was superb and 'The beauty of the movements of McMenemy, Quinn and Somers is unsurpassed in football', was the opinion of the writer in the *Glasgow Herald*.

The opponents in the final at Hampden were to be Hearts who were of course the current holders of the Scottish Cup. Both finalists had won the Scottish Cup on four occasions, Celtic in 1892, 1899, 1900 and 1904 while Hearts had triumphed in 1891, 1896, 1901 and 1906. 1901 had been the only time the two teams had clashed in the final and it was a painful occasion for Celtic supporters, Celtic having lost 3-4, and supporters maintained that they would have won the game had it not been for poor goalkeeping. Hearts were a well supported side and had some fine players, notably defender Charlie Thomson and inside-forward Bobby Walker, generally agreed to be the best forward for sheer artistry in Scotland, even though Jimmy McMenemy of Celtic was now pushing him hard for that honour.

There was also a little of the Edinburgh v Glasgow issue at stake here. Edinburgh may have been the capital of Scotland, but there was little doubt that Glasgow was the football centre. Three huge stadia had been built there in the past fifteen years, as Celtic, Rangers and Queen's Park competed with each other for the right to host the Scotland v England game. Edinburgh lagged behind. There had been internationals played at both Tynecastle and Easter Road in the past, but never the England game. In addition, the last international played at Tynecastle had been the previous year and it had been Tynecastle's misfortune to host Scotland's first ever defeat to Wales on Scottish soil. For this reason Tynecastle would be considered an unlucky ground for Scotland, and it was certainly true that it was not as big as the Glasgow grounds – nor was it ever likely to become so, as it was hemmed in by railways, schools, breweries and churches. And sadly for Hearts, their board of directors lacked the vision to build a larger ground, which might have, in time, become Scotland's national stadium.

The crowd of 50,000 at Hampden Park on 20 April 1907 contained an estimated 20,000 from Edinburgh who had travelled on one of the many Football Special trains which left Waverley, Princes Street and Haymarket stations that morning. Indeed the streets around Hampden were so thronged with fans from Edinburgh and Glasgow that Hearts goalkeeper Tom Allan was delayed in the traffic of horse-drawn trams and cabs. Why he did not travel with the rest of the party is not clear, but he did not arrive in time for the kick-off and Celtic sportingly agreed to delay the start for 15 minutes until he arrived, as Hearts did not have a specialist goalkeeper among their reserves and would have had to deploy an outfield player as a deputy goalkeeper. The delay also allowed more of the latecomers to gain entrance.

The 'capitalists' in the crowd, most of them on their first visit to Hampden (last year's Scottish Cup Final having been at Ibrox), were dismayed to see that Charlie Thomson, their brilliant centre-half, was not playing. Everyone had known that he was injured, but they had all nurtured a secret hope that he might yet make it for the big occasion. He didn't, and the Edinburgh men worried how the defence would cope with the Celtic forwards in his absence. Celtic fans felt that this merely balanced things, as Celtic had been without Willie Loney for most of the season.

Celtic supporters were upbeat and noisy, singing their Irish songs, music hall ditties with added bits and an adaptation of a Victorian nursery rhyme:

Oh, dear what can the matter be?
Rangers got beat by Celtic last Saturday!
Two goals from Quinn, and one from McMenemy
Oh, what fun it was there!

It was a typical April day; not particularly cold, bright and breezy but with the occasional violent storm of rain. It was on these occasions that one felt that Hampden, for all its size and magnificence, had one fatal flaw – there was no shelter, unless you were one of the very rich fans who could afford to go to the stand. Queen's Park supporters would have no problem but 'the rest of us simply have to get wet', muttered those of an egalitarian persuasion. To be fair to Queen's Park, however, it was not normally in the mindset of Edwardian football clubs or stadium designers to consider the welfare of their spectators!

The game was a good one, but half-time came with no goals. Both sides had had chances, but neither team had as yet exerted any sort of dominance over the other. Ominously for Hearts however, the Celtic forward line had not yet been seen at their best. The feeling was expressed that if Celtic went ahead, they would be very difficult to dislodge.

The second half was less than ten minutes old when Celtic struck, the goal coming from the penalty spot. Some sources say it was Jimmy Quinn who was fouled, others say it was Alex McNair (including McNair himself). Although Hearts and their supporters would claim for years after that it was a soft award, soft or not, Willie ORR took the penalty and scored.

Hearts now lost heart, as it were! As Hearts fans feared, when Celtic went ahead it looked impossible to pull them back. There was also not a little of the Edinburgh paranoia and inferiority complex (which has continued unabated for the next 100 years) which increased the feeling that Glasgow cannot be beaten, for they are favoured by referees. This conveniently ignored the fact that the referee came from Dunfermline, but depression and pessimism were definitely factors as Hearts dropped out of the game.

Celtic now took command and scored two goals which were more or less carbon copies of each other. They were scored in the 70th and the 80th minute and both were supplied by Alec 'The Artful Dodger' Bennett on the right wing. In the first case, Bennett beat his man and crossed for Quinn who stepped over the ball as two men converged on him and Peter SOMERS coming up behind scored. Then ten minutes later, Bennett crossed again and Jimmy Quinn acted as decoy, running in the opposite direction taking a couple of panicky defenders with him so that SOMERS once again had the easiest of tasks to put the ball past Allan, who must have wished by now that he had still been stuck in that traffic jam.

Celtic finished the game well on top with most of the Hearts supporters having left to catch one of the trains back to Edinburgh. This was a truly immense Celtic side which could have scored more but had no desire to humiliate their opponents. A sign of a great side is that they are not over upset when they lose a player to injury and this clearly happened here with Alec McNair more than adequately covering for Willie Loney.

As was the tradition in those days, both teams adjourned to the Alexandra Hotel in Bath Street for a meal and the drinking of toasts to each other. One of Celtic's committee men Mr J.H. McLaughlin stated that the reason for Celtic's sustained success since 1904 had been the ability to hold on to their own youngsters, also mentioning the importance of team spirit and playing for each other. The Scottish Cup was then held aloft to the hundred of fans waiting outside.

A few days later at Meadowside, the home of Partick Thistle, Celtic, with the Scottish Cup on show, won the Scottish League. The double had been achieved, something that many commentators had doubted the possibility of. In fact it was a treble if the Glasgow Cup was to be counted, and it might even have been a quadruple a month later, but Celtic played one of their rare bad games and lost to Rangers in the final of the Glasgow Charity Cup.

If this Scottish Cup triumph was a significant victory for Celtic, the same could not be said for Hearts, for it was the start of their trophy famine which would last through two wars and endure for nearly 50 years. They would always be a force in the land with many fine players and would consistently provide difficult opposition, particularly at Tynecastle, to both Celtic and Rangers, but they would take a long time to recover from their defeat in the 1907 Scottish Cup Final. Both they and Hibs were destined for a long barren spell, and this is perhaps why Edinburgh now began to pay more attention to rugby than football.

v St Mirren 5-1

Scottish Cup Final, Hampden
18 April 1908

CELTIC	ST MIRREN	REFEREE
Adams	Grant	Mr Ferguson, Falkirk
McNair	Gordon	
Weir	White	
Young	Key	
Loney	Robertson	
Hay	McAvoy	
Bennett	Clements	
McMenemy	Cunningham	
Quinn	Wylie	
Somers	Paton	
Hamilton	Anderson	

IT WAS a beautiful day as 60,000 made their way to a sun-drenched Hampden Park. 'God's happy that he's getting tae see Jimmy Quinn the day,' said the irreverent, but there was a spring in the step of the faithful. Last year their team had won three of the four available trophies.

This year it was possible that they might even lift all four. Already the Glasgow Cup had been won in October, and the team was well ahead in the Scottish League and only St Mirren stood between Celtic and the Scottish Cup. The Glasgow Charity Cup would, of course, be played in May.

It was St Mirren's first appearance in a Scottish Cup Final. They were not a bad side, but games between them and Celtic had shown a tendency to be rough and unpleasant in the past. Yet there seemed little reason to believe that this would be the case on Scottish Cup Final day, especially on such a beautiful afternoon. The occasional shower of rain seemed possible, however, for it was April in Glasgow.

The health of the former Prime Minister would be much discussed. Sir Henry Campbell-Bannerman had resigned in early April through ill health, and was so weak that he could not be moved from 10 Downing Street where his successor Herbert Asquith should by rights now have been living. Campbell-Bannerman would die the following Wednesday (22 April), and he was a Prime Minister who was responsible for a great deal of progressive social legislation. His true value was not unlike that of Clement Attlee 40 years later, in that he led and moulded a Cabinet of massive talent but disparate temperaments whom he managed and blended to good effect. His Cabinet contained men like Asquith, Lloyd George and Churchill, and he got the best out of them. He was from Glasgow and was respected, if not loved, by his fellow Glaswegians. His successors, Asquith and Lloyd George, would be less popular.

'This is Jimmy Quinn's hame,' said a wag as he caught his first sight of the massive Hampden. Indeed it would be the third Saturday in a row that he had played there. The previous week, Celtic had beaten Queen's Park at Hampden in a league match and the week before that Quinn had been in the Scotland side that had drawn 1-1 with England before a world record crowd of over 120,000.

Quinn was indeed the centre of attention in 1908. A month previously in Dublin he had scored four goals for Scotland, compelling all Ireland to sit up and take notice and remark that he was of Irish ancestry. Less happily at places like Dens Park and Pittodrie, he had been singled out for rough treatment on the grounds that 'if you stop Quinn, you stop Celtic'.

This was rubbish, of course. For one thing, Jimmy could look after himself and frequently did, and for another, this was a superb Celtic forward line with Alec Bennett, the speedy and talented right-winger who loved Rangers but was adored at Celtic, Jimmy McMenemy, to be nicknamed 'Napoleon' because of his tactical genius, Peter Somers, that impish character full of tricks both on and off the park, and the often grossly undervalued Davie Hamilton on the left wing, a shy, retiring man who never courted popularity – but such was his skill that it followed him around anyway! Indeed such was the strength of the forward line that even though Quinn had been out of the side for a lengthy spell with a septic toe at the start of 1908, the team kept winning anyway!

And behind the forward line were the Three Musketeers of Young, Loney and Hay – a magnificent half-back line, which frequently had the erudite scribes of the *Glasgow Herald* searching for even more classical and biblical allusions to do them justice. Willie Loney was the attacking centre-half, but also known as 'The Obliterator' or 'No Road This Way' as he gobbled up everything that came down the middle; then there was Sunny Jim Young with the inch-perfect passes and the gritty determination that no-one in any circumstances would ever say that they got the better of him; then came the calmer element of captain James Hay, called 'Dun' for some obscure reason, always the leader of the team on the field and a born diplomat, making sure that the wilder elements in the team never got totally out of hand.

But the man who made it all happen was manager Maley, now a few days away from his fortieth birthday and at the height of his powers. He had been appointed secretary-manager more than a decade ago, and although in theory he had no power over things like team selection, in practice it was he who called the shots. In a real sense he was the man who made Celtic. He had been a good enough player, although not a great one. He loved football and had a thorough tactical knowledge of what was required to win games.

He devoted his life to the club; his private life had been difficult and unhappy, but he enjoyed the therapy of looking after his football team. He combined idealism – he did genuinely want the impoverished Irish in Glasgow to have something to be happy about – with a shrewd knowledge of how to make money. He also enjoyed with a relish the internal politics of the game, making alliances with teams like Aberdeen and Dundee if it suited his purpose to win a point over Rangers or Queen's Park. His man-management skills were a matter of some dispute. As with Jock Stein, if a player played regularly in the team, that player loved Willie Maley; those on the margins of the team were less fulsome in their praise. But no-one doubted Maley's status in the game, and he was genial and forthcoming to the press with the result that his name and that of his beloved Celtic were seldom off the back pages.

The referee, Mr Ferguson of Falkirk, had had an unpleasant experience (as had Celtic) in the semi-final at Pittodrie where the recently-formed Aberdeen team had given Celtic a run for their money. Their tactics had been rough, but Celtic, as we have said, did not lack those who could dish out the raw meat as well, and the crowd had reacted unfavourably to Celtic's late winner. The cab carrying Mr Ferguson back to the railway station had been stoned, as had the Celtic charabanc – conduct for which the embarrassed *Aberdeen Press and Journal* had no tolerance, blaming it all on 'irresponsible young ragamuffins' and the 'prevalence of cheap ale on sale in the environs of the ground'.

The Glasgow police may have worried about disorder at the Scottish Cup Final, but a large police presence and the careful filtering of spectators all around the ground (which had, of course, a fortnight previously contained twice the 60,000 estimated attendance) ensured that everything was under control. A wind sprang which prevented the sun getting too hot, as Celtic playing towards the Mount Florida end had to cope with the bright sun, which the St Mirren forwards exploited by using the high ball, hoping that Davie Adams in the Celtic goal might struggle with the glare. But Davie was wearing a bonnet, pulled well down over his forehead, and dealt competently with the few early potshots that came his way.

It was Alec BENNETT who opened the scoring in the 10th minute after a fine movement involving Jimmy McMenemy. Celtic remained on top for the rest of the first half and in the 36th minute Jimmy QUINN scored the second, although St Mirren would claim that the ball had been 'fisted through' to him by Young. Half-time came with Celtic well on top, and the Celtic fans happy and content.

The interval brought some real-life drama for the 60,000 crowd. It came from the press box, situated on top of the sloping Hampden stand at an angle, so that the impression was that one could fall over onto the field. The writer of the *Evening Times* had finished his handwritten half-time report which he was about to send (using that new device called the telephone that not everyone yet trusted in 1908) into his office, when a gust of wind came in through the window and blew the paper out of his hand onto the roof and then into the gutter at the foot of the roof.

It was just too far for him to stretch his hand out to, and fearing a row from his editor if no half-time report could be phoned in, he realised that he had no option but to crawl out onto the roof to grab the paper before a further gust of wind could blow it away for ever. The crowd gasped in admiration at first, but then in fear for the man as he intrepidly crawled over the corrugated roof. A cheer rose when he reached the piece of paper, another one as he crawled back again and a huge outburst of applause and relief as his colleagues in the press box grabbed him and pulled him back in!

All this happened without the Celtic players being aware of it, for they were emerging from the pavilion, confident but grimly determined to get the job done. Green favours were waved as they appeared, and three minutes later the crowd erupted once again as Alec BENNETT scored his second and Celtic's third. Rumours that Alec was to get his lifelong wish to join Rangers had been spreading through Glasgow for the past four or five years, but this week they had been more prevalent than usual. If this were the case, Alec was going to go out on a high note, and it would have been nice to see him get a hat-trick.

St Mirren at last rallied and CUNNINGHAM took advantage of a little momentary slackness in the Celtic defence to pull one back. This gave the large Paisley contingent something to cheer about and encouraged the hope that the huge civic reception scheduled for that night might not have to be cancelled after all. But their confidence was short lived, for Davie HAMILTON scored a few minutes later, and the crowd, particularly the 'Buddy boys' were streaming out, long before Peter SOMERS scored the fifth and final goal in the 85th minute.

It had been a superb display of football from a fine Celtic team. Next week, after a nasty game at Ibrox, they confirmed their status as league champions for the fourth successive year. A month later they won the Glasgow Charity Cup as well, meaning that they had won every trophy they entered. It was difficult to dispute the contention that Celtic were 'the greatest show on earth'. Ironically the only one member of the forward line who had not scored in the Scottish Cup Final was Jimmy McMenemy, but no-one was in any doubt that he was the instigator of it all. Jimmy, was a master tactician and was the man who made it all happen for Celtic in that great year of 1908, earning the particular approval of Willie Maley. 'Without Napoleon, it would be less eventful,' he would say.

v **Hibernian** 4-1

Scottish Cup Final Replay, Ibrox
16 April 1914

CELTIC	HIBERNIAN	REFEREE
Shaw	Allan	Mr T. Dougray,
McNair	Girdwood	Barrhead
Dodds	Templeton	
Young	Kerr	
Johnstone	Paterson	
McMaster	Grossert	
McAtee	Wilson	
Gallacher	Fleming	
McColl	Hendren	
McMenemy	Wood	
Browning	Smith	

THE GREAT thing about Willie Maley was his ability to replicate success. His sublime Edwardian side had now clearly aged and moved on, but after three years in the wilderness (some wilderness, they won the Scottish Cup in two of these three years!), Maley was back for the 1913/14 season with a team that was at least the equal of that of 1907 and 1908. It all centred on a magnificent little Irishman by the name of Patsy Gallacher, still reckoned to be the greatest player there has ever been, even though any who saw him play in the flesh have now departed this vale of tears.

Three men remained from the Edwardian side: Alec McNair, called 'the icicle' for his cool defending, James 'Sunny Jim' Young, that ferocious defender and tough tackler, and Jimmy McMenemy, evergreen and called 'Napoleon' for his ability to lead the line.

In goal they had Charlie Shaw, the start of the immortal triangle of Shaw, McNair and Dodds. Charlie had a superb season and also enjoyed a magnificent rapport with the supporters who named 'brake clubs' (the prototype of supporters' buses) after him and made flags and banners with his picture on them. Modest, gentle and good-natured, Charlie smiled a lot and enjoyed his football, looking like everyone's favourite uncle in his thick yellow polo-necked sweater which must have caused problems on warm days. Opposition forwards seldom caused him problems though: from 13 December 1913 until 28 February 1914, he did not concede a single goal.

But there did seem to be a problem at centre-forward. No adequate replacement had yet been found for Jimmy Quinn. Maley had rather foolishly allowed Davie McLean to leave in 1909, and the said Davie was having a great season for Sheffield Wednesday when he might have been doing the job for the team that he still had a hankering for. At the moment, a red-headed Englishman with the unlikely name of Ebenezer Owers was doing the job, although most supporters felt that in Jimmy McColl, who had joined the club the previous September from St Anthony's, they had a better bet. But poor Jimmy had suffered a terrible shock on 21 March when he returned home after a friendly game against Middlesbrough to find his mother dead, and his form had suffered accordingly with Maley keeping him temporarily out of the limelight.

Celtic, however, were enjoying a good season. They had lost the Glasgow Cup semi-final replay to Third Lanark in October because their forwards were 'stingless', but apart from that their form had been inspired. They were well ahead in the Scottish League as a 4-0 drubbing of Rangers on New Year's Day at Parkhead had indicated, and had not lost in 1914 apart from a game at Falkirk in late February when Dodds, McMenemy and Browning were playing for Scotland. The winning of the Scottish League was more or less a formality for Celtic, because Rangers and Hearts (who had briefly threatened) had now collapsed.

The Scottish Cup Final was reached by wins over Clyde, Forfar, Motherwell and Third Lanark. Their opponents were to be Hibs, a team whose season had been mediocre, but who felt that they could cause an upset. Their supporters, including the writer of the Edinburgh-based *Scotsman*, were not slow to remind Celtic that Hibs had defeated them in the final of 1902 in a situation where Celtic had been the favourites.

The 'all green' final or the 'Irish Cup final' as some newspapers described it was scheduled on 11 April at Ibrox, which had surprisingly won the vote over Hampden, the ground which had done such a great job in hosting the previous week's Scotland v England game. As a result of Scotland's emphatic 3-1 win (Jimmy McMenemy being generally regarded as the best man on the field), football was much talked about and the cup final much anticipated. The huge crowd delayed the start because the Hibs charabanc was caught up in the crowds, and this added to the great atmosphere which was not without its political component, because Irish Home Rule was a huge issue at this time, and one report tells of the 'lung bursting' rendition by both sets of supporters before the game of:

High upon the gallows tree
Hang the noble hearted free
Whom vindictive tyrants cut down in the prime
But we met them face to face
With the courage of our race
And now we march undaunted to our doom
God Save Ireland, cry our heroes
God Save Ireland, cry we all
Whether on the scaffold high
Or the battle field we die
What matters it when for Ireland dear we fall?

The game was a damp squib with Celtic underperforming and the luckless Ebenezer Owers (whose name suggested that he really should belong in a Dickens novel rather than the ferociously passionate atmosphere of Scottish football) unable to convert the chances that Gallacher and McMenemy made for him. In fact, if anything, Hibs might just have won the game at the end, for the luckless Willie Smith in the last minute picked up a long ball, beat (for once) Alec McNair and ran in on goal. Charlie Shaw came out, and Smith rounded him, but Charlie had forced him wide and he was unable to convert a goal which would have made a great difference to the subsequent history and folk culture of both teams.

This did not disguise the fact that it had been a poor game, nor did it lessen the mutterings about a 'fix for another big gate' as always happened after a drawn cup final. The replay was scheduled for Ibrox again at the unlikely time of 5.45 pm (so that it could finish in daylight) on Thursday 16 April. This was because Celtic had a game on the Monday and (incredibly) Hibs had one on Wednesday, and there was no budging of schedules because the season had to finish by the end of April. Hibs, to no-one's surprise, fielded their reserve team against Dumbarton on Wednesday and drew the meaningless fixture 1-1, after Celtic on Monday had taken another step towards the league title with a 5-0 defeat of Queen's Park. Significantly, Jimmy McColl replaced Ebenezer Owers and scored twice.

Thus it was that McColl retained his position for the Scottish Cup Final replay. The crowd was smaller than the Saturday but still a respectable 40,000, some 20,000 down on the first game but not surprising given the cost of rail fares from the capital on a day when no cheap Football Specials were run. In addition, Thursday was of course a working day. Hibs had made a half-hearted bid to have the game played at Tynecastle, but there was little likelihood of that as Glasgow, with its larger population and obsession with football, always did call the shots over Edinburgh. Celtic similarly talked vaguely about Hampden being a better venue, but Ibrox it was once again.

This time it was immediately clear that Celtic meant business, and the presence of McColl made a huge difference. Inside the first quarter of an hour (and before many of the crowd had got from their work to the ground) Celtic were two up. The first was from a corner kick on the left. Johnny Browning took it and the ball came across the goalmouth to the right-winger Andy McAtee. Young McAtee was waiting for this purpose and headed the ball back to the unmarked Jimmy McCOLL who did the needful. Two minutes later with the crowd in turmoil and the Hibs defence reeling, Celtic scored again when McCOLL netted from a rebound after the goalkeeper could only palm the ball out to him. It had been McColl who had shot the first time and in so doing had fallen, but quick as lightning he recovered and got there before two defenders converged on him. It was a great triumph of courage, worthy of Jimmy Quinn, who, now bedevilled by injuries but still a member of the Celtic squad, was seen to rise from his seat in the stand to applaud.

There was now no way back for Hibs, and Gallacher and McMenemy simply took over and played superb football with the Hibs defence due some credit for the way that they held out until almost half-time before surrendering another goal. This time it was left-winger Johnny BROWNING who scored with a low fast shot, and the same BROWNING scored again after 15 minutes of the second half after picking up a brilliant crossfield pass from Andy McAtee.

A belated trainload of Hibs fans arrived from Edinburgh at this point. They were allowed in free, but must have wished that they hadn't been, for there was little left to see. Hibs did pull one back through Willie SMITH, but Celtic were content to entertain rather than score more goals and humiliate a team for which they still felt some affinity. As the triumphant songs of 'God Save Ireland' and 'The Wearing Of The

Green' resounded round Ibrox, the Hibs fans joined in! Willie Maley in the stand was seen on several occasions to rise from his seat to indicate to referee Tom Dougray that enough was enough to save Hibs from further torture, but Dougray, professional to the last, allowed the full 90 minutes to elapse.

As the Scottish Cup was presented for the ninth time to the Celtic directors in the Ibrox board room after the game, the march back to the east end now began with songs of triumph rending the air, with banners wafting in the breeze and the rest of the Glasgow population staring in awe and not a little resentment from some quarters, although the main emotion would have been benign amusement.

This was indeed a great night for the supporters. There seemed to be little in the following few years that could prevent further joyous occasions. There really was, once again, a magnificent side in place with Jimmy McColl seeming likely to solve the centre-forward problem left by Jimmy Quinn. And what about Patsy Gallacher? Born in the Milford Poor House in Ramelton in Donegal, he had taken the Scottish game by storm since his arrival on the scene in 1911. Would there ever be a better player? Even on a broader front things looked good, with the passing of the Irish Home Rule bill looking a certainty.

We could even go back to Ireland then, some reckoned, for there would be no more English landlords and rack renting – but no, far better to stay in Glasgow and watch Patsy Gallacher and Jimmy McMenemy!

> Though slight of build, you are super skilled
> With amazing control of the ball
> Though your star may set, we will never forget
> Wee Pat from Ould Donegal!

Further joy would come to the green and white brigade two days later when the Scottish League was clinched mathematically in a 3-0 win at Parkhead against – incredibly – Hibs. The summer saw another victory in the Glasgow Charity Cup before a tour of Germany and the Austro-Hungarian Empire. Willie Maley was a little perturbed about the amount of men he saw in military uniform but there seemed to be no problem. Celtic were well received by their hosts, and they arrived back home in early June ... several weeks before the assassination in Sarajevo that would change the world.

v Rangers 5-0
Scottish Cup Semi-Final, Hampden
21 March 1925

CELTIC	RANGERS	REFEREE
Shevlin	Robb	Mr P. Craigmyle,
W. McStay	Manderson	Aberdeen
Hilley	McCandless	
Wilson	Meiklejohn	
J. McStay	Dixon	
McFarlane	Craig	
Connolly	Archibald	
Thomson	Cunningham	
McGrory	Henderson	
Gallacher	Cairns	
McLean	Morton	

THERE WAS little doubt who the favourites were for this game. Rangers were well on their way to winning their third successive Scottish League championship, and had already dished out three hefty beatings to Celtic this year. Their forward line in particular attracted much excitement and envy with the left wing pair of Tommy Cairns and Alan Morton generally reckoned to be the best in the business. They now had a huge support, swelled by the influx of Ulster shipbuilders since the war who naturally settled in the Govan area and gave their support to the local side now seen as the Protestant answer to the Catholic Celtic who had dominated Scottish football before the Great War.

It would of course be totally unfair to assume that all Rangers supporters were religious bigots, for there were other factors as well that would encourage one to support Rangers, not least the many fine players who were at Ibrox at the time, but religion was now a factor in Scottish football, and hardly discouraged by the Rangers establishment, themselves all loyal to the Church of Scotland and the King, and who (cynically) saw in all this a tidy little earner.

Celtic on the other hand had struggled since the war. They had fine players, notably Patsy Gallacher, now approaching the end of his career, a fine young wing-half in Peter Wilson and a young man called McGrory who could score goals, but they had struggled to find a successful team.

So many players had found Maley's abrupt and dictatorial style of management hard to handle; Johnny Gilchrist, Willie Cringan, Joe Cassidy and Tommy McInally might have stayed in other circumstances, but they had moved on to be lesser players at lesser clubs. Celtic had won the Scottish League in 1919 and 1922, the Scottish Cup in 1923, and several successes in the two Glasgow tournaments, but they were undeniably in early 1925 second best to Struth's Rangers.

There was however one factor that might help Celtic as they approached the semi-final (which they reached, incidentally, after a prolonged struggle to beat St Mirren) and that was the irrational, almost psychic and definitely scary talk about jinxes and hoodoos. Rangers, for all their successes in other tournaments, simply could not win the Scottish Cup. Their last success had been in 1903. Some 22 years had passed, with the Great War and many other things happening since that time. It was even quite widely believed in the 1920s (when belief in the occult and the super-natural was more prevalent than it is now) that there was some sort of curse on Rangers, perhaps connected with the Ibrox Disaster of 1902.

Very few people in the cold light of day will ever really admit that they believe in any sort of jinx or curse, but a football field is far from a rational place, and the feeling that 'we are not meant to win today' can very easily take hold after an early reverse or two. This feeling certainly affected Celtic in the early 1960s when they simply could not beat Rangers; it affected Dundee United in the 1980s when not even Jim McLean could persuade them to win at Hampden; and it has affected more than 100 years of Hibs players and supporters as far as the Scottish Cup is concerned. In this case in 1925, on the Monday after the game, the *Evening Times* is sufficiently affected by hoodoos to ask the question in its headline 'Did Funk Beat Rangers?'

The pressure was thus all on Rangers to deliver the Scottish Cup for their supporters, and to put an end to all this nonsense. They would be nervous men in front of the huge crowd (the first time that over 100,000 appeared at Hampden for any game other than a Scotland v England international) and no-one appreciated that more than Celtic's precocious and charismatic Patsy Gallacher. This was quite simply to be Patsy's day.

The six-figure crowd was massive, and it was really a very big day in sport in Scotland with Edinburgh attracting huge attendances as well. In the first place there was the other semi-final between Dundee and Hamilton Accies at Tynecastle, but across the railway line at a new ground called Murrayfield, Scotland were playing their first ever rugby international at this fine, well appointed stadium. They would hansel it with a 14-11 winning start.

In the Celtic dressing room before kick-off, Willie Maley had delivered his usual homilies about playing the game well, entertaining the crowd, being a credit to Celtic etc ... and had departed to talk to the Rangers directors, leaving captain Willie McStay in charge. McStay said his bit, but then Gallacher asked if he could say his piece. He expatiated on the Rangers hoodoo, telling the Celtic players to keep mentioning it on the field, he outlined a few weaknesses about the two Irish full-backs Manderson and McCandless that he knew well, he suggested an initial policy of defence and containment on the grounds that the longer the game went on without Rangers scoring, the more panicky they and their support would become. He also reminded them that a week past Wednesday they had gone down 1-4 to Hibs at Easter Road, sending their bewildered and unhappy supporters out of the ground to catch an early train back to Glasgow.

But then he also told Celtic how good they were. Young Peter Wilson of the bucolic looks and gait was singled out as the key man for his ability to pass the ball. Young Alec Thomson was told that this could be his day, wingers Connolly and McLean that they were equals of Archibald and Morton, and how the Rangers two were picked for Scotland before them was beyond him... And then he turned to the nervous youngster beside him called James McGrory. 'You can head a ball like a bullet, Jimmy.'

The referee was Peter Craigmyle of Aberdeen who had been involved in a curious incident involving Celtic in the quarter-final on the previous Monday. Celtic were leading 1-0 when McFarlane brought down Gillies late in the game on the edge of the penalty box. St Mirren claimed a penalty kick but after Craigmyle had gone down theatrically on his knees to examine the precise spot, a free kick was awarded. But St Mirren refused to take it, still wanting a penalty, and as the Celtic defence waited, Craigmyle took out his watch and watched the seconds tick away until he blew for time, picked up the ball and walked off! Some spectators thought that he had sent off all the St Mirren players, but all he had done was to allow the time to elapse. The *Evening Times* is of the opinion that he did the right thing, both in the awarding of a free kick and in what followed. He would have no such problems on this day, for it was a very easy game to referee.

It was a bright spring day but rather cold with an east wind blowing as Rangers started off playing towards their followers behind the Mount Florida goal. Celtic did as Gallacher had suggested and dropped back to contain Rangers. Willie and Jimmy McStay were immense in the middle of the Celtic defence and left-half Jean McFarlane (whose real name was John, but was called Jean because of a couple of cartoon characters in the *Weekly News* called 'Jock an' Jean') having won a few jousts over his immediate opponent Andy Cunningham, now came into his own and began to release the Celtic wingers, Connolly and McLean.

It was still however against the run of play when Peter Wilson brought the ball out of defence and passed to Gallacher who then found Paddy Connolly on his wing. Paddy beat McCandless, charged to the dead ball line, crossed and found Jimmy McGRORY to do the needful. It was a brilliant goal, a visionary one, but it did not disguise the fact that Rangers were the better team and that Celtic were fortunate to go in at half-time one goal to the good.

The Celtic dressing room was upbeat, although Patsy Gallacher's claims that 'we were about to give Rangers a real hiding' were looked upon as a trifle optimistic. Nevertheless it was obvious that the Celtic crowd were the ones who were doing all the shouting and the singing during the break, while the Rangers end was more subdued, their fans' singing more sporadic and half-hearted.

It is often said that there is a moment which defines a football match. This one came within a few minutes of the start of the second half as Rangers pressed forward. Davie Meiklejohn found himself with a little space on the edge of the penalty box. He shot and hit the crossbar to the relief of the Celtic crowd behind that goal, but then the ball rebounded to Tommy Cairns. 'Tireless' Tommy, normally so deadly in such circumstances, lost concentration and headed the ball weakly into the hands of Peter Shevlin in the Celtic goal.

It was at that moment that the thoughts of jinxes and hoodoos took over, and Rangers visibly lost heart. Celtic on the other hand played with renewed vigour and their four key midfield men: Peter Wilson, Jean McFarlane, Alec Thomson and the wizard himself, Patsy Gallacher, took over and gave Rangers such a roasting that they took about two years to recover.

A corner was forced on the right after Connolly robbed the hesitant Dixon. Paddy Connolly, deservedly called 'the greyhound' for his speed and tenacity, sent over a high one. McGrory rose for it, taking at least three Rangers defenders with him – but Jimmy was only the decoy. It was Adam McLEAN whose head Connolly found! The third goal was a brilliant triangular move – a pass from Gallacher to McGrory, McGrory fed Connolly on the wing, Connolly beat the wretched Billy McCandless again and crossed to the unmarked McGRORY who had beaten the Rangers defence for speed.

By now 70 minutes had gone, and Rangers were beat. Their supporters turned nasty, wondering how this could have happened. It was all blamed not so much on hoodoos but on corruption, with several of their own men accused of being in league with bookmakers. In truth they had simply become too complacent. Huge gaps appeared among the Union Jack wavers at the Mount Florida End as 'Erin's Green Valleys' was belted out from the other as the Celtic faithful enjoyed a rare day of euphoria. The song was really a hymn called 'Hail Glorious St Patrick' but had been emended to include such geographical absurdities as:

'Where Erin's green valleys Look down on Parkhead!'

Celtic's triumphant fans, frantically waving their flags of Ireland of the green background and the yellow harp, would have settled for 3-0, but Willie Robb in the Rangers goal, clearly unsettled and even traumatised by recent events, gifted another two goals. He missed a high ball and allowed Alec THOMSON to score a fourth, and then Adam McLEAN scored a fifth when Manderson and Robb misunderstood each other with a pass back.

'Waverley' of the *Daily Record* has no doubt where the glory all lies. Patsy Gallacher, he said, had shaken off the shackles of Anno Domini and remained 'a star in the football firmament'. But the greatness of Patsy that day was not so much his own play, which was superb, as the way that he was able to motivate others – McFarlane, Wilson, Connolly, Thomson were all superb – and convincing Celtic that Rangers really could be beaten.

It was a triumph as complete as it was unexpected; a day on which Celtic shook off their inferiority complex and decided to play the way that they could play. And of course they had Patsy Gallacher! It would be a result never to be forgotten by those who experienced it, with some people in distant parts of Scotland querying their evening newspaper about whether they had got the score the right way round!

There are those who associate the song 'Hello! Hello!' with Rangers. Not so! The 'Marching Through Georgia' anthem of the American Civil War would be used for decades after to commemorate this game as Celtic supporters arrived in Dundee, Falkirk, Edinburgh and Aberdeen to the strains of:

Hello! Hello! We are the Tim Malloys!
Hello! Hello! You'll know us by the noise!
We f***ed the Rangers in the cup
Twas great to be alive!
Not one, not two, not three, not four but five!

v Dundee 2-1

Scottish Cup Final, Hampden
11 April 1925

CELTIC	DUNDEE	REFEREE
Shevlin	Britton	Mr T. Dougray, Bellshill
W. McStay	Brown	
Hilley	Thomson	
Wilson	Ross	
J. McStay	W. Rankine	
McFarlane	Irving	
Connolly	Duncan	
Gallacher	McLean	
McGrory	Halliday	
Thomson	J. Rankine	
McLean	Gilmour	

THE CELTIC supporters in the 75,317 crowd that approached Hampden on that dull and dour spring day of 11 April 1925 were optimistic, but their optimism was qualified with a certain disquiet about the inconsistency of their team's performance. But perhaps the inconsistency was in the past, for following the spectacular 5-0 win over Rangers in the semi-final three weeks previously, the team had won another three games against Morton, Raith Rovers and Falkirk, with the young goalscoring prodigy Jimmy McGrory having found the net on four occasions in the Falkirk game.

There were other reasons for happiness as well. A week before the cup final, Scotland had beaten England 2-0 at Hampden and it was difficult not to join in the general euphoria, for Scotland had thus beaten all three British sides that season. Willie McStay had been the right-back of the Scotland side and his play had been superb.

But there were rumours as well of the return to Celtic Park for next season of the charismatic and controversial Tommy McInally. Tommy, a superb entertainer and naturally gifted forward, had lit up Celtic Park in the years immediately after the war but in 1922 had fallen out with the club and had gone his reluctant way to Third Lanark – a move that had helped nobody. It had been no secret that Tommy had long been 'pining for home' and as Third Lanark were now apparently doomed for relegation, it seemed that the logical return would take place.

But this would have to be in the future. The immediate present demanded that Celtic win the Scottish Cup, or another unhappy season like 1924 would inflict its own degree of misery on the Celtic fans whose demands for success had not been met as often as they would have liked. The opponents in the final would be Dundee. The men from the Jute City, where football was almost as much a passion as it was in Glasgow, were a difficult side to beat, although they lacked the flair of Celtic. Interestingly enough, they now contained a man by the name of Davie McLean, who had played for Celtic between 1907 and 1909 (nearly 16 years ago!) and had also appeared for a variety of different clubs, one of them being Rangers!

Many supporters thought that Maley had made a mistake in getting rid of McLean (whom he apparently did not like) because McLean's career had been a varied, interesting and fruitful one. He was now however in his mid-30s, and had moved from centre-forward to inside-right, but this did not mean that he could not still score the goals nor that he lacked the desire to put one over on his old mates from Celtic. He was stocky, determined and was famous for his cannonball shot which had once inflicted serious damage on the back of Celtic's Joe Dodds when Joe had got in the way of a free kick!

Dundee had won the Scottish Cup in 1910, and the feeling was that they could do so again this year, as Celtic, in spite of their great and much heralded 5-0 win over Rangers, were perceived as being no great shakes. The Jute Mills, boring, repetitive and monotonous as they were, were lightened by the claims about how the cup would be coming to the city by the River Tay once again. The Dundee players themselves with the benefit of the major propaganda institutions of the local press – the *Courier* and the *Advertiser* – talked in a quietly confident way about how they would beat Celtic. They were frequently photographed in the local swimming baths, and on the Carnoustie golf course or the Angus glens as they prepared for the game which had all of Dundee and the surrounding area in such excitement.

Yet Tayside confidence was hardly justified by results, as until the New Year Dundee had been flirting with relegation and their two games against Celtic this year had hardly provided them with any great grounds for optimism. The game at Dens Park was a 0-0 draw on the first Saturday of the season, but the return match at Parkhead at the end of February had seen a 4-0 win for Celtic and that had been without Willie McStay and Patsy Gallacher, both on international duty!

Celtic were calm in their approach to this game. Maley knew that in Patsy Gallacher, for all his occasional thrawnness and cussedness, he had a match winner. But Patsy was now getting old and may have been upset by all the rumours of the imminent return of Tommy McInally whom he would have seen as a rival for his position. In fact Celtic had another great inside-forward as well in Alec Thomson, a young man who had appeared recently from Buckhaven in Fife and had shown tremendous talent, not least in his ability to interchange position with Patsy, for the pair of them could play at inside-right or inside-left, according to the demands of the situation.

Dundee started off playing towards the King's Park end of the ground, the end which was traditionally populated by Celtic fans. It was closer to 'their' end of the city of Glasgow in the same way as the Celtic dressing room was traditionally the one to the east end of the south stand. The *Evening Time*s is impressed by the Celtic crowd: 'It seems that the Celts possess the biggest choir of all the clubs' and mention is made of the presence of 'green and white turbans [sic]' in the crowd. Before the game the band played a catchy tune called 'Chilli Bom Bom' and veteran Celts like Jimmy Quinn, Charlie Shaw and Alec McNair were seen to join in.

The first few minutes were nervous, as was likely to happen in a Scottish Cup Final before a huge crowd, but as play settled down, Dundee began to have the better of the exchanges. Indeed it was Dundee who scored first after 30 minutes. The Celtic defence failed to deal with a cross from the right and the ball came to inside-left John Rankine who shot for goal and hit the bar. The ball however rebounded to none other than Davie McLEAN who was on the spot for a goal that must have given him particular satisfaction considering that it was now some 15 and a half years since Celtic had allowed him to join Preston North End!

The Dundee supporters, a noisy and enthusiastic minority, celebrated well and half-time was spent by the Celtic supporters in quiet contemplation of how they must fight back, but at the moment, apart from the occasional flash from Patsy Gallacher, not much was happening for the Celtic team. There had been pressure, and lots of it, but no inspiration, and too often the ball ended up in a hopeful punt into the centre of the defence where the young McGrory, apparently overawed by the occasion, was as yet making little impact on the Dundee defence.

But there is no greater sight or sound in football than the Celtic crowd in full cry as their team 'chase' a game. The rabidly pro-Celtic *Glasgow Observer* describes the roar of the Celtic crowd as 'deafening, unending, tempestuous as the growl of the wrathful sea' as Celtic pressed for the equaliser. But this time, there was more control. Gallacher was of course superb – the *Sunday Mail* calls him 'the little wizard' and on the Monday after the game the *Dundee Advertiser* would have as one of its headlines: 'Wonderful Patsy' – but now the wing-halves Peter Wilson and Jean McFarlane came into their own, prompting and supplying ammunition for the forwards.

Yet the Dundee defenders held out, and with the second half now well advanced, the Dundee supporters began to feel that they might well have weathered the storm. Another goal for their team would have made them feel more comfortable however, but there was little chance of that for McLean, Rankine and Halliday were required for defensive duties against the mighty green and white onslaught.

Something special was needed to break down this Dundee defence, in which goalkeeper Jock Britton was outstanding, and something special was forthcoming. Indeed it became the most talked about goal of all time, yet the sources do not always agree as to exactly what happened. It is clear than not every reporter saw the incident, or perhaps saw it but could not believe it! 'John O'Groat', for example in the *Sunday Mail* says simply that: 'Amidst a crowd of players, Patsy Gallacher scraped the ball over the line.'

If one merges all the newspaper reports and eyewitness accounts, what seems to have happened is this. Patsy GALLACHER got the ball just outside the Dundee penalty box on the left. He then beat several defenders (the numbers vary!) found himself in the box, even pushed his own man Jimmy McGrory out of the way and when he found himself confronted with two burly Dundee defenders, did not pass to a colleague as one would have expected, but with the ball between his feet, somer-saulted into the goal, and had to be disentangled from the net by his exultant team-mates!

Hampden took a while to realise that this was in fact a legal goal. It was only when he was disentangled from the net that some spectators and indeed journalists realised that the ball was with him! Some thought that the ball was still underneath goalkeeper Britton or had rolled past the post but the reality was that Celtic were now back on level terms and as time slipped away, a replay on Wednesday seemed to be the most likely scenario. But there was more to come yet.

Celtic won a free kick about halfway inside the Dundee half on the left. As Jean McFarlane shaped to take it, pulling up both his socks before he did so, a line formed on the edge of the penalty area with the Celtic forwards keen not to be caught offside, something which had frustrated a few earlier attempts. McFarlane floated the ball in. There was little wind at Hampden that day (unusually!) and the ball seemed too high for the line of attackers and defenders. It would have landed in the Dundee goalkeeper's arms, but for the mighty leap of Jimmy McGRORY. A 'green and white figure catapulted forth' according to one eye witness, connected with the ball, headed it into the far corner, then hit the ground with such a bump that he was momentarily stunned. When he came round, he wondered why there was such a noise and why everyone was pummelling him on the back. He had scored the winner and Dundee had no time to recover.

It was a particularly significant Scottish Cup victory for Celtic, for they had now won the trophy on 11 occasions and had overtaken Queen's Park's record. Moreover, Celtic had now won the Scottish Cup twice since the Great War, and it was particularly sweet as Rangers were in the midst of their hoodoo years. Willie McStay said 'Grit did it. Sheer Celtic grit'. He was right of course, but there was more than that. There was also a little genius as well in the scoring of the two goals which will be talked about for as long as there is a Celtic. Maley himself insisted that they should 'Give young McGrory the Cup' to show off to the hordes as the omnibus returned that night to Celtic Park.

v **Motherwell** 2-2
Scottish Cup Final, Hampden
11 April 1931

CELTIC	MOTHERWELL	REFEREE
J. Thomson	McClory	Mr P. Craigmyle,
Cook	Johnman	Aberdeen
McGonagle	Hunter	
Wilson	Wales	
McStay	Craig	
Geatons	Telfer	
R. Thomson	Murdoch	
A. Thomson	McMenemy	
McGrory	McFadyen	
Scarff	Stevenson	
Napier	Ferrier	

CELTIC HAD had a bad few years. Since the loss of the Scottish Cup in 1928 and the subsequent departure of men like Tommy McInally and Adam McLean, life had been impoverished – in every sense of the word. Maley, now over 60, had given every indication that the job was getting too much for him, so obsessed was he with money. Admittedly, the new stand which opened in 1929 had had to be paid for, but that was no excuse for his attempt to sell Jimmy McGrory and John Thomson. Fortunately both men were true Celts, one by birth and the other by adoption, and refused to go anywhere other than the club they loved.

1929 and 1930 had passed without any significant victories but there were signs at the start of the 1930/31 season that things were beginning to pick up. In particular there was the development of some fine forwards to supplement McGrory. On the right wing was Bertie Thomson, a wild boy but absolutely teeming with talent, on the left was Charlie 'Happy Feet' Napier, a different character who dressed flashily and attracted the attention of the fashion conscious. In the inside positions, to supplement the ever reliable Alec Thomson had come a hardworking ball winner called Peter Scarff.

Tangible evidence of the improvement of the team came in October 1930 when Celtic beat Rangers 2-1 to win the Glasgow Cup. It was a tough game, inadequately refereed, and outside-right Bertie Thomson had been sent off for retaliation after much provocation, but Celtic had shown the grit and determination to win through even with ten men and to give their fans some silverware. The Scottish League campaign had been an improvement as well, although the New Year game against Rangers had been a very unlucky 0-1 defeat and Rangers held the edge in the championship race … just. But another team was appearing. This was Motherwell.

Motherwell had had a fairly undistinguished history before 1931. Their distinctive claret and amber strip (which they had adopted in 1911 in conscious imitation of

Bradford City who won the English Cup in that year, largely because they were fed up of having to bring a change strip as everyone else in Scotland seemed to wear blue!) had seen little success. But they did have a reputation for playing good football, and incredibly in view of its reputation today, the Fir Park pitch was considered to be one of the best playing surfaces in the country!

Their manager was an astute character called John 'Sailor' Hunter (so called because of the rolling way that he walked), a man who had had a successful playing career with Liverpool and Dundee, where he was still considered a hero for his part in Dundee's winning of the Scottish Cup in 1910. At Motherwell, Sailor had built up a good team on a limited budget, and in particular the left wing pair of George Stevenson and Bobby Ferrier had attracted a great deal of admiration. Centre-forward Willie McFadyen rivalled even Jimmy McGrory in his ability to score goals, and at inside-right there was John McMenemy. John had of course great Celtic connections in that he was the son of Jimmy 'Napoleon' McMenemy and had himself played for Celtic, his finest hour being the medal that he won in the 1927 Scottish Cup Final.

The clubs had played each other twice in the league this season. The first in October at Fir Park had been a thrilling 3-3 draw with honours even, but when the 'Well appeared at Parkhead on 4 March, Celtic had turned it on with Bertie Thomson and Alec Thomson supplying the ammunition for McGrory to score all four in a 4-1 win. It was decisive and seemed to give Celtic a psychological advantage for the Scottish Cup Final. Clearly a key factor in the game would be how Motherwell's centre-half Alan Craig managed to cope with the menace posed by Jimmy McGrory.

104,803 turned up to see this final. For John Thomson and Jimmy McGrory of Celtic and George Stevenson of Motherwell, a six-figure crowd was nothing new. A fortnight previously they had played before a crowd of 129,810 at Hampden for Scotland v England. They had been introduced to Labour Prime Minister Ramsay McDonald (still considered a Socialist Messiah in some quarters) before the game, and it seems almost otiose to add that McGrory scored for Scotland in the 2-0 victory (George Stevenson of Motherwell scoring the other).

The crowd, although predominantly pro-Celtic, contained a large contingent from Motherwell, and Sailor Hunter was by no means the first manager to wonder where all these people in their claret and amber favours went on a normal Saturday when the team were playing at home! The Mount Florida end of the ground had clearly been influenced by America, in particular Hollywood, as some scantily clad female cheerleaders appeared with a row of people with huge placards of the letters of the Motherwell name. Thus someone would shout: 'Give us an M' and the letter 'M' would appear, then 'Give us an O' etc. until the whole end would ask: 'What have we got?' and the answer came: 'MOTHERWELL'.

This was new to Scottish football in 1931, but there was another more sinister element obvious at the Motherwell end that day. Rangers had no game, so many of their supporters turned up at Hampden, some of them intent on trouble, to lend their support to Motherwell whom they persisted in calling 'The Protestants' and 'The Scotsmen' to the embarrassment, one presumes, of the genuine Motherwell supporters who were well aware that John McMenemy and several other Motherwell players were Roman Catholics, and that Bobby Ferrier was an Englishman!

The weather was pleasant and sunny, and Motherwell started playing towards the King's Park end of the ground, obviously relishing the occasion, and after 20 minutes they were two goals up, both of them deflections off Celtic's centre-half and captain, Jimmy McStay. The first was only a slight touch-on of a STEVENSON drive – but enough to deceive John Thomson – and the other was a far more obvious one when a McMENEMY shot cannoned off McStay's leg. It would be interesting to have known the feelings of McMenemy's father at this point – torn as he was between his love for the Celtic and family loyalty.

The rest of the first half and the half-time interval were spent with the Motherwell supporters in a fervour and the Celtic fans, so noisy and raucous before the start, in brooding introverted silence, their banners drooping sadly and their attempts to sing and rouse their team sporadic and unsuccessful, as depression reigned. Two goals were a lot to pull back against this strong Motherwell side.

But Celtic had fought back to win the Scottish Cup on two famous occasions before in 1904 and 1925 and in the second half with the benefit of a breeze which had sprung up from west to east, began to put pressure on the Motherwell defence. But it was hysterical pressure, devoid of any great flowing football, and the Motherwell defence although 'prodigal of fouls' as one account put it, were holding out. Meanwhile the huge Hampden clock on the South Stand ticked away relentlessly to the dismay of the Celtic fans on the North and East terraces. The game would finish at 4.40, and the minute hand kept moving downwards towards the half-hour mark.

Several claims for penalties were turned down by referee Peter Craigmyle, a man who was also clearly, being the extroverted show-off that he was, enjoying the occasion. At one point he ran away round the back of the goal to avoid being manhandled by Scarff and Bertie Thomson who assailed him with their importunate demands for a penalty when Alan Craig had seemed to handle, and later when the howl for a penalty went up, he paused, and in a moment of pure theatre, waved both arms in front of his body in the 1930s Hollywood gesture which meant 'No Deal'.

The weaker brethren of the Celtic support were already suggesting an early exit to avoid the crush and the inevitable traffic jams (loads of supporters had come by car, an indication perhaps that 1931 was not necessarily quite the year of universal poverty that it has been depicted), and the minute hand on the clock had now reached the perpendicular when a glimmer of hope was offered to the Celtic hordes. A free kick was taken by Charlie Napier. He made as if to 'have a go' himself and the Motherwell wall braced itself for a cannonball shot, when very craftily he lobbed the ball up in the air over the heads of the wall and the ever eager McGRORY lunged forward and prodded the ball home off goalkeeper McClory's left post.

This gave Celtic some relief, but as yet no ecstasy. It did at least stay the trickle to the exits, at least temporarily. McGrory himself ran back to the centre of the field, shrugging off the hugs and kisses of his team-mates and pointing very obviously towards the clock, where seven or possibly eight minutes remained. Anxiety had crept into the Motherwell ranks and it was now their defending that became hysterical, with wild clearances in all directions, the willingness to concede a corner, to give away a foul if necessary… but at all costs to keep the ball away from McGrory!

The minute hand on the clock now began its slow and inexorable upward journey and seemed to have reached the 4.40 mark. Time now appeared to be up, but

Craigmyle, clearly still relishing the moment, obstinately refused the demands of the Motherwell players and fans. Bertie Thomson had the ball on the right in front of the main stand, but several Motherwell men were on him, so he just pumped over a 'hope for the best' ball. With McGrory around there was always a chance. But then came Hampden's most dramatic moment, and the one that was recalled by eyewitnesses well over 60 years later with horror or joy as appropriate. Motherwell's centre-half Alan CRAIG, who had been outstanding all game, rose to head the ball clear. He may have been distracted by a cry from someone of 'Go for it, Alan!', he may have been distracted by his goalkeeper's hesitation, he may have hesitated himself as to whether to head the ball clear or put it out for a corner (he certainly was well aware of the lurking presence of Jimmy McGrory), but for whatever reason, he rose and misheaded the ball into his own net.

Hampden was silent for a split second while the crowd took in the enormity of what had happened. The Mount Florida end was stunned and would remain in a catatonic trance for minutes, unable to say anything other than the odd curse or cry of 'b******s'. The Celtic fans went crazy. The *Glasgow Observer* reporter, unable to contain his glee, wrote: 'Talk about earthquakes, landslides, tidal waves and what not? … Men, utter strangers, seized each other, thumped each other, wrestled, danced, shook hands, shouted, laughed, cried and, in a word, went plumb crazy with joy.' And to his dying day more than 60 years later, one humane Celtic supporter would recall the sight of Alan Craig, lying prone on the Hampden turf, prostrate with grief, thumping the ground again and again, ignoring the attempts of his team-mates to comfort him, and even the words of consolation of men like referee Craigmyle and the ever gentlemanly Jimmy McGrory. Football always has been and always will be a cruel game. It was never more so than to Alan Craig that bright April day of 1931.

Celtic had thus earned a replay. It is often erroneously assumed that they then won that fixture the following Wednesday night with no trouble. This is not true. It was a hard fought game, but Celtic's 4-2 victory owed a great deal to the psychological advantage given to them by the dramatic and traumatic events of the previous Saturday in what must surely be the most poignant Scottish Cup Final of them all.

v **Motherwell** 5-0

Scottish League, Celtic Park
14 March 1936

CELTIC	MOTHERWELL	REFEREE
Kennaway	McClory	Mr P. Craigmyle,
Hogg	Grant	Aberdeen
Morrison	Ellis	
Geatons	Wales	
Lyon	Blair	
Paterson	Telfer	
Delaney	McGillivray	
Buchan	Bremner	
McGrory	Wylie	
Crum	Stevenson	
Murphy	Stewart	

THINGS WERE happening at Celtic Park in 1936. At long last, after some of their supporters had despaired of them ever rising again, Celtic had hit back, and there were signs that winning the Scottish League championship might be a possibility. A decade had passed since this had happened, when Celtic, with Tommy McInally at his best, had won the league in 1926. Since then it had been the exclusive property of Rangers, other than in 1932 when a fine Motherwell side had won it.

Such things sit ill with the Parkhead faithful. Crowds and enthusiasm had dropped. To an extent this could be blamed on the worldwide recession, but only to an extent, because Celtic fans will do anything to go and see their favourites if they consider them worth going to see. Poverty and unemployment will not necessarily be barriers to the determination of the Celts to see their team – as long as the end product is worth watching.

Lack of success and mediocre performances are severe deterrents, though, and in 1934 crowds had dropped to less than 15,000 on average, putting Celtic well below teams like Rangers, Hearts and even sometimes Dundee and Motherwell. Maley, who took a long time to recover from the untimely deaths of John Thomson and Peter Scarff, would thunder in the programme and the yearbook about the 'lack of Celtic spirit', apparently oblivious to the fact that to a certain extent he was also responsible for what was going on.

But slowly things began to get better. Players like Jimmy Delaney, Johnny Crum and Willie Buchan began to emerge, and in October 1934 the club had had one of its rare brainwaves in the appointment of Jimmy 'Napoleon' McMenemy as coach. In practice, this means that although, in theory, the brooding Maley remained manager, Napoleon in fact ran the team, picked the players, organised the training and became the *de facto supremo* of the team. McMenemy had the good fortune to get on well with Maley (he had been one of Maley's best ever finds 30 years ago) and he also was well loved and respected by the players with the ability to get the best out of them.

McMenemy had of course been part of a great forward line. One of the features of their play had been their ability to interchange position at speed. This can only really work of course if all the players are versatile enough. Bennett, McMenemy, Quinn, Somers and Hamilton all had this ability, and McMenemy soon realised that Delaney, Buchan, McGrory, Crum and Murphy were also adequately skilful, with the young Delaney on the right wing particularly able to cut inside if necessary and even exchange wings with Frank Murphy. These tactics would now be employed to devastating effect.

In the 1935/36 season Celtic were quite clearly the form team of the league. By the New Year they had lost only three games – the opening day fixture at Aberdeen, the Glasgow Cup Final to Rangers and an unaccountable lapse of form at East End Park in early December, but apart from that, not only were they winning, but they were also playing excellent football. The team was full of youngsters, with maybe one exception. But that exception certainly did prove the rule! We are talking about Jimmy McGrory.

McGrory had failed to score in only four league games that season, and the reason freely given for Celtic's strange loss at Dunfermline in December was that McGrory wasn't playing. He scored with both his feet and his head, with so many coming from headers that he was given the title 'The Golden Crust'. All this was good enough in the eyes of the Celtic fans, but what made him special was that he was an exceptionally modest and humble man, a total gentleman who loved the game and loved the club. Apart from a year early in his career when he had been farmed out to Clydebank, he had been with Celtic all his life and never wanted to go anywhere else, even when Maley made a despicable attempt to sell him to Arsenal.

On 19 October 1935, McGrory overtook Steve Bloomer's goalscoring record and then on midwinter's day in a 5-3 defeat of Aberdeen at Parkhead, he became the record goalscorer of all time when he reached 366 goals, now two ahead of the late Hugh Ferguson. This was on a hard pitch on a cold day in front of an attendance given as 40,000. If the amount of spectators was anything like accurate, the size of the crowd gave a clear lie to any idea that Celtic's support had disappeared.

Indeed the fans were coming back. Industry was picking up again, for the recession was over, although most people were able to see a sinister reason for the rise in employment. The funny little man with the moustache and silly walk in Germany had ceased being a joke, and it was beginning to look as if Germany might one day try to have 'another go' at world domination. In early March 1936, Hitler flagrantly ignored the Treaty of Versailles by marching troops into the demilitarised Rhineland with the obvious intention of being a little closer to France. France and Great Britain did nothing other than protest, and even tried to rationalise their lack of activity by saying that it was the equivalent of 'Hitler moving furniture about his own house', for the Rhineland was undeniably all in Germany. The Allies would have cause to regret their lack of action.

Back in Scotland, by the time that Motherwell appeared on 14 March 1936, Celtic were at the top of the Scottish League, but only just, in a close fight with Rangers and Aberdeen. They had appalled their fans by being ousted from the Scottish Cup by St

Johnstone at Parkhead, but had since fought back, and McGrory had scored 40 goals in the league so far that season.

Motherwell were a strong going team – as they had been consistently through the 1930s, having won the Scottish League championship in 1932 and reaching two Scottish Cup finals, losing to Celtic in 1931 and 1933. John 'Sailor' Hunter, who had won an English League medal as a player with Liverpool in 1901 and a Scottish Cup medal with Dundee in 1910, was Motherwell's manager for the astonishingly long period of 1911 until 1946, and he was renowned for his ability to produce good football players. They were destined to finish fourth in the league this year, and in spite of the loss of Bobby Ferrier, were always considered to be tough opponents.

Play for the first 20 minutes was even, but then Jimmy DELANEY began to show the form that had some supporters rating him as the best in Great Britain. On 22 minutes he ran though the left part of the Motherwell defence, cut inside and scored. Five minutes later, he played a part in Willie BUCHAN adding a second, as the Parkhead crowd of 'about 30,000' showed their pleasure. It was the second half however which proved to be the talking point of the whole season.

Celtic were well on top in spite of an injury to Bobby Hogg (Ellis of Motherwell had also been injured) and Jimmy Delaney was causing havoc wherever he went. It was from one of his charges down the field when the defenders were expecting him to cut inside that he passed to the ever ready McGRORY to beat his marker and score in the 65th minute. It would be an unusual Saturday if McGrory did not score, the supporters reckoned. Those who then went to the toilet missed something special.

More or less straight from the kick-off, the ball came to left-winger Frank Murphy. Frank was only marginally less effective than his right-wing partner Jimmy Delaney. Like Delaney he was quiet and modest, but he had little reason to be diffident about his achievements. Murphy beat his man, realised that the Motherwell defence were still reeling from the loss of the previous goal, went to the corner flag and crossed a high ball for McGRORY to 'rise like a bird' and head homewards into the net. The Celtic faithful could hardly believe their luck in seeing their hero scoring twice in two minutes, when, to everyone's astonishment, absolutely the same thing happened again. Murphy did his stuff on the left wing again and McGRORY was there again to score this 43rd goal of the season, and what must surely be the fastest hat-trick of all time.

> And on the wing Delaney's speed
> Created goals for Jimmy's heid!
> A Cleland boy, so fast and true
> A loyal Celt, straight through and through
>
> But wait a bit, don't be so fast!
> We've left the star turn, till the last
> There in the midst o' a' his glory
> Goal a minute, James McGrory!

On 15 August 1959, Ian St. John of Motherwell would claim to emulate this feat in a League Cup game against Hibs, but in the absence of any exact method of measuring the times, it would be difficult to say which was the quicker. They were both very fast however and St. John would be flattered and delighted to be compared with the valiant Jimmy McGrory who would finish the season with 50 league goals.

The euphoria about the McGrory performance must not cloud anyone's judgement about the rest of the team, and allow anyone to think that this was a mediocre Celtic side who were totally dependent on McGrory. The half-back line of Geatons, Lyon and Paterson were fit enough to be mentioned in the same breath as Young, Loney and Hay of old, and the forward line had few weakness. 5-0 against Motherwell was an excellent result and it said a lot about Celtic who that day took a rather large step towards winning their first league championship in a decade.

McGrory's performances, however, were the thing that galvanised the support once again. Celtic's crowds had dwindled as we have seen, but those who recall the enthusiasm in 1998 as Celtic rallied to thwart Rangers' attempt to win ten championships in a row will appreciate a little of how their fathers and grandfathers felt in 1936 as a superb side, spearheaded by the genius from Garngad, rose to restore Celtic to greatness.

> Tell me the old, old story,
> A hat-trick for McGrory!
> A victory for the Celtic
> He will carry us through!
> He'll carry us through the hue
> We'll beat the b******s in blue
> Look forever to McGrory
> He will carry us through!

v Aberdeen 2-1

Scottish Cup Final, Hampden
24 April 1937

CELTIC	ABERDEEN	REFEREE
Kennaway	Johnstone	Mr M. Hutton, Glasgow
Hogg	Cooper	
Morrison	Temple	
Geatons	Dunlop	
Lyon	Falloon	
Paterson	Thomson	
Delaney	Benyon	
Buchan	McKenzie	
McGrory	Armstrong	
Crum	Mills	
Murphy	Lang	

SCOTLAND'S (and Glasgow's in particular) love of the game of football surprised even its own devotees in spring 1937. A world record crowd was set up on 17 April 1937 when 149,407 (and some sources give a lot more than that) attended the Scotland v England international, and then a week later 146,433 (at a conservative estimate) came to see the Celtic v Aberdeen Scottish Cup Final. In both cases thousands climbed over the wall, and indeed there were some spectators who attended both games and claimed that the cup final actually housed more. No-one will ever know, but when one considers that there were also 76,000 at the Celtic v Clyde Scottish Cup semi-final a few weeks earlier, it would be fair to say that Scottish football was enjoying a boom.

1937 was Aberdeen's first ever Scottish Cup Final. Under ex-Celt Paddy Travers, the Black and Golds (they didn't adopt the now more familiar red until after the Second World War) had built up a fine side and had mobilised their huge, albeit normally latent support for this game. As early as Thursday evening, shoals of buses had left the Granite City and the surrounding villages hoping to see their favourites Willie Mills and Matt Armstrong beat the mighty Celtic whom they usually did well against at Pittodrie but seldom lived up to their capabilities in Glasgow.

Football had come late to Aberdeen. Aberdeen themselves had been founded as late as 1903, an amalgamation of sundry small clubs, and the city had arguably suffered in that, unlike the other three large Scottish cities, there was no significant Irish population. This meant that no 'Celtic' had emerged, and therefore no rivalry against a 'Rangers' as was the case in Edinburgh and Dundee as well as Glasgow, but it did mean that Aberdeen Football Club enjoyed the more or less undivided love of the whole city. Their nearest rivals were 65 miles away in Dundee, and this probably meant that the difference between home form and away form was far more accentuated in Aberdeen than in any other team. Success had been difficult to come by, but it was the unanimous opinion in the Granite City that this was to be their year.

Celtic had slipped slightly from their brilliance of 1936, and the support was divided on Jimmy McGrory. By some distance the greatest goalscorer ever to have donned the green and white (or indeed any other colour), McGrory was now into his 30s. Yet Maley still believed that he could yet produce the goods, and was reluctant to axe him. 1935/36 had in fact been an *annus mirabilis* for McGrory when he had over-taken the records of Steve Bloomer and Hughie Ferguson. It did however seem to be clear that this would have to be McGrory's last Scottish Cup Final. Could he score in this one as he had done in 1925, 1931 and 1933?

Celtic had some great players – Jimmy Delaney on the right wing was as good as one would get, and it was hard to spot any weakness in Willie Buchan, Johnny Crum or Frank Murphy. Behind them was the mighty half-back line of Chick Geatons, Willie Lyon and George Paterson, with Lyon, in particular, proving to the word that not being born a Celt was no obstacle in gaining the love and affection of the Celtic fans. He was an Englishman, and had joined Celtic from the unlikely source of Queen's Park, but he was a commanding centre-half and captain.

Full-backs Bobby Hogg and Jock Morrison were grim, rugged, determined characters in the traditional Scottish mould, and in goal was the much underrated Canadian called Joe Kennaway. Joe had taken over the mantle of the late John Thomson after the tragic events of 1931 when Thomson was accidentally killed in the game against Rangers at Ibrox, and had performed so well in the Celtic goal that he had been capped for Scotland, and some felt that he should have been given more international honours than the solitary cap that he had won.

Glasgow had groaned under the influx of visitors the previous week for the international. This week was the same, as Aberdeen and Celtic supporters (some of them from Ireland, England and parts of Scotland other than Glasgow and its immediate environs) mingled happily together, joking in friendly banter, exchanging drinks and listening with respect to the ardent speeches of the soapbox orators who were inviting everyone to join the International Brigades and fight against the Fascists in Spain. 'The bombs that fall on Madrid today will fall on London and Glasgow tomorrow', proclaimed the posters with chilling accuracy.

But even that consideration took second place to Celtic v Aberdeen. As a rule, there was a tremendous respect between supporters of both these clubs, simply because their traditions are so radically different. It was also true that this particular combination of teams in a Scottish Cup Final always has produced more interest worldwide than any other combination, simply because of the diaspora of the Glasgow Irish and of the douce folks of rural Aberdeenshire in the early years of the 20th century.

The Irish had had no monopoly of suffering and poverty in the 19th and early 20th centuries. Life had been hard in the north-east of Scotland as well, as one can deduce from reading the books of Lewis Grassick Gibbon. Emigration had been a common phenomenon and the result was that in places like Canada and Australia, news of this match would be awaited with much interest. Some places could hear the BBC commentary, others would depend on newspapers the following day, but the game would be important to those who still dreamed of home. Aberdeen, indeed, planned to tour South Africa after the cup final and would dearly love to take the Scottish Cup with them as Celtic had done to the USA and Canada in 1931.

Half an hour before the start, the decision was taken to close the turnstiles. The result was that thousands were left outside, including many who had travelled some considerable distance to attend this game. They could do little else in this era before television and the portable radio than hang about outside, judge the progress of the game by the noise of the crowd and wait for the opening of the exit gates so that they could rush in and see the last ten minutes.

The decision to close the turnstiles was the right one, for even the huge Hampden was clearly struggling to cope with the massive crowd, swaying danger-ously at several points on the higher areas of the terracing. There was probably enough room near the bottom, but such is the obstinacy of human nature, the crowd would not move down, even when it was so obviously in their interests to do so.

Willie Buchan, Celtic's inside-right, who was destined to play a crucial part in the destination of the Scottish Cup tells about the 'wall of sound' that met the players as they emerged from the tunnel. The noise was intense, ferocious and would have been quite intimidating had it not been for the fact that at least half the crowd was supporting his side. The division was possibly 50/40 in favour of Celtic with the other ten per cent made up of those who were, quite simply, football fans, and went to see the game without any clear commitment to either side.

It was indeed Willie Buchan, according to the *Glasgow Observer* who won the game for Celtic, for he 'orchestrated a change of tactics that kept Aberdeen guessing and unsettled.' One suspects that he did this on the prompting of the wily old Jimmy McMenemy, the Celtic trainer who of course knew and had played with Aberdeen's manager Paddy Travers. Travers had been a good enough player for Celtic in the early 1910s but had not been able to displace the young Patsy Gallacher at inside-forward and had moved to Aberdeen in summer 1912. If Travers had any fault, it was that he had a plan and stuck to it, whereas McMenemy was far more flexible and had the players who could interchange at will. By this time it was the astute but self-effacing McMenemy who made most of the onfield tactical decisions, leaving the brooding, despotic but still incredibly vain Willie Maley to reap the rewards and bask in the glory.

Celtic opened the scoring at the Mount Florida end of the ground when a Paterson free kick found the head of McGrory but the ball rebounded off a defender to Buchan. Buchan drove hard, the goalkeeper could only parry it and the ball broke to the gallus Glaswegian Johnny CRUM who put Celtic in front. Hampden erupted, and it exploded again a minute later when the Dons equalised. Matt ARMSTRONG picked up a cross from Benyon and tried a snap shot which Kennaway would have saved if it had not hit the unfortunate Lyon on the way and deflected into the net.

Thus the score remained until half-time with the huge crowd in perpetual fervour as the game ebbed to and fro. The second half saw a lessening in the inten-sity of the play, but not so in the commitment of the players. McGrory was tirelessly belying his 32 years by foraging for the ball when he had to, by being in the penalty box for whenever the ball might break to him and lurking ever dangerously at free kicks and corner kicks. It was Chick Geatons's best ever performance in a Celtic jersey as he kept surging forward, almost himself an extra forward as he left George Paterson and Willie Lyon to deal with the menace of Mills and Armstrong.

It was about the 70th minute when McGrory chased Temple for a ball near the corner flag. McGrory won the ball fairly with his chest, but Aberdeen made the fatal mistake of appealing for handball, and lost a few vital seconds as McGrory slipped the ball to Willie BUCHAN who ran through the defence and scored what would prove to be the winner.

The Celtic fans roared their appreciation of all this, but knew that Aberdeen would now throw everything at their team's defence. It would have been nice for McGrory to score in his last final, but that would have been a luxury, as Jimmy was required (as was everyone else) to man the barricades and keep out the Black and Golds. But the Canadian accent of Joe Kennaway and the English tone of Willie Lyon (in a few years' time he would become an excellent officer in the British Army) calmed the troops, and the steady tackling of Hogg and Morrison kept the Aberdeen forwards at bay.

After what seemed to be an eternity, Mr Hutton blew his whistle and the players shook hands and trooped off. Aberdeen fans were naturally disappointed but knew that they had been present on one of the really great occasions of Scottish football. Celtic received the trophy in the committee room at Hampden and then after the huge crowd had gone home, had their photographs taken in the now empty stadium with only a few seagulls watching them. It was a shame that the huge crowd did not see the cup being presented, but they did bring Glasgow to a standstill that night as they thronged Willie Maley's restaurant – The Bank – hoping to catch a glimpse of their heroes and the piece of silverware which they had now won for the 15th time.

As for Aberdeen, they went home disappointed but with every right to feel proud of what they had achieved. Very sadly, there were to be two tragic aftermaths for the Dons. Director Bill Hay died the following day, and then a month or so later when the team were on their tour of South Africa, their Welsh right-winger, Jackie Benyon, who had played well in the final without ever totally getting the better of Jock Morrison, contracted peritonitis and died. It was a dire time for men from the North, but for a long time after this game, they retained the affection of the Celtic support.

v Everton **1-0**

Empire Exhibition Trophy, Ibrox
10 June 1938

CELTIC	EVERTON	REFEREE
Kennaway	Sagar	Mr T. Thompson,
Hogg	Cook	Northumberland
Morrison	Greenhalgh	
Geatons	Mercer	
Lyon	Jones	
Paterson	Thomson	
Delaney	Geldard	
MacDonald	Cunliffe	
Crum	Lawton	
Divers	Stevenson	
Murphy	Boyes	

In 38 there was a show
Glasgow was the place to go
A model of the tower was football's prize
England sent four of the best
They didn't meet with much success
For the trophy ended up at Paradise

1938 WAS a strange year in Great Britain. On the one hand there was the welcome return of full employment and a degree of prosperity, on the other there was the by now obvious danger from Europe as Germany was clearly girding itself up for another attempt on world domination. Only 20 years had passed since the last world war, and a walk along any street in any Scottish town or city on any day would inevitably cause one to meet a man with missing limbs, or disfiguring facial injuries – all testament to the folly of war.

The Empire Exhibition was held in Bellahouston Park, near Ibrox. It was a much needed propaganda riposte to the vulgar, raucous, strident displays of nationalism in Germany, and it was a celebration of the British Empire with Tait's Tower at the very centre of it. More importantly, perhaps, it was a way of attracting money to the city of Glasgow, and in the summer of 1938 there was more money around than there had been for years.

Football, appropriately for this 'fitba-daft' Second City of the Empire, played its part. There were eight teams. Four from Scotland (Celtic, Rangers, Aberdeen and Hearts) took on four from England (Everton, Chelsea, Sunderland and Brentford) in a straight knockout tournament with the prize being a cup in the image of the Tait's Tower. All games would be played at Ibrox Park because of its proximity to Bellahouston Park. This annoyed Queen's Park who might have offered Hampden, but was very much to the delight of the Rangers Establishment who saw themselves as the home of the Scottish branch of the British Empire. They would be less happy with the way that things turned out!

Celtic had had a fine season. They were league champions and winners of the Glasgow Charity Cup and the only blot on the copybook had been a surprise defeat to Kilmarnock (now managed by, of all people, Jimmy McGrory) in the Scottish Cup. 1938 was also their Golden Jubilee season and a dinner had been planned at the Grosvenor Hotel for a few days after the end of the Empire Exhibition Tournament. Willie Maley, the manager of the club and one of the very few survivors of the early days, would be there, and what a great thing it would be if the team could lift the trophy that would make them the unofficial champions of Great Britain!

The loss of McGrory (to become manager of Kilmarnock) and Buchan (to Blackpool for £10,000) had been hardly noticed, for Johnny Crum had been moved to the centre-forward position, and two new inside-forwards had been introduced in John Divers and Malky MacDonald. MacDonald in particular had been a revelation. He had been with the club for a few years and had been tried in the defence and the half-back line without any great success, but now at inside-right alongside the great Jimmy Delaney, he had taken on a new lease of life, becoming in the opinion of many, the best player of pure football that Celtic had ever had. That would be an ambitious claim considering that that would make him better than the likes of Jimmy McMenemy and Patsy Gallacher, but 'Callum' (as he was nicknamed) was worthy at least to be mentioned in their company. Jimmy Delaney himself, ever modest and shy, when told that he was the best player in the Celtic team, replied: 'Hoo could I be, when Malky MacDonald's in that team?'

Celtic's first opponents were Sunderland on Wednesday 25 May 1938 before a large crowd of 53,971. Without MacDonald from the start, Celtic soon lost Jimmy Delaney to injury, and with MacDonald's deputy Joe Carruth limping all of the second half, they were probably lucky to get off with a 0-0 draw, being indebted to the fine defensive work of the ever calm Willie Lyon and the immaculate goalkeeping of Joe Kennaway.

The replay was held the following night in torrential rain – often conditions in which Celtic play their best football. This time MacDonald had returned, and Matt Lynch played well in place of Delaney. But it was the inspirational play of John Divers ('Divers played the sort of football that money can't buy', says the *Glasgow Herald*) which won the game for Celtic, as he scored twice himself after Crum had cancelled out Sunderland's early strike.

The semi-final was against Hearts on Friday 3 June. Johnny Crum scored the only goal of the game, largely dominated by Hearts who had a goal disallowed. Hearts fans alleged discrimination (they often do!) but the result meant that the final on Friday June 10 1938 would be contested by Celtic and the most illustrious of all the English teams, Everton.

Everton had been known as the 'Bank of England' team because of their riches. Clearly the better team on Merseyside, their stadium, Goodison Park, was generally reckoned to be the best in England. The immortal Dixie Dean had now retired but they still had fine players like Tommy Lawton, Joe Mercer and of course ex-Celt Willie Cook at right-back. Cook had of course played at Ibrox before, not least on that terrible day in 1931 when John Thomson had met his death. Everton had won the English League in 1928 and 1932 (and this fine side were destined to win the league again in 1939) and the English Cup in 1933.

Over 82,000 made their way to Ibrox that beautiful summer Friday evening. The fine conditions sparked off a debate about why football was not played more often in conditions like this rather than the grim winter conditions so prevalent in Scotland. The answer was provided in the other main topic of conversation that evening, namely the progress of the England first innings at Trent Bridge that day. Len Hutton had scored a century. Was he the answer to Australia's Bradman? Even in Scotland, Test Matches were followed avidly.

For those unable to attend the game, a commentary was broadcast by the BBC to all of Great Britain, the commentator being Rex Kingsley of the *Sunday Mail*. By 1938 most houses could afford a 'wireless' as they were called, although it would be another couple of decades before the transistors or portable radios would make their debut. Reception was now better than it had ever been and Celtic fans, therefore, who lived some distance away from Glasgow, clustered round their wirelesses and felt every bit as much of the action as those who were at the game.

Celtic were given a great boost by the return from injury of Jimmy Delaney to the right wing. Jimmy was fast and intelligent with the ability to 'skin' a defender, leave him for dead and then deliver a telling cross. Arguably he missed McGrory to take advantage of his openings, but he was still the best winger in the business. Torry Gillick, a Scotsman who would later play for Rangers, was out for Everton, but this was hardly a disadvantage because Everton had so many fine reserves.

Tommy Lawton, the centre-forward, was the key man for the Liverpool side, but not for the first time Celtic realised what a great centre-half they had in Willie Lyon (ironically an Englishman from Birkenhead which is not too far away from Liverpool). Willie was immense as he led by example, getting to the ball before Lawton did, keeping himself between the striker and the goal and inspiring his defenders to do their utmost.

This was indeed a fine Everton side, and it was generally agreed that they had the better of the first half. In the second half though they were handicapped by the injury to inside-right Cunliffe who (as usually happened in those days when there were no substitutes) played on the right wing and Celtic gradually took command with wing-halves Geatons and Paterson slowly gaining control of the midfield, without however being able to manufacture the goal that the supporters craved so much. Full time came with the score at 0-0.

Extra time was played and the stalemate continued. Celtic, clearly by now the better side, pressed and pressed. The menace of Lawton had now been snuffed out, but Everton retreated more and more into defence, hoping for the full-time whistle which would give them a replay and the chance to have Gillick and Cunliffe recovered from injury.

But Celtic finally broke the deadlock, the goal coming from the hard-working John Divers seven minutes into extra time. He picked up a loose ball in midfield, beat a man, feinted to send a long ball over to Delaney on the wing, but then slipped the ball through to the alert CRUM who had made some space for himself. Crum's shot was parried by goalkeeper Sagars, but was so powerful that it spun behind him into the net. There then followed a great Celtic moment (albeit much disapproved of by the Establishment) when Crum, with the crowd in ecstasy, ran behind the goal and performed an impromptu Highland fling before being engulfed by his team-mates.

The game indeed was not over, for Everton now redoubled their efforts against the mighty half-back line of Geatons, Lyon and Paterson but with no success other than when, almost at the death, Stevenson scored for Everton but was 'well offside' as the *Scotsman* put it. Rex Kingsley, broadcasting to the nation, said the immortal words: 'It's a goal … no it's not,' to those who were unable to see how 'well offside' Stevenson was.

The final whistle blew, the crowd went delirious and then in a moment unusual for the time, the cup was presented to Willie Lyon on the field of play as Ibrox resounded to the cheers and the 'revolutionary songs' (as BBC TV commentator Kenneth Wolstenholme would put it years later) of the Celtic fans. The team were, in all but name, the champions of Great Britain. It was a wonderful way to celebrate a Golden Jubilee. The Jubilee Dinner the following Wednesday was a double celebration for the hero of the hour, Johnny Crum; he had been married earlier that day!

The real significance of this game for supporters lay in what came later. Some 13 years would pass before Celtic would win another major honour, and these years would be momentous in world history. The grim days in Africa, Italy, Normandy, Burma and on the high seas would now and again be lightened for at least a moment or so by recollections of this famous game. The cricket writer E. W. Swanton says that his awful days in a Japanese POW camp were rendered endurable by his possession of a 1939 *Wisden* and his reminiscences of cricket games he had attended. The memory of the Empire Exhibition Trophy performed a similar service for thousands of Celtic supporters.

v Dundee 3-2
Scottish League, Dens Park
17 April 1948

CELTIC	DUNDEE	REFEREE
Miller	Brown	Mr F. Scott, Paisley
Hogg	Follon	
Mallan	Irvine	
Evans	Gallacher	
Corbett	Gray	
McAuley	Boyd	
Weir	Gunn	
McPhail	Pattillo	
Lavery	Stewart	
Gallacher	Ewen	
Paton	Mackay	

IT WOULD be fair to say that the Second World War was not good to Celtic. Unlike the First World War, where Maley's contacts managed to keep most of his good players out of the forces and in the munitions industries near Glasgow and therefore still available to play for Celtic, by 1940 Maley and Celtic had parted company. It had been such a symbiotic relationship that neither functioned particularly well without the other. Maley was never seen at Parkhead (but he was occasionally at Cathkin and even Ibrox) and Celtic lapsed into a seemingly terminal decline which lasted all the war years and for a few seasons after the end of hostilities.

In 1948 the great Jimmy McGrory was manager and was struggling. He was clearly far too nice a man for the nasty and unpleasant side of football management, and was putty in the hands of the powerful directors who seemed to lack ambition for the club. They certainly knew little about how to construct a football team. And it cannot be stressed too much that the years after the Second World War were emphatically NOT difficult years for Scottish football!

Indeed the irony, as far as Celtic fans were concerned, was that these were boom years for Scottish football with attendances high, and Celtic's as good as any. Everyone was just so glad to be alive and there was a general determination that things must get better.

On the political side of things a new society was being created rapidly and efficiently with the new National Health Service due to start in the summer of 1948. There was full employment, a tolerable degree of progress and prosperity ... but it was simply not happening for Celtic on the football field.

1947 had been bad, but 1948 was worse. The first two games of the New Year saw defeats to Rangers at Parkhead and then to Hearts at Tynecastle, and a word that had started as a joke or a rhetorical exaggeration now began to take on an ominous reality. The word was relegation.

Relegation and Celtic simply had never gone together. Along with Rangers, Hearts, Partick Thistle and Aberdeen, Celtic had the distinction of never having been relegated. It is of course not unknown in England for 'big' teams to go down. Manchester United in 1974, Tottenham Hotspur the following year and Newcastle United on frequent occasions have had to countenance the horrors of a move downstairs, but Celtic in the 'B' Division of the Scottish League? This was surely too bad, even to contemplate?!

But why were Celtic so bad? They had some good players: John McPhail, Bobby Evans, Jock Weir, veteran Bobby Hogg and the man whom many supporters would have considered one of the best of them all if he had been in a better team – Pat McAuley. In the goal was Scotland international Willie Miller, well worthy of being mentioned in the same breath as Charlie Shaw, John Thomson and Joe Kennaway. But there were also too many ordinary players: Jimmy Mallan, Willie Corbett and Danny Lavery, for example, would not have featured in other Celtic teams. There was also the fact that they were not well trained. The players were still part-timers after the war, and training sessions were not well run, simply because there was no-one at Parkhead with the expertise to organise them.

It was now almost a decade since the departure of Willie Maley. Given Maley's age (he had been well into his 70s before he left the club) his departure was perhaps inevitable, but little thought appears to have been given to a successor. The board had appointed Jimmy McStay in 1940 and Jimmy McGrory in 1945; good players both, but not manager material, with little idea of how to run a club as huge as Celtic. The club had festered.

Now as winter gave way to spring, the relegation scenario seemed increasingly possible. Thankfully, however, Willie Corbett's ability to take penalties brought victories against Aberdeen and Falkirk, and this seemed to guarantee survival. But then two defeats by Third Lanark and one by championship-chasing Hibs as March turned to April meant that Celtic would really have to beat Dundee at Dens Park. Failure would not necessarily mean relegation, but it would mean that their own destiny was out of their hands.

It was a situation rich in irony. Dundee themselves had just come up from Division 'B' the previous season, and on 25 January 1947 at the same ground of Dens Park, the Scottish Cup had seen what has to be described as a giant killing, as 'B' Division Dundee had defeated 'A' Division Celtic. Celtic supporters remembered that game and shivered with apprehension. Was Dens Park to be the scene of Celtic's demise?

Such a scenario attracted some attention away from the build-up to the Scottish Cup Final between Rangers and Morton that was to be played on the same day (April 17), but the reality of the situation was that, although supporters of some clubs would want Celtic relegated, directors and officials of those same clubs were far from convinced. James Handley in *The Celtic Story* talks about the hysterical pressure on Dundee from all of Scottish football to beat Celtic and relegate them, and in *A Lifetime in Paradise* Jimmy McGrory claims that Dundee were on a huge bonus to beat Celtic. Both these statements must be looked at critically, for they are divorced from reality.

Rangers, for example, certainly did not want to see Celtic relegated. They wanted to beat Celtic, yes, and possibly even enjoyed their discomfiture, but there would be no New Year Old Firm game with Celtic in the 'B' Division, and Glasgow would be considerably impoverished if there were no counterblast to Rangers. It would be the same thinking that would prevail at Ibrox a few years later when small-minded blazerati of the SFA tried to make Celtic take down the Irish flag. Rangers would support Celtic! If Celtic were to be relegated, the Ibrox men almost certainly would have tried to restructure the Scottish leagues or even to secede along with Celtic and those who would miss the huge income that Celtic generated even in bad times.

The pressure was therefore on Dundee NOT to beat Celtic, in spite of what the press said. Mysteriously, Dundee's left-back Bobby Ancell did not play in this game. Those of the cynical inclination took what they wanted out of that, but perhaps more significant was that Jimmy McGrory had a brainwave. He made Willie Gallacher (Patsy's son who was not doing all that well at right-half) and Bobby Evans (the red-headed inside-left who always seemed to be capable of more than he actually produced) change places. This move would of course be the making of Bobby Evans and in so doing, it saved Celtic from relegation.

Dens Park was full with 31,000 fans (there looked to be even more than that) as Celtic kicked off. Patsy Gallacher, who had a son playing for each side – Willie for Celtic and Tommy for Dundee – was there and was given a huge cheer as he took his seat in the stand. Those who believed that referee Mr Scott of Paisley wanted to see Celtic relegated would have grist to their mill, for within the first quarter of an hour he had disallowed three Celtic goals! All of them were however for clear infringements – two fouls and an offside – and, although they looked like good goals to the punters desperate for the opener, no great objection was raised by the Celtic players.

But after about 20 minutes Celtic did go ahead, and it was Jock WEIR, Celtic's 'utility' man who did the job. He was so called because in the years immediately after the war, such was the pressing need for things like new houses that sometimes folk had to settle for something that was good enough but less than what one would have liked in an ideal world. These were 'utility' houses. Weir was very much like that, but he proved his value on that day when after an 'Aunt Sally' type of shoot in which three Celtic shots were blocked before Weir scored with the fourth attempt!

But as the action raged back and forward at both ends, Celtic began to throw more men forward than they should have done, and just on half-time, slackness in the Celtic defence allowed 'Piper' MacKay through, and after Miller had saved brilliantly, Ernie EWEN netted the rebound. A draw at half-time was fair reflection of the scoreline and would probably have suited McGrory's men, but after the break, following a period of sustained pressure from Celtic, Dundee broke and ran up the field, and MacKAY scored from close quarters on the hour mark.

Defeat and possible relegation now faced Celtic, but now that the pace of the game had slackened, they took control and began to build up pressure in an organised way rather than the hysterical mayhem that had prevailed previously. Evans and McAuley now took a grip of the game with the red mop of Bobby Evans being particularly conspicuous as he was ubiquitously diligent, winning balls and spraying passes.

It was from one of these passes that the equaliser came in the 67th minute. An Evans pass found John McPhail whose fierce shot could only be parried by goalkeeper Jock Brown and WEIR nipped in to score. Eyebrows would be raised in local circles about this goal for years afterwards because it was felt that Brown was suspiciously dilatory in getting to the ball after he had stopped it, but this does less than justice to the energy and determination of Jock Weir.

2-2 would have saved Celtic's Division 'A' future and everyone's honour. It would have to be said that Dundee gave every indication of settling for that scoreline, but then almost at the death Celtic decided to 'mak siccar' with a winning goal, from WEIR again, this time after some good work from McAuley who found Weir on the wing and who squeezed the ball home from what seemed to be a very difficult angle.

One would have thought that Celtic had won the league or the cup from the joy exhibited by their supporters that day, and their prolonged celebrations in the city before they got their buses home or headed to Dundee West station. It did not mask the fact that Celtic were an ordinary team, a poor team, in fact, but at least the ultimate humiliation had been averted.

And what about Dundee? Did they try as hard as they might have? Certainly those who had few arguments to back their case would say for decades after that Dundee were given the same bonus for losing as they would have received for winning, that manager George Anderson had been seen talking to Jimmy McGrory in a secretive sort of way and that one Dundee defender told his friends when he was drunk that, if he had had to, he would have scored against himself, etc. etc!

In whatever way, Celtic's status was secured.

v **Motherwell** 1-0
Scottish Cup Final, Hampden
21 April 1951

CELTIC	MOTHERWELL	REFEREE
Hunter	Johnstone	Mr J. Mowat,
Fallon	Kilmarnock	Rutherglen
Rollo	Shaw	
Evans	McLeod	
Boden	Paton	
Baillie	Redpath	
Weir	Humphries	
Collins	Forrest	
McPhail	Kelly	
Peacock	Watson	
Tully	Aitkenhead	

FOR CELTIC supporters the dreadful 1940s continued into the 1950s. Even as the war began to recede into the memory and more and more things like clothing and sweets were beginning to come 'off the ration', Celtic's quota of trophies was restricted to the Glasgow Cup in 1948 and the Charity Cup in 1950. No national honour had been lifted since 1938, and the new trophy called the Scottish League Cup had seen some of Celtic's worst performances.

But the Scottish Cup still had Celtic as the record winners on 15 occasions, and was often regarded as Celtic's special trophy. Those with long memories recalled 1925 and 1931, and those with even longer ones talked about 1904, but since 1937 the tradition had not been lived up to. In early 1951, a Scottish Cup triumph looked unlikely given the shocking form of the team. For example, in January Celtic lost four league games out of four, drew a cup game at East Fife and eventually, on the last day of January on a Wednesday afternoon, scored their first success of 1951 with a 4-2 defeat of East Fife in the replay at Parkhead! The team then promptly 'celebrated' in front of 60,000 fans by losing their next game against Hibs!

Yet there were some straws in the wind betokening a brighter tomorrow. The crowd had stayed unbelievably and irrationally loyal to the cause. There were 60,000 to see Celtic v Hibs, as we have mentioned, and the replay against East Fife with a 2.30 pm kick-off on a January afternoon had attracted 36,185 spectators! Such commitment demanded success, and a few key players had emerged or were emerging. Charlie Tully, although infuriatingly inconsistent and inclined to play to the gallery rather than win a game, was a personality player whom the crowd loved. John McPhail, although injury prone and sometimes slow could score some great goals, Bertie Peacock was proving to the world that an Orange background in Coleraine in Northern Ireland was no handicap to becoming a Celtic legend, and in the last two years, the crowd had fallen in love with the 'wee Barra', the diminutive, but tigerish Bobby Collins.

But the best of them all was the red-headed Bobby Evans. Immediately recognisable, his presence was ubiquitous and he was quite simply a superb player. He had started off a moderately good attacker in the forward line during the war years, but once he moved to right-half in 1948, like Bobby Murdoch some 20 years later, his career never looked back. He had already won ten international caps for Scotland, and had been outstanding in the victory at Wembley the week before.

The league was given up as a lost cause (it would be won by Hibs that year) but as the Scottish Cup campaign developed, optimism began to grow at Celtic Park. Duns presented no problem, and then at a dangerously overcrowded Tynecastle with the crowd in excess of 50,000 with break-ins and the climbing over of inadequate walls, Celtic's goals by Jock Weir and John McPhail were enough to beat Hearts 2-1. McPhail's goal was the result of a brilliant piece of combined play between himself and Charlie Tully, but the hero of that game was 20-year-old goalkeeper John Hunter whose concentration was never distracted by the fact that there were supporters sitting on the back of his goal net, allowed there by the police who feared that youngsters could otherwise be crushed to death on the terracing!

The team then really turned it on in the quarter-final at Parkhead where over 76,000 saw a 3-0 win over Aberdeen, who now had the legendary Jimmy Delaney in their ranks, and then grim determination saw them get the better of Raith Rovers in the semi-final, the winning goal of the 3-2 tussle coming late in the game and the result (as all Kirkcaldy from the Provost downward claimed) of a foul by McPhail on the goalkeeper to prevent him jumping and thus allowing Tully to score.

And so it was Motherwell in the final. Some 20 years earlier (and what a lot had happened in those intervening years!) in 1931 Celtic had beaten Motherwell in the cup final and had taken the Scottish Cup with them to America. This year a tour was organised to the new world as well, and it would be nice if the cup could go with them, as it had done on that previous occasion.

Motherwell were generally reckoned to be one of the best football-playing sides around in those days. They had a tradition of good football, but tended to be a little trophy shy. They had still not won the Scottish Cup, although they were the proud possessors of the League Cup, a competition from which they had dumped Celtic at the quarter-final stage. They had also been one of the teams who had beaten Celtic during Celtic's dreadful January, and it would have to be said that on form, Motherwell were the better team. Their star player was left-half Willie Redpath who had played so well for Scotland against England at Wembley a week previously that he was generally described as the best in Britain.

Against that Celtic had, in addition to the good players already mentioned, a few mediocre foot soldiers, honest journeymen – Alec Rollo, Joe Baillie, Jock Weir, Alec Boden, Sean Fallon – and their not-so-secret weapon in their support. The lack of success brings with it an insatiable thirst for it, and seldom had Celtic mobilised such a support. Every town in Scotland seemed to send those who were willing to buy from the vendors at the railway stations and street corners the green and white favours, the sprigs of lucky white heather wrapped in green foliage, the rosettes, the tammies, and the rattles with 'C'way the Celtic' scrawled over them.

Old friends, sometimes ex-comrades in arms, would meet each other again in Buchanan Street or Lewis's Polytechnic in Argyle Street with a handshake, an embrace, an enquiry about wife and family, and reminiscence about barracks and tents and Cairo, then the urgent all-important question: 'Do ye think we are gonnae do it the day?'

The weather was good, the attendance was 131,943 (as always there seemed to be much more than that) the atmosphere was colourful and friendly with the green and white colours outnumbering Motherwell's claret and amber by about 25 to 1. The game started with Celtic playing towards the traditional Celtic End, the King's Park end of the ground, amidst constant noise and raucous singing:

> There's Weir and Collins
> And big captain John
> With Peacock and Tully
> To carry us on!

Indeed, it was 'big captain John' who opened the scoring for Celtic in the 15th minute. After the nervous opening exchanges had passed, the game was settling into a pattern of Motherwell, the better team, passing the ball to each other in a way which delighted the football purist and won the admiration of the neutral, while Celtic with their few flair players and honest determination from everyone else creating more chances. Then Alec Boden won the ball out of defence and punted a long high ball up to John McPHAIL who beat his man in the air, headed on, evaded another tackle and when goalkeeper Johnstone came out to narrow the angle, lobbed the ball over his head from about the edge of the penalty area.

It was moments like this which elevated McPhail to almost divine status among the fans, and the pity was that he did not do it more often. Hampden went mad for a few minutes after that, but those Celtic fans who expected a goal rush were to be disappointed, for Motherwell now fought back and the first half came to an end with the claret and amber side perhaps a little unlucky not to be on level terms.

The second half was long and tense. The game was even, for Evans was beginning to dominate the midfield but Celtic could not yet grab the second goal which would guarantee the cup. Motherwell, for their part, continued their fine football with good passing and running off the ball, but came up against a determined half back line in Evans, Boden and Baillie with the two uncultured but hard-tackling full backs in Sean Fallon and Alec Rollo, their hair brushed back in the style of the early 1950s, who 'kicked everything that came over the half way line – paper bags, stray dogs, trainers and their own men included' in the words of one fan clearly given to hyperbole. 'The wind didnae even get by them!' added his friend.

Not only was the contest enjoyed by the fans (if one can ever 'enjoy' a cup final when so much is at stake) but the BBC Home Service was relaying it to the rest of the country and indeed the world on the World Service where thousands and thousands of Celtic fans were spending their morning or evening (as appropriate, depending where in the world they now lived) wearing away their carpets as they paced their living rooms like caged lions.

Once it seemed that Motherwell must equalise, when George Hunter, to the relief of all those on the terracing behind him, dived to save a crisp shot from Wilson Humphries which seemed destined for the top corner. On other occasions they came close as well, but after the 80th minute, the impression began to grow that they had shot their bolt. Celtic now had more of the play and Baillie, a rough and tumble character but possessing a good football brain, began to distribute passes on the left hoping to find the two Irishmen, Peacock and Tully, who formed the left wing.

The noise grew in intensity as the final whistle approached, everyone too aware that a single mistake could ruin it all and deprive the support of the sight of the Scottish Cup once again bedecked in green and white ribbons. Mr Mowatt, strictly fair and generally regarded as being the best referee in the world, added a generous amount of injury time. This was, of course, long before a fourth assistant would appear to show how much injury time there was to be, and everyone simply had to guess. But the final whistle came, and Hampden erupted, not so much in joy and rapture as relief that Celtic were back among the honours once again.

John McPhail received the trophy from Lady McGowan at the end, as tears ran unashamedly down the cheeks of those who had waited so long for this day. Veterans of Africa, Italy and D-Day were quite prepared to admit that this event made it all worthwhile, and that night for the first time since VE Day in 1945, there was singing and dancing in the streets of the Gorbals, Garngad, Holytown, Cleland, Croy and the other Celtic strongholds.

v Hibernian 2-0

Coronation Cup Final, Hampden
20 May 1953

CELTIC	HIBERNIAN	REFEREE
Bonnar	Younger	Mr H. Phillips,
Haughney	Govan	Motherwell
Rollo	Paterson	
Evans	Buchanan	
Stein	Howie	
McPhail	Combe	
Collins	Smith	
Walsh	Johnstone	
Mochan	Reilly	
Peacock	Turnbull	
Fernie	Ormond	

Coronation time was here
'53 that was the year
Another four from England met their doom.
They said we'll have to try again
For like before it was in vain
And the trophy's in the Celtic trophy room

CORONATION TIME certainly was here in 1953, as the whole nation prepared to join in the celebration of the young monarch with her Greek husband and her two charming children. Celtic supporters are normally little given to royalty because members of the Roman Catholic faith are barred by some archaic law from that strange and unnatural society, but even they were caught up in the mood of national euphoria, involving as it did extra holidays, free chocolate bars for children (a huge treat in 1953!) and a mug with a picture of the Queen on it given to every family in the land.

Celtic supporters did need something to cheer them up in 1953, for the performances of the team had been dire. Mid table mediocrity in the league, dismal exits from the Glasgow Cup and the Scottish League Cup, and in the Scottish Cup, a disappointing 0-2 exit to Rangers at Ibrox after a few more encouraging displays. After this defeat, Celtic, as often happens in the wake of an Ibrox reverse, lapsed into introverted self doubt and the league season finished abysmally.

Celtic's mediocre league position meant that they could consider themselves to be very fortunate to be invited to participate in the Coronation Cup at all, and indeed they wouldn't have been if it had not been for their huge support and the fact that all the games were to be played in Glasgow. Celtic, Rangers, Hibs and Aberdeen represented Scotland while England provided Arsenal, Manchester United,

Tottenham Hotspur and Newcastle United. On league form, it could be argued that Celtic were the worst of the lot.

But they were not as bad as they appeared. There were good players: Evans, Tully, Collins, Fernie and at centre-half a man called Stein, from a distinctly non-Celtic-minded background. He was by no means the best centre-half in the world – he would describe himself in one of his lighter moments with deliberate ambiguity as 'passable' – but he did work hard and he was determined. More than that, he was clearly a leader and a fine captain.

Many supporters were of the opinion that if the team came good, they would be very good, but the problem was that the Scottish season was now over, and Celtic had now completed seven post-war seasons with just one Scottish trophy to show for themselves, the Scottish Cup in 1951, after which the promise of better things had not been fulfilled.

Before the Coronation Cup was the Glasgow Charity Cup. This trophy was often looked upon as an afterthought for the season and wasn't always taken seriously. But it was always for good causes (in the early days the players had been expected to play for nothing, as it was all for charity) and a good performance could give supporters something to be happy about over the summer.

Celtic began this tournament on a night of heavy rain at the end of April when Clyde came to Parkhead. The play was an absolute revelation with lovely fast football as Celtic defeated Clyde 4-0. It made everyone wonder why there had not been more of this earlier on in the season, but then in the semi-final against a good Third Lanark team, they had lapsed a little and were lucky to beat Thirds on the toss of a coin after a spirited but uninspired performance.

Then on Friday 8 May, the day before the Charity Cup Final, they did something very unusual and moved into the transfer market to buy Neil Mochan from Middlesbrough. In 1953 Celtic were not a buying club as a general rule, but Mochan was a Celtic fan who had played for Morton in the late 1940s and jumped at the chance to return to Scotland from Ayresome Park where his career had been stagnating. He was put straight into the forward line for the Glasgow Charity Cup Final the following day where he scored twice as Celtic beat Queen's Park to win the cup.

Mochan thus won a medal on his first outing for the club. This belated piece of silverware gave Celtic heart. Celtic supporters can be naïve sometimes and have always been very keen to believe that they have a great team when in fact they don't (the acquisition of Charlie Tully in 1948 had led to similar, and ultimately unfounded euphoria) but their newfound optimism would soon be put to the test two days later when the Coronation Cup tournament opened on Monday 11 May at Hampden when Celtic played Arsenal.

Arsenal had won the English League that season, and there were no great rational grounds for optimism, but 59,500 stood in amazement and awe on Hampden's slopes as Celtic scored first through Bobby Collins and held onto their 1-0 lead for the rest of the game. In the words of the *Glasgow Herald*: 'Celtic taught them how to play football. Had Arsenal lost by 5 or 6, they would have had no valid complaint. Celtic's shooting was a revelation.' Indeed, the acquisition of Mochan seemed to have made all the difference, for there was a confidence about the forward line which had been missing all season.

This was euphoric, rapturous stuff for a Celtic support starved of success all season, and more was to come in the defeat of Manchester United in the semi-final in the rain the next Saturday. It was a narrower victory however, but Celtic were just the better team, scoring through Bertie Peacock and that man Mochan again before Jack Rowley pulled one back for Manchester United and Celtic were compelled to defend desperately at the end.

And so it was Hibs in the final. Not to put too fine a point on it, this was hardly the combination that the Establishment had wished. It was *meant* to be Rangers v Arsenal, the two most notably royalist teams of them all, both rich and with supporters who waved Union Jacks. Instead it was Celtic v Hibs, the Glasgow Irishmen against the Edinburgh Irishmen, or as someone cruelly put it, 'The IRA v The Fenians'. The singing of 'The Soldiers' Song' was heard from the 117,060 crowd and one wonders what Her Majesty, had she been there, might have made of one of the lines of 'Kevin Barry' which ran:

Another martyr for old Ireland,
Another murder for the crown!

Hibs were the favourites. As Scottish League champions in 1951 and 1952 and with the Famous Five forward line of Smith, Johnstone, Reilly, Turnbull and Ormond at their peak, this tag was justified, for although Celtic had improved phenomenally of late, their basic standard was still a peg or two below that of Hibs. Lawrie Reilly had been the hero of Scotland in April when his last minute strike had saved Scotland from defeat at Wembley, and it was hard to see him not scoring against the Celtic defence which had conceded so many goals this season. In addition, Charlie Tully had been injured in the semi-final against Manchester United, and would not be able to play, his place going to yet unproven Fifer, Willie Fernie.

Celtic started playing towards the heavily-populated King's Park end. It was a fine clear evening with the sun setting over the Mount Florida end likely to trouble defences. Heavy rain had fallen for much of the day, indeed for much of the whole month of May, but the skies had cleared and the night was more or less ideal for football. Celtic, with the sun behind them, had the better of the first half, and on the half-hour mark, opened the scoring. It was a punt from Stein to Fernie who slipped a ball through to MOCHAN who surprised everyone by shooting from well over 25 yards. No photographic record appears to exist of that goal to do adequate justice to it, but the terracing behind was an eloquent testimony to Celtic's new hero.

The second half has been described as the longest in Celtic's history, as Hibs moved into gear, swamping Celtic's midfield and raining down on the beleaguered Celtic goal in which Johnnie Bonnar, who had never been too convincing so far in his stop-start Celtic career, was called upon by destiny to play the game of his life. With Stein in front of him preventing too much damage from Reilly, the main danger came from the inside men, Eddie Turnbull and Bobby Johnstone. It was nervous stuff, the tension shared by the densely packed masses behind the goal and the tens of thousands listening to the BBC Home Service that beautiful Wednesday evening when the garden should have been tended to or children put to bed instead.

Eddie Turnbull would wonder how Bonnar saved one of his 'specials' or a Bobby Johnstone header that he really should, by the laws of dynamics, never have sniffed, and Willie Ormond, while manager of Scotland in 1977, would tell people on a train that the biggest disappointment in his playing career was not getting 'one by that bugger Bonnar'. One in particular he recalled saying to himself, 'that's a winner', but somehow Bonnar got to it.

Corner kicks, free kicks, charges down the wing, the crosses from the silky Gordon Smith (by some distance a better player than his direct opponent Alec Rollo) all came to naught against Bonnar. Slowly the tide eased as Celtic gained more and more confidence. Stein, sensing a change of mood, now radiated command and assurance, and then came the blow which Hibs did not really deserve, but which guaranteed the 1953 side a place in Celtic immortality. Fernie found Collins who ran up the right wing, and crossed for the ever dangerous Mochan. Mochan might have tried himself but found Jimmy WALSH instead. Walsh then shot, beat the goalkeeper, saw the ball cleared by a defender but scored the rebound.

At the distant end, this sight came like Manna from Heaven to the Celtic hordes who had braved the second-half barrage, saving every shot and kicking every ball off the line. To use clichés like 'Hampden erupted' and 'bedlam reigned' does little justice to the scenes all over the stadium, for as Jock Stein collected the Coronation Cup, it joined Celtic's other two permanent all-British trophies – the British League Cup of 1902 (sometimes also called the Coronation Cup) and the Empire Exhibition Trophy of 1938. The miseries of the post-war years were almost all wiped out on that glorious summer evening of 1953, and Neil Mochan in particular must have wondered if he was already in heaven. It was certainly not 'paradise' for he had now won two medals for his new club ... but had not yet played a game at Parkhead!

So, alas for the hopes of the true Royal Blues
The Celtic beat Manchester and Arsenal too
Then Hibs in the Final, see, lo and behold!
All Hampden was covered in green white and gold!

v Aberdeen 2-1
Scottish Cup Final, Hampden
24 April 1954

CELTIC	ABERDEEN	REFEREE
Bonnar	Martin	Mr C. Faultless,
Haughney	Mitchell	Giffnock
Meechan	Caldwell	
Evans	Allister	
Stein	Young	
Peacock	Glen	
Higgins	Leggat	
Fernie	Hamilton	
Fallon	Buckley	
Tully	Clunie	
Mochan	Hather	

IT WAS great to be alive if you were a Celtic supporter in 1954. The team had just clinched the Scottish League on 17 April with a 3-0 win over Hibs at Easter Road – a tremendous achievement considering that on their previous visit to Edinburgh to Tynecastle in early February the team had lost to Hearts and had seemed out of contention for the championship. But then Celtic had hit a rich seam of form and kept winning as everyone else faltered. They would eventually finish the season five points clear of Hearts.

This was the first winning of the league since 1938, and now there was the Scottish Cup. The path to the Scottish Cup Final had been difficult. Three games had been played away from home at Falkirk, Stirling Albion and Hamilton Accies, and in each case, at small grounds with the crowd on top of them in a frantic atmosphere, it had been a stern test of character as Celtic had won by the odd goal: 2-1 at Brockville, 4-3 at Annfield and 2-1 at Douglas Park.

Old cup-tie foes Motherwell now faced them in the semi-final at Hampden. Celtic were 2-1 up with Jock Stein immense in the centre of the defence as Motherwell, the better team on the day, rallied and scored through Aitken, following a moment's hesitation in the Celtic defence. The replay was held on a Monday afternoon at Hampden before an astonishing crowd of 92,662, and Celtic played much better to win 3-1 with goals from Willie Fernie, Neil Mochan and an own goal by the luckless Motherwell player with the unlikely name of Willie Kilmarnock!

It was now therefore possible for Celtic to do something that they had not done for 40 years and that was to win a league and cup double. They had been the first to do this in 1907, then did it again in 1908, but 1914 was often regarded as the best Celtic team of them all with men like Jimmy McMenemy, Patsy Gallacher and 'Sunny Jim' Young on board. Could this Celtic team emulate that great side? Were they good enough?

Opinions were divided even among the Celtic support on the value of their current side. There were some fine players like Willie Fernie, Bobby Evans and Bertie Peacock – no-one disputed this – but Charlie Tully had the ability to infuriate as well as to charm and entertain. On his day he was one of the best in the world, but other days could be selfish and uncooperative with the occasional sulky refusal to chase a ball that was well within his reach. Often a little goal-greedy in that he would try to score from an impossible angle rather than pass to a colleague who was better placed, nevertheless he also did have the ability to score difficult and unusual goals and he remained, like Tommy McInally a generation ago, the great hero of the crowd, who tended to forgive and forget his unfortunate foibles.

But there were other players of lesser ability who had done well for the team. Full-backs Haughney and Meechan (Haughney had just recently won an international cap in a disastrous 2-4 defeat to England) were honest hard workers, as indeed was centre-half and captain, Jock Stein, who had slowly won the Parkhead fans over. He had not started well, but Celtic fans will always forgive and cheer on a player willing to go the extra mile for the cause. He had had a superb season, not least for the fact that he was a great captain, knowing exactly when to chastise and when to sympathise – knowing the difference between when a player was simply having a bad game, when he was not trying 100 per cent, and when he, quite simply, would not make it.

Supporters were much divided on who should be the centre-forward. In the absence of John McPhail, Jimmy Walsh and Bobby Collins, the management had been forced to turn to Sean Fallon. Sean was of course a rugged defender, a no-nonsense tackler and a player who would be prepared to die for the cause, but to put him at centre-forward seemed a strange decision, and yet it was working – up to a point. He had for example scored twice in a crucial game at Partick Thistle in March, and in the first semi-final against Motherwell, but the feeling persisted that centre-forward was not Sean's position.

The obstacle to Celtic winning a league and cup double came from the North. Under the management of Davie Halliday, Aberdeen had developed into a fine side with good players in wingers Graham Leggat and Jackie Hather, veteran George Hamilton and centre-forward Paddy Buckley. They were men of real talent and it was felt that they would get the better of the Celtic defence which contained so many honest journeymen, but no great silky defenders.

Aberdeen had of course played in the 1937 Scottish Cup Final against Celtic, in the final that was generally reckoned to be the best of them all, and since then they had changed their colours from black and gold to red and had won the Scottish Cup in 1947. They had beaten Hibs in that first post-war cup final and been considered unlucky in 1953 to lose to Rangers in a replay. They were a fine side, and as in 1937, they would be well supported.

They had also caused the sensation of the tournament so far when they had beaten Rangers 6-0 in the semi-final, ripping the famous Iron Curtain defence to shreds. Joe O'Neill had scored a hat-trick that day but he was now injured and unable to play in the final, thus perhaps relieving his family of a difficult decision. Joe O'Neill was as much a Celt as his name would suggest ('as Irish as the pigs of Docherty', as the saying went), so his family could now go to Hampden to support Celtic and say that Aberdeen would have won, if only Joe had been playing.

81

Celtic and Aberdeen supporters have always got on well together, and the huge crowd was well integrated, although the King's Park end was heavily decorated in green and white. Aberdeen must have contributed some 50,000 spectators to the 129,926 crowd, and it had seemed most of Aberdeen's population had moved to Glasgow that weekend, judging by the amount of trains and buses that left the Granite City all day Friday and particularly overnight on the Friday, full of people (including a higher than average amount of women and children) bedecked in red and white and singing the new song that seemed to be sung on every radio programme and on every variety show – 'The Northern Lights of Old Aberdeen'. This was of course 1954, when the welfare state had made its appearance and even the traditionally (supposedly) tight-fisted, sour-faced Aberdonians were now able to make a trip to Glasgow!

The ticket arrangements had been puzzling. Nominally all-ticket, because the previous encounter between these two in the final had seen a record crowd in 1937, there were nevertheless some 'cash turnstiles', and the *Sunday Mail* was delighted to note the discomfiture of the profiteers and ticket touts who had tried to sell tickets at about three times their value, and then had to give them all away after 3.00 pm! Some lucky punters, therefore, managed to gain entrance for nothing if they kept their nerve until kick-off time.

The first half on a dull but dry day, with Celtic playing towards their own supporters at the King's Park end, was keen, fast, entertaining, but goalless. Celtic's tactics had been to concentrate a couple of defenders – Evans and Stein – on the dangerous Paddy Buckley, with Sean Fallon (who was of course by nature a defender) coming back to help out as well, while Tully and Fernie roamed all over the field trying to create openings. Aberdeen's fast and dangerous wingers Graham Leggat and Jackie Hather were well policed by full-backs Mike Haughney and Frank Meechan, and the half finished with the Dons having slightly the better of things in midfield, but not enough to create a breakthrough.

But a goal came early in the second half and it was a tragedy for Aberdeen's centre-half Alec YOUNG. Neil Mochan made ground on the left and sent in a low drive across the penalty area, and the ball cannoned off the luckless centre-half into the net past an astonished Fred Martin. Yet scarcely had the roars of acclaim died down from the green and white rainbow at the far end of the ground, than Aberdeen were level. A long ball from defence found Hamilton who headed on to Paddy BUCKLEY who for the first time in the game got the better of Stein, beating him for pace (as he was always likely to do) and firing past John Bonnar.

One flash of brilliance was enough to win this final fought between two evenly matched teams and this was when Willie Fernie went on a mazy run down the left, drawing several defenders towards him, then crossing a brilliant ball for Sean FALLON to score what must have been the easiest goal of them all.

Once again the green and white roar took over Hampden Park, but there was a long way to go, the best part of half an hour to hold out against this talented Dons side. Aberdeen pressed forward, but Stein was magnificent against the untiring Buckley. Bonnar, the hero of the Coronation Cup of last year, was once again in fine form, clutching and grabbing high balls, radiating command in the goal and enjoying a perfect understanding with his defenders.

At the other end, Charlie Tully would treat the crowd to some dribbles and tricks to use up the time, and full time came with 22 exhausted players shaking hands with each other with Aberdeen players swallowing their disappointment as they congratulated their Celtic counterparts. It was a scene mirrored on the terracing as supporters did likewise. The *Sunday Mail* called both teams a 'credit to the competition', for the standard of their play and their sporting demeanour.

Celtic had now won the double, and on the following Monday night before a meaningless game against Hamilton Accies, the Scottish Cup was paraded in green and white ribbons for the fans to see. It was the 17th time that Celtic had won the Scottish Cup, but those who supposed that this was to be a permanent return to winning ways would be in for a bitter disappointment. Nevertheless, 1954 was a glorious summer.

v **Partick Thistle** 3-0
Scottish League Cup Final Replay,
Hampden, 31 October 1956

CELTIC	PARTICK THISTLE	REFEREE
Beattie	Ledgerwood	Mr J. Mowat,
Haughney	Kerr	Rutherglen
Fallon	Gibb	
Evans	Collins	
Jack	Crawford	
Peacock	Mathers	
Tully	McKenzie	
Collins	Wright	
McPhail	Hogan	
Fernie	McParland	
Mochan	Ewing	

THE SCOTTISH League Cup and Celtic had not been good bedfellows since that trophy's inception at the end of the Second World War. It had originally been a war time trophy called the Southern League Cup, and became an official trophy in season 1946/47. It was normally competed for at the start of the season, and Celtic, traditionally poor starters to a campaign, had never done well. Incredible as it may seem, a whole decade had passed without Celtic having even been in the final (and only once in the semi-final) until season 1956/57. During this time East Fife had won the trophy three times and Dundee twice!

But season 1956/57 had begun well. The team had lost the Scottish Cup Final the previous April in an astonishing and bewilderingly lacklustre performance to Hearts, and perhaps the club felt that the supporters were owed at least something to cheer about. It was not that the team lacked talent. Indeed there were at Parkhead players the equal of and perhaps better than previous generations, but they seemed to lack direction, were infuriatingly inconsistent and had a particular and distressing tendency to 'bottle' the big, important occasions.

The League Cup was played on a sectional basis, and Celtic, playing good football, won a strong section of Aberdeen, East Fife and Rangers. The tightness of the section could be seen however in an analysis of the results. Celtic won five out of their six games by a single goal margin and the sixth game was a 0-0 draw with Rangers. They thus qualified for the quarter-finals where they waltzed past Dunfermline and then got the better of Clyde in the semi-final to set up a final appearance against Partick Thistle.

Celtic had recently changed McPhails. On virtually the same day that John, a big, lumbering disappointment (not without his moments, but far too injury prone) went out the door, his younger brother Billy, a slimmer more athletic version, came in, and it was Billy who had scored the two goals against Clyde in the semi-final. At centre-half, replacing Jock Stein who had never really recovered from a bad ankle injury a year previously, was a young man of Lithuanian descent called John Jack. This would be Jack's moment of glory in his brief Celtic career.

The first game of the final was played on Saturday 27 October and was a massive disappointment to the Celtic fans in the 58,794 crowd. It was a 0-0 draw, and if anything Partick Thistle had come closer to breaking the deadlock than Celtic – and that was in spite of playing with only ten men, for their inside-right Smith was taken off injured. It was one of those days when Celtic supporters began to wonder why their team, with so many fine players, could play so badly and whether there was some sort of jinx or hoodoo on them ever winning the Scottish League Cup. The more cynical pointed out that the replay would bring another large attendance. In this respect, however, they were wrong, for in terms of atmosphere, this was a strange cup final.

The replay was scheduled for Wednesday 31 October at Hampden with a 2.15 pm kick-off, and it was played with the backdrop of an international calamity with Great Britain apparently on the point of invading Egypt in what became known as the Suez Crisis. Israel and Egypt had already been at war for two days, and Great Britain was about to side with Israel (an unlikely combination, perhaps, but they were both united in their hatred of Egypt). It was hardly coincidental that the Soviet Union was taking action at this time (when the attention of the West was diverted elsewhere) to crush a rebellion against their dictatorship in Hungary where the great Hungarian footballer Ferenc Puskas, who had attracted widespread attention and praise in the World Cup of 1954, was rumoured to be one of those put to death. He wasn't, in fact, and he went on to play brilliantly for Real Madrid in years to come.

In these circumstances, it was hardly surprising that a meagre crowd of only 31,156 appeared for the replay. By the standards of the 1950s, this was poor for a cup final, and could only partly be explained away by the world crisis and the afternoon kick-off. (The following week, double that amount – 62,035 – would appear at the same ground to see Scotland v Northern Ireland). The real reason for the poor crowd was the indifference of the Celtic crowd. It was not a boycott, exactly, but a decision deliberately taken by supporters. They reckoned that taking a day off work, possibly losing one's job, was simply not worth the risk to see such a poor performance as they had seen in the first game.

But Bob Kelly or Jimmy McGrory or whoever picked the team made one wise decision. That was the re-introduction of Neil Mochan. Mochan 'the Smiler' was never consistently given a run in the team, yet when he did play, he was very often the talisman required. He was a fine forward and scorer of goals, but his face never quite fitted at Parkhead. Playing him that day instead of the unpredictable and frequently disappointing Jimmy Walsh and the subsequent re-jigging of the forward line proved to be Celtic's salvation.

Partick Thistle, managed by ex-Ranger Davie Meiklejohn, an inveterate foe of Jimmy McGrory and Celtic, also had to change their team. Smith, injured on Saturday, had to be replaced but a more serious blow was sustained when centre-half and captain Jimmy Davidson, who had been one of the few stars of the game on the Saturday, had to be withdrawn because he still had stitches in his head wound. Yet Thistle supporters remained confident that this could be their day. The Jags were commonly referred to as 'The Unpredictables' because their supporters never knew where they were with them. But of course the same thing could have been said in 1956 about Celtic.

The crowd was of course small in a huge stadium, but it did grow throughout the first half as quite a few schoolboys in school uniform began to appear about half-time. Clearly some schools had decided to turn a blind eye to a little absenteeism – but perhaps not. Perhaps a good belting with the tawse would follow the following morning! In addition, as shifts ended, more and more men appeared with piece bags. These were men who had been working since about five or six in the morning, and it was a clear indication of the feeling and love that some people still held for the club. They would receive some sort of reward that day.

The first half was a far better, more urgent performance than Saturday's had been, but still lacked the inspiration that Celtic fans demanded of their team. They started off playing towards the under-populated King's Park end, and with Collins and Fernie in the inside-forward positions and feeding the fast young McPhail, one would have expected a goal before half-time, but although Celtic were far more technically proficient than they had been on the Saturday, they could not break through the Thistle defence in which reserve centre-half Crawford was playing a blinder. It was not that Celtic overwhelmed Thistle, however, for the Maryhill men also had their moments. Yet the longer the game went on, young Jack at centre-half seemed to settle. As the lacklustre first half came to an end, it began to look as if the side which scored the first goal would win the game.

But then in a ten-minute spell at the start of the second half, Celtic showed the small crowd just exactly what they were capable of. The first goal came from Neil Mochan who made ground on the left and passed to Billy McPHAIL who evaded the challenge of Crawford and hooked the ball over goalkeeper Legerwood who had been caught in no-man's-land. It was a fine goal, and was followed a couple of minutes later by another as Mochan, on the right wing this time, crossed for McPHAIL to score a crisp goal. This was the stuff that the fans had been waiting for, and eight minutes later, any chance that Thistle might have had of a comeback vanished when Celtic scored again. This time it was Bobby Evans, injured a few minutes earlier and put on the right wing in order to recover (as often happened in the 1950s) passed to Bobby COLLINS who may have been marginally offside. Certainly the Thistle defence thought so, for they froze as if waiting for the whistle, as the 'wee barra' ran on and scored the third goal.

All this before the hour mark had been reached, and the game was over. Those who came into the ground late in the second half hoping to see a little of the action were to be disappointed as Celtic now killed the game stone dead and Thistle lacked anyone who could bring them back into the game. Credit was due to the fine performance of John Jack who thus deserved his first ever and indeed only cup medal. The game finished with the minuscule Celtic support in good voice, for they were now destined to see green and white ribbons on this League Cup. Even before the final whistle went, Thistle manager Davie Meiklejohn had been seen to shake hands with his old opponent and good friend Jimmy McGrory, now puffing away contentedly at his pipe.

Thus it was that Bobby Evans, now recovered from his injury, collected the Scottish League Cup for the first time, but Jim Rodger of the *Daily Record* was unimpressed. 'No doubt Celts are in seventh heaven over this victory – but they cannot be happy about the way they achieved it. They were a patchy, poor imitation of the great cup-winning Parkhead teams of the past.' Maybe so, but it was at least a start to this particular trophy. There would be many more winnings of this trophy in years to come, but the first was always an important one, and it killed off any sort of hoodoo that might have been believed to exist. Next year would see a far better and more famous triumph, but this one was at least something to be going on with.

'Euphoria' and 'rapture' and indeed Jim Rodger's 'seventh heaven' would perhaps be an exaggeration in describing the emotions of the support as they stood among the autumn leaves in the crepuscular mellow light as darkness slowly fell over the queue for the trains at Mount Florida station that Hallowe'en evening, but there was a certain contentment. It certainly went a little way to redeem Celtic for their awful performances in this tournament up to this point, and indeed for the Scottish Cup Final fiasco against Hearts the previous April.

The world crisis ended almost as soon as it began with Britain and France committing a few dastardly deeds against the Egyptians, then realising that they were earning almost universal worldwide condemnation for so doing and having to withdraw. They tried to claim a victory, but impressed no-one, and Prime Minister Sir Anthony Eden suffered a nervous breakdown and was compelled to resign.

v Rangers 7-1
Scottish League Cup Final, Hampden
19 October 1957

CELTIC	RANGERS	REFEREE
Beattie	Niven	Mr J. Mowat,
Donnelly	Shearer	Rutherglen
Fallon	Caldow	
Fernie	McColl	
Evans	Valentine	
Peacock	Davis	
Tully	Scott	
Collins	Simpson	
McPhail	Murray	
Wilson	Baird	
Mochan	Hubbard	

THIS GAME is probably the most talked about and written about in Celtic domestic history, rivalled only by the European Cup Final of a decade later. Obviously who the opponents were is one of the reasons, another is the extent and the scale of it all and yet another is the sheer unexpectedness of the result. It was generally believed in autumn 1957 that Celtic were perhaps marginally the better team of the two Glasgow giants (they had already beaten Rangers 3-2 in the league a month previously) but on the morning of the game, most newspapers were predicting a tight encounter with extra time and a replay strong possibilities.

Celtic had suffered from what might be termed a 'domestic dispute' on the Thursday before the final when the normally very cool Bobby Evans and the mercurial Charlie Tully had come to blows over an article that Tully had written in a newspaper concerning a recent game between Scotland and Northern Ireland in which Evans had been indirectly criticised.

Two weeks before the League Cup Final on 5 October, Evans had played in a miserable 1-1 draw for Scotland against Northern Ireland. It was generally admitted that this had not been a great performance by Evans (nor indeed anyone else in the Scottish team), but things were hardly helped when Tully (not playing in that game) said in his 'Tullyvision' column of the *Evening Citizen* of Saturday 12 October that only two Scottish players would ever be likely to be considered for a Great Britain team, namely Younger and Parker. 'The rest lack class.'

There is a suggestion that this feud had been simmering for some time, for both men were of different temperaments, with Evans, the hardworking professional, becoming increasingly frustrated by Tully's overuse of the ball and general playing to the gallery. Indeed the previous summer Evans had lost the captaincy of the club to Bertie Peacock, and it may have been that his inability to get on with Tully would have been one of the reasons.

However that may be, the two men had to be separated and the diplomatic skills of captain Bertie Peacock were pressed into service. Peacock had of course played in the game in question for Northern Ireland and was able to laugh it off, saying things like 'I'm glad Charlie didn't say anything about me! I was the worst player on the park!' Half-hearted apologies were said, hands were grudgingly shaken and the promise was made that there would be no more of it, at least until Saturday's game was over. Peacock did well to hush this up, but inevitably the story leaked out and, Glasgow being Glasgow, grew arms and legs.

Such things do, of course, happen at football clubs. Tully in his book *Passed To You*, published about a year later, gives a candid account of the incident, but it is in a chapter, the first paragraph of which reads: 'I've seen some good players in my time at Celtic Park – played with and against them – and without question the best of the lot is Bobby Evans.' Tully, while admitting that Evans was by no means his best buddy, goes out of his way to praise the commitment and professionalism of the man who was generally regarded as being one of Scotland's best players in the 1950s. The spat certainly had no effect on the way either of them played in the League Cup Final.

Celtic's form had been good. The previous year's winners of the League Cup, they had qualified from the sectional stage with only one defeat – and that was at the difficult venue of Easter Road – and then they had beaten Glasgow opposition in Third Lanark and Clyde to reach the final. The form of some players had been encouraging. Bobby Collins who had had a difficult patch previously was now in top gear for both Celtic and Scotland, and the move of Willie Fernie to right-half was a stroke of genius, for he loved the midfield position where his visionary passing was put to good effect. Evans, previously a brilliant right-half while Jock Stein was centre-half, had now settled into the position vacated by Jock where he was immense. 'Evans, as usual, was superb' was the much-used cliché of the writers of the *Evening Citizen* and the *Evening Times*.

And it was beginning to be thought of by the ever-optimistic Celtic supporters that the new McGrory had been found in Billy McPhail. He was fast, hard-working and played with the elan that betokened a man who enjoyed his football. Beside him was Sammy Wilson, a quiet but grimly determined man who enjoyed the nickname of 'Slammin' Sammy' and who had joined the club in the summer from the unlikely source of a free transfer from St Mirren. On the left wing, just edging the spot ahead of the precocious young Bertie Auld, was Neil Mochan, the 'cannonball kid', that grossly undervalued player whose presence often made all the difference.

Scotland was in the throes of a flu epidemic in October 1957 and this is why the crowd was only 82,293 when six figures might have been expected for the first national cup final between Celtic and Rangers since 1928. The weather was fine and autumnal as the game kicked off at 2.45 pm, slightly earlier than normal, to allow for the possibility of extra time. Party songs were inevitably sung by both sets of supporters as they queued at the turnstiles, but so too was one of the current 'hits' – Paul Anka singing 'Oh, please, stay by me, Diana.'

This game turned out to be a personal disaster for Rangers' centre-half John Valentine. Rangers had struggled to find a centre-half since the *sine die* suspension of Willie Woodburn in 1954 and the retirement of George Young. Valentine had been recruited from the unlikely sources of Buckie Thistle, Queen's Park and the Army, and would struggle this day. But he was by no means the only culprit for the full-backs stayed obsessively in their wings to counteract the threats of Tully and Mochan even when it became obvious that the big problem was down the middle. In addition, the much-admired Ian McColl simply had an off day, and Korean War veteran Harold Davis was never in the game.

On the other hand, no team on earth could have lived with Celtic that day. It was quite simply one of those days when everything went right for Celtic, and made the supporters realise that Celtic could be a world-class side. The best team on earth in 1957 was apparently Real Madrid. Celtic might have disputed that claim that day. The wonder was that Rangers got off with going in at half-time only 0-2 down. It should have been a lot more as wave after wave of Celtic attacks poured down on that King's Park end goal to the delight of their own fans, hitting the woodwork on several occasions and scoring when WILSON drove home a McPhail header and then when MOCHAN scored with a screamer just on half-time.

Yet the mood at the Celtic End at half-time, though upbeat and noisy, was tinged with a little anxiety as well. Surely Rangers would stage some sort of fightback? In truth it was difficult to see where such a revival could come from, for Rangers had been absolutely overrun in all departments. But Celtic had rather too often in the past pressed the self-destruct button and could do so again. There was a feeling that this couldn't last. It was so good. But clearly their counterparts at the other end of the ground did not fancy their side's chances of a revival, for they spent the interval throwing bottles at the police and fighting each other!

Celtic, now playing towards the Rangers end began where they had left off, with McPHAIL heading home a Collins cross. Then the torch of a Rangers revival did flicker briefly when Billy SIMPSON scored with a good header on the hour mark, but it was only the briefest momentary ray of hope for the Ibrox faithful, because Celtic once again took command, and ten minutes after Simpson had scored, McPHAIL added his second when he was on hand to squeeze home a Wilson drive which the Rangers defence could only parry. That was now 4-1 and the Rangers End, realising the game was up, began to empty, thus avoiding more torture for themselves.

There was simply no stopping the green and white tide. Number five came in the 75th minute with a MOCHAN piledriver which left Niven and the rest of the Rangers defence rooted to the spot, and then came possibly the best goal of the lot when McPHAIL, now oozing confidence, ran almost the whole length of the Rangers half to complete his hat-trick, leaving the luckless John Valentine nowhere in sight.

That made it six, and the Celtic End was now a sea of delirium and included the frenetic waving of an Irish tricolour which was technically banned from public display at Rangers v Celtic matches but which the police made no attempt to seize. Then just on the full-time whistle, Celtic made it seven. Bobby Shearer ('Captain Cutlass' as they affectionately called him) who had hardly had a kick of the ball all afternoon, downed McPhail. A more compassionate referee than Jack Mowat might have waved play on, but grimly and relentlessly fair as always, he awarded a spot kick which Willie FERNIE slotted away.

Thus ended Celtic's second most famous victory (the European Cup Final of 1967 beats it, but not by much!). It is one of the few games which has merited having a book written about it on its own. Several songs were written about it (one sharing its title with the book called *Oh Hampden·In the Sun*) and of course it created the myth that the BBC were irreconcilably anti-Celtic.

There was of course some truth in this for BBC Scotland were for a long time notorious for their reluctance to employ Roman Catholics. Peter Thomson, the BBC commentator, would admit to being a Rangers fan and enjoyed the nickname of 'Blue Peter', his demeanour and countenance often giving away the score of a Rangers game before he actually said it! But on this occasion it was a mistake by BBC London where a technician forgot to remove a lens cap from a camera, and the whole BBC record of the game was lost. Or so they said... Not that it really mattered to Celtic fans, for they were in dreamland for the next few weeks, but it is a shame that the only record of the game is an amateurish and rudimentary one from an old-fashioned cine camera.

But there is a tragedy here as well. This was Celtic at their best. It was arguably the only occasion when that immensely talented side all played to their full potential to show the world what life could have been like. As it was, that team imploded almost immediately after, winning nothing else in the 1957/58 season and indeed nothing else until 1965. It became an almost pathetic riposte to the jeers of Rangers fans who spent the early 1960s mocking Celtic for their dreadful performances, that all we had was this game to harp back to. But it was a good one...

v Rangers 3-1

Scottish League, Celtic Park
5 September 1964

CELTIC	RANGERS	REFEREE
Fallon	Ritchie	Mr H. Phillips, Wishaw
Young	Hynd	
Gemmell	Provan	
Brogan	Greig	
Cushley	McKinnon	
Clark	Baxter	
Johnstone	Henderson	
Divers	McLean	
Chalmers	Forrest	
Gallagher	Brand	
Hughes	Wilson	

1964 HAD been a bad year for Celtic. Rangers had won a domestic treble, and Celtic had often seemed paralysed in the face of them, even at times when Celtic were the better team. There seemed to be some divine law that Rangers had to win – and the infuriating thing was that Celtic seemed to believe it as well. Each of the five games against Rangers in 1963/64 followed the same miserable pattern of Celtic being on top for the first half-hour, yet failing to capitalise on pressure, then something unfortunate happening in the shape of a defensive error or a refereeing decision, Celtic going all to pieces and subsiding woefully in the second half. Yet Celtic were not a bad team. 1964 had seen an immeasurable improvement from 1963. In April 1964 they had even reached the semi-final of the European Cup Winners' Cup where they had gone 3-0 up in the first leg to a Hungarian side called MTK before collapsing miserably in Budapest and naïvely blaming everything on the referee – as if they expected anything else in Europe!

Thus summer 1964 had not been any easier than the previous ten summers, but the start of the season had seen a distinct improvement in that the team qualified from a difficult League Cup section of Hearts, Kilmarnock and Partick Thistle, playing some good attractive football and scoring plenty of goals with Steve Chalmers in particular impressing everyone with his speed and ability to be in the right place at the right time for the passes from Divers, Murdoch or Johnstone. There was even a spectacular, although ill-thought out, attempt to sign Alfredo di Stefano from Real Madrid! Jimmy McGrory flew to Spain with Spanish teacher John Cushley (the reserve centre-half) to talk to the great man. Sadly Cushley was only able to talk to him on the telephone, had problems with his Argentinian accent, and the whole thing was a distinct failure.

It was however a good exercise in knocking Rangers off the back pages for a few days, and in any case in the form of the team there was enough cause for optimism to justify the *Scottish Daily Express*'s contention that it was 'Stevie, not Steffie' who could solve all Celtic's problems, such was the prolific goalscoring of the gentlemanly Steve Chalmers who in his demeanour and behaviour reminded everyone so much of Jimmy McGrory himself.

But everyone was well aware that this team which had started the season so well had not yet met the cause of the previous year's psychiatric disorder. The first game of the season between the two big Glasgow rivals was scheduled for 5 September at Parkhead, but before then Celtic had the misfortune to run into a vindictive Kilmarnock side at Rugby Park in a meaningless League Cup fixture. The section had been won by Celtic on the previous Wednesday night when Hearts had been put to the sword to the tune of 6-1 (and that was with Chalmers having an off night and not scoring!).

Willie Waddell's Kilmarnock were, frankly, a disgrace that day and a stronger referee might well have even abandoned the game, such was the ferocity of the tackles. The motivation seemed to be little other than sheer spite and revenge. McNeill and Murdoch were both carried off, with McNeill badly injured and likely to be out for a considerable part of the season. Destiny now crooked a finger and called to the Hispanist John Cushley to show that he would be more successful at preventing Rangers from scoring than he had been at persuading di Stefano to come to Celtic!

But there were other problems as well, and young Jim Brogan had to be drafted in too. He had a brother Frank who was now with Ipswich (having foolishly been allowed to go when quite a few old timers saw a bit of the old-fashioned Frank Murphy/Adam McLean type of left-winger there) but Jim was an unknown quantity to most of the Parkhead crowd who gathered in the rain to see what everyone realised was going to be a very important game in Celtic history. They really had to beat Rangers sometime or else accept permanent second-best status and admit that the 'inferiority complex' was justified. (This phrase was the buzz word of the 1960s and much used by educational psychologists to explain underachievement in the classroom. In later years it would become 'low self-esteem'.)

Of more immediate concern to the fans that September day was the rain. It pelted down all morning, and it said a great deal for the Parkhead drainage system that the game was never in doubt. But those of us who ventured into the old Jungle were soon very aware of its deficiencies with the holes in the roof, and decided that the 'Celtic End' or the 'Railway End' with the shelter that annoyingly only covered half the terracing was a better bet.

The rain however was good news for Celtic and for one player in particular – big John Hughes, the man who divided the support more than any other player. He was a great player on his day but his day didn't necessarily come round all that often. Yet he was a good 'bad weather' player in both ice and rain, as indeed was John Divers, a fine distributor of the ball but a little on the slow side. But the rain slowed other players down as well and John often revelled in the wet.

Celtic started off playing towards the Rangers end of the ground (where there was no shelter at all), and clearly started with the intention of attacking. Within five minutes the ground erupted in joy as John Hughes ran the length of the Rangers half, having got the better of Rodger Hynd and scored what looked like a brilliant goal only to have it chalked off for a mysterious infringement on the halfway line by referee Hugh Phillips. This was cruel for it had looked to be a great goal, and we wondered what effect this might have on the sometimes emotionally insecure 'Yogi Bear', as he was lovingly called by his supporters.

It had little effect, for Hughes continued to rampage past Hynd as if he didn't exist, and with Jimmy Johnstone equally on song on the other wing, Celtic fans were in rare good voice with the much vaunted Jim Baxter unable to make any impact at all on the Celtic midfield. But then desolation settled over the Celtic end again as Celtic missed a penalty. It was Charlie Gallagher who took it, beating the goalkeeper but only to see the ball hit the post and rebound out to the far side of the field, as Celtic once again began to wonder whether there was some cosmic influence at work to guarantee that Celtic would never beat Rangers.

But then with half-time approaching, Celtic did go ahead. Some fine work involving Hughes and Divers found Jimmy Johnstone who crossed low and hard and found the diving head of Steve CHALMERS. It was a great goal, and greatly celebrated by the Celtic end who thus spent the half-time interval with much song, joy and laughter. If the team could continue to play like this, Celtic would win comfortably. But this was 1964, a year in which nothing could be taken for granted.

And yet how nice it was to see at the other end the silent, morose fans, their blue scarves wrapped round their heads to ward off the incessant Glasgow rain, gazing sullenly and impotently at the green and white rainbows of colours of the Celtic fans. A more ominous and threatening sight was the glint of glass in the air, the terracing opening to allow the police in and the dragging away of some scrofulous, misshapen, despicable character whose frustration had caused him to throw beer bottles in rage … at his own fans at the bottom of the terracing! The Celtic supporters roared their approval of the police action and suggested unlikely and extreme punishments for such behaviour.

The one-way traffic continued in the second half, as Celtic, now playing towards their own fans, revelled in the conditions, with John Divers in particular playing one of his best games for the club, distributing passes to both wingers – the diminutive Johnstone and the burly Hughes who were creating havoc on each flank. The second goal came in the 50th minute from Johnstone who had a great run down the wing and crossed for CHALMERS to score again. The bedlam of noise and dancing had not yet died down when Celtic were three up as HUGHES charged down his wing, cut inside, beat a man or two then hit a shot, not in all honesty as crisply as he would have liked, but Billy Ritchie in the Rangers goal allowed the wet ball to slip through his hands into the net.

By the time that the BBC Home Service joined the game at 4.10 pm Celtic were thus three goals up and their supporters were in full song. At the Celtic end the crowd danced and sang, as total strangers embraced and hugged each other and all the old favourite songs about Charlie Tully 'Putting on the agony, putting on the style' mingled with 'Sure it's a grand old team to play for' and rebel songs like 'We will cha-a-nt the soldier's song' came thundering out.

The terracing at the far end was like a cake crumbling as supporters deserted in droves. One could not really blame them for they must have been very wet across there. For once, they were the team that had been humiliated, they were the people who could not bear to stand and watch what was happening, they were going to be the ones who would change the subject when football was mentioned! One would recall the Irish rebel song of Barry's Flying Column which went:

Oh, but isn't great to see
The Tommies and the RIC
The Black and Tans and Staters flee
Away from Barry's Column!

But the game was not of course finished, and indeed the Celtic end was forced to have a collective intake of breath when Davie WILSON pulled one back, but that was already well within the last ten minutes, and although Celtic fans were glad to hear the final whistle, the truth was that Rangers were a beaten team, on the wrong end of their first defeat from Celtic for four years in national competition. And, oh how it hurt!

The significance of this game was that Celtic could now beat Rangers. The unfortunate thing was that they didn't keep doing it, and threw away the opportunity almost as quickly as they had grabbed it. Incredibly on the following Wednesday, Celtic went to Methil and lost to Second Division East Fife in the League Cup quarter-final first leg (fortunately they repaired the damage in the second leg) and then in one of the most tragic days of them all, went down 1-2 to Rangers in the League Cup Final in October. Once again the death wish had taken over, and Celtic were not 'allowed' to beat Rangers.

But the punters who marched proudly along the Gallowgate that wet night on 5 September 1964 with their banners flying in the breeze were not to know that. They had beaten Rangers, and the talk was already of a league and cup double. The *Daily Record* caught this mood saying that this might be Celtic's year, singling out Jimmy Johnstone and deputy captain Jim Kennedy who had had an excellent game at left-back for special praise and quoting Jimmy McGrory as saying that 'Celtic did not have a single failure'.

It was as well that no-one knew what the winter would bring, but things had to get worse before they could get better. The Stein revolution was just round the corner but this result guaranteed that some players at least knew what it was like to beat Rangers.

v **Dunfermline** 3-2

Scottish Cup Final, Hampden
24 April 1965

CELTIC	DUNFERMLINE	REFEREE
Fallon	Herriot	Mr H. Phillips, Wishaw
Young	W. Callaghan	
Gemmell	Lunn	
Murdoch	Thomson	
McNeill	McLean	
Clark	T. Callaghan	
Chalmers	Edwards	
Gallagher	Smith	
Hughes	McLaughlin	
Lennox	Melrose	
Auld	Sinclair	

SUPPORTING CELTIC was not easy in 1965. Life was grim for the lovers of the great side who had now watched seven years go by without a major honour, and 11 years since the lifting of the Scottish Cup. These barren years had been full of heartbreaks – four Scottish Cup finals had been lost (incredibly, the common factor being a faulty team selection) – but the really disappointing thing was that, apart from 1955, the team had never been really in contention for the Scottish League. The 1964/65 season had seen the team reach the final of the Scottish League Cup in October (some nine days after Harold Wilson's Labour Party had won the 1964 General Election and a sign perhaps that things were changing) but after much 'bubble and squeak' (as a supporters' handbook put it) in the first half the team lost two goals to the professional Rangers in the second half, and although Celtic pulled one back, luck was simply not with them.

Depression now reigned and the collapse immediately after that was far more profound than anyone could have anticipated, for Celtic went into freefall, losing to teams like Kilmarnock, St Johnstone, Dundee, Dunfermline, Rangers, Dundee United and Hearts before, at the end of January, chairman Bob Kelly admitted that he had been wrong all along and appointed Jock Stein to the manager's job.

Stein, of course, had a proven record at Dunfermline and Hibs, and had been Celtic's captain a decade earlier when they last won the Scottish Cup. He had then played a part in Celtic's youth policy by bringing on players like McNeill, Crerand, Clark and others. A few mischievous journalists tried to make capital out of the fact that he was a Protestant. Such attempts failed, for a man's religion never cut any ice with anyone at Celtic Park. The important thing was whether Stein could bring any success and silverware to the fans, some of whom in that dreadful winter of 1964/65 had given every sign that they had had enough and they would find something else to do on a Saturday afternoon.

Stein was appointed at the end of January but did not take up office until the beginning of March. By this time, although league form continued to be haphazard and unpredictable, some progress had been made in the Scottish Cup with the defeat, of St Mirren and Queen's Park. And then on 6 March, the very eve of Jock's arrival, Celtic reached the semi-final with a good win over Kilmarnock at Parkhead while Jock Stein, in his very last game as manager of Hibs, dealt his new club a huge favour by disposing of Rangers with a late goal.

Thus in the semi-finals, Celtic faced Motherwell and Hibs played Dunfermline. Dunfermline beat Hibs while Celtic struggled to draw with Motherwell before disposing of them in the replay. Thus it was Dunfermline, and Celtic fans had bitter memories of 1961, of that awful night at a drizzly and dull Hampden when Celtic pounded and bombarded the goal of Celtic supporter Eddie Connachan – but could not score, and the cup went to Fife. But this time there was a key difference – and he was called Jock Stein, then with Dunfermline but now with Celtic.

In the run up to the cup final, Celtic's league form became even more sporadic and unpredictable. They lost to St Johnstone at Parkhead, they lost to Hibs at Parkhead, they beat Hibs at Easter Road, they received a real thumping at Falkirk, and the week before the final lost at home to Partick Thistle before a miserable crowd of 11,000 with the rest of the supporters clearly saving their money for the following week's cup final.

This was dire stuff, but Stein was experimenting. In the lucky position of knowing for certain that even a defeat of the most substantial proportions would not lose him his job – for he was only recently appointed – he tried various ideas for the final. In particular, he hit on the idea that many fans had felt for a long time, namely that Bobby Murdoch, a sadly underperforming inside-forward would make a world class right-half. Moreover, he considered that the talented Jimmy Johnstone was not quite there yet, that John Fallon was the best available goalkeeper, that the forward line should revolve around Bertie Auld, and that John Divers, Jim Kennedy and Hugh Maxwell should not be considered for the final.

Meanwhile the more prescient and perspicacious of the support picked up one thing, which was the form of the team was poor, but what about Dunfermline? The week before the final they could more or less have won themselves the Scottish League, but could only draw at home with St Johnstone. In other words it seemed they couldn't win when they had to! Centre-forward Alex Ferguson had had a bad day and was dropped for the Scottish Cup Final. Was pressure telling on them and their Northern Irish manager Willie Cunningham? Already that season, Rangers had collapsed under the media campaign orchestrated by Stein himself about what Celtic were going to do in the next few years. Would Dunfermline also crack under this propaganda onslaught?

On the day of the game itself, in the lunchtime edition of the 'Souvenir Special' in the *Evening Citizen*, Stein delivered his final volley by saying that there would be changes at Parkhead, 'even if, by some unkind quirk of fate, the Cup is not wearing green and white ribbons to-night'. It was a way of telling supporters that whatever was going to happen, it would be good for Celtic.

The crowd of 108,806 probably contained 90,000 Celtic supporters. Dunfermline supporters were in the minority to that extent, and there were as always in these days a smattering of neutrals who just happened to like football. How long could these 90,000 wait? There was clear desperation as well as optimism in the air. 'We'll forgive everything, Celtic, everything – as long as we win the day!' screeched a man with a face that looked as if he had a lot to forgive.

Celtic started playing towards the King's Park end of the ground where most of their supporters were congregated. It was the Pars who drew first blood in the 15th minute when the veteran Harry MELROSE hooked a ball into the net after some hesitation in the Celtic defence. The support sank into depression, but soon rallied for there was a long time to go, and it was now that the wisdom in bringing back Bertie Auld from Birmingham City (almost at the same time as Stein arrived and it was said on Stein's suggestion, even though he was still manager of Hibs) became apparent. A pass was picked up in midfield by Charlie Gallagher, one the most under-rated players in Scottish football at the time. Charlie was a visionary passer, but also had a mighty shot. He fired the ball from about 30 yards; it looked a winner, but hit the bar. Scarcely had the groans of disappointment died away when it was noticed that the ball had gone straight up into the air, and was blown back by the capricious Hampden wind into play and the alert Bertie AULD rushed in to head home, ending up in the back of the net himself in doing so.

1-1, but then just on half-time Dunfermline went ahead again, thanks in part to the loudspeaker announcer who clearly did not see what was going on. A free kick from Melrose was passed to John McLaughlin, the loudspeaker burst into action, the Celtic defence momentarily hesitated and McLAUGHLIN fired the ball past the diving Fallon whose concentration had clearly been affected.

Half-time was thus passed in melancholic silence tempered by the thought that Jock Stein must have something up his sleeve for the second half. But all Stein said was 'Keep going. You might get the breaks yet!' Indeed they did, for early in the second half came the best developed goal of the game with a fine one-two involving Bobby Lennox and Bertie AULD who levelled for Celtic for the second time in the game.

Battle now raged for all the second half. Fallon had two fine saves from Edwards and McLaughlin, and then there was a moment when John Clark cleared off the line in a slightly unorthodox way as the ball rolled up his body before disappearing over the bar. At the other end Chalmers and Gallagher came close for Celtic, while in the centre John Hughes, although by no means at his best, was a constant source of concern for the Dunfermline defence.

As the game entered the last ten minutes, it looked as if a draw and a replay the following Wednesday was to be the outcome, but then Celtic won themselves a corner kick on the stand side of the ground. Across trotted Charlie Gallagher to take it. The Dunfermline defence, well marshalled as always by Harry Melrose, stood firm, with every Celtic forward marked. But then from halfway inside the Dunfermline half Billy McNeill began his run for his appointment with destiny. Charlie sent over a hard ball, and McNEILL charged forward, almost knocking Bobby Lennox out of the way, and headed home what was perhaps the most signifi-cant goal in Celtic's history.

From high on the terracing at the other end of the field, it looked as if it might have been Tommy Gemmell who scored, but McNeill it was and the crowd erupted in a way seldom seen even in Hampden's long history. But a long nine minutes remained. Words fail the chronicler as he tries to recall the agony of these nine minutes – begging the game just to finish there and then, cheering every time a Celtic player kicked a ball upfield, smiling when a throw-in was given for Celtic, groaning with fear and anxiety whenever the worthy Dunfermline side crossed the halfway line, looking at referee Hugh Phillips as he signalled to his linesmen, trying hard not to think of the previous 11 years of low self-esteem and the unhappy childhood that had been our lot, beseeching the clock to go round, praying to God (or even to Satan if necessary) just to let us win...

It was Mr Phillips who decided that Celtic had won their 18th Scottish Cup Final, and joy was unconfined. Harry Andrews of the *Scottish Daily Express* put it brilliantly when he wrote: 'This is not the Hampden Roar. It is charged with deeply felt personal emotions. It is choked with the wonderful relief that ends years of frustration ... Parkhead is Paradise once more.'

A man who had 20 years earlier played a glorious part in the liberation of Italy from the Fascist jackals said in measured tones that he had never seen anything like this, and the memory abides of the man, totally sober and dressed in a soft hat, shirt and dignified tie – a lawyer perhaps, or a teacher, certainly an educated and professional man – collapsing over a hedge in Aitkenhead Road and telling the world, quietly and without a single word of foul language, 'I couldn't have stood it, if we had lost today!'

v Dundee United 4-0

Scottish League, Tannadice Park
25 August 1965

CELTIC	DUNDEE UNITED	REFEREE
Fallon	Mackay	Mr R.H. Davidson,
Young	Millar	Airdrie
Gemmell	Briggs	
Murdoch	Munro	
McNeill	Smith	
Clark	Wing	
Chalmers	Carroll	
Divers	Gillespie	
McBride	Dossing	
Lennox	Mitchell	
Gallagher	Persson	

SUMMER 1965 saw Celtic fans on a high that they had not been on for years. They had won the Scottish Cup and the future seemed bright under Jock Stein, whose energetic management made sure that Celtic were never far from the headlines that summer. They had signed Joe McBride from Motherwell, they had arranged a pre-season game at Sunderland (now containing Jim Baxter from Rangers) and had beaten them 5-0. A new newspaper, the *Celtic View*, had been launched, and things had never been so upbeat as they were in that glorious summer of 1965 as the football season was impatiently waited for.

But it had all gone a little pear shaped when the season opened on 14 August. Celtic had been drawn in a League Cup section with Dundee United, Motherwell and Dundee. They would play each of these three teams, then a league match in midweek (and by coincidence this was Dundee United at Tannadice), then they would play the three teams of their League Cup section again, this time with venues reversed.

The season thus opened at Tannadice in glorious weather. Great was the disappointment among the huge travelling support when Dundee United edged it 2-1, a game in which Celtic could feel justified in saying that a draw would have been a fairer result. This was not in itself an irretrievable blow however, and when Celtic beat Motherwell at Parkhead on the Wednesday night 1-0 with a goal from John Divers, things looked as if they were returning to what the pre-season build-up had promised us. It was the following Saturday however when Dundee defied all the odds by winning 2-0 at Celtic Park that we began to wonder whether Celtic were all that they were cracked up to be.

But the league season started, as the League Cup campaign had done, at Tannadice and 18,000 travelled to the game this Wednesday night in which Dundee United were the firm favourites, as they had not only beaten Celtic in the League Cup but had also drawn with Dundee and beaten Motherwell 4-0. There was indeed a touch of arrogance about them, fuelled by the local press, for they were traditionally a difficult team to beat on their own ground, which was so tight and compact with the fans almost on top of the players.

Ten years previously Dundee United had been a poor Second Division team. They owed their rise to several things. One was an energetic manager called Jerry Kerr, the other was the imagination shown by their setting up of a lottery (long before anyone else had this idea) called Taypools, and they also owed a little, in a funny sort of way, to the mediocrity of Celtic in the late 1950s and early 1960s.

The Irish in Dundee had founded their team in 1909 called the Dundee Hibernians. They changed to Dundee United in 1923 but failed to make much impact. As a result, those of Irish descent in Dundee tended to follow Celtic, but when in the late 1950s Celtic began to slide, the Dundee Irish transferred their allegiance back to their own local team, particularly after United's promotion to Division One in 1960 and other signs of ambition like a curious L-shaped stand which was unusual for its day, and indeed the cause of not a little mirth and ridicule, especially when they brought out a song which contained the embarrassing lyrics of

> We've a grand stand
> The finest in the land
> At Tannadice!

Dundee United had held their own (and more than that) in the First Division, and Celtic fans would have a taste of the commitment of the United team in January 1962 when a young and inexperienced Celtic side were 5-1 up at the start of the second half, fatally relaxed and ended up desperately hanging on to get a 5-4 victory! The following year, between the 1963 cup final and its replay, a feckless Celtic team had gone down 0-3 to Dundee United, a result that did absolutely nothing for their confidence and was a contributory cause, one felt, of their annihilation at the hands of Rangers in the replay.

And now this energetic Dundee United club had followed Morton's lead by introducing Scandinavians in Mogens Berg, Lennart Wing, Finn Dossing and Orjan Persson. They had made a difference and Dossing in particular had already given Billy McNeill a hard time on more than one occasion, although it was generally agreed that midfielder Lennart Wing was the best of them all. The optimists in the Dundee United support were already talking about the 'Tannadice terrors' winning their first ever piece of silver this season, something that they felt they needed for they were gnawingly aware that their near neighbours Dundee had won the Scottish League as recently as 1962, and had followed it with a good European run. Celtic and Rangers did not always relish their visits to Tayside.

But this was a different Celtic, a Jock Stein-led Celtic, combining youth with common sense and football knowledge. The reverses sustained had been learned from, and they now knew, if they didn't know it before, that success has to be worked for. Occasionally a blow to the chin has to be taken and recovered from. Sometimes a battle has to be lost if the war is to be won.

Celtic, with a different pair of wingers from Saturday in Stevie Chalmers and Charlie Gallagher, started off playing toward the Shed end of the ground. The Shed of course still exists and is nowadays used by visiting supporters. In 1965 it was all-standing terracing, and the crowd was well mixed, for segregation was not practised in 1965. In any case the two sets of fans normally got on quite well – until this particular Wednesday night when relations turned a little less harmonious.

In the sixth minute Charlie Gallagher rattled the crossbar. That set the pattern of the play, for this was a Celtic side with a point to prove, a Celtic side that was determined to attack. Murdoch, now revelling in his right-half role supplied the ammunition as Celtic, even without the injured Bertie Auld, surged forward in waves to the roars of their appreciative supporters.

It was John DIVERS who opened the scoring in the 15th minute after a sustained spell of Celtic pressure. Supporters often wondered what would be the future for Divers at Parkhead under Jock Stein. He had pointedly been left out of the Scottish Cup Final team the previous April, and it was felt that he lacked pace. Yet he was a great ball player and had now scored twice in the three games that he had played. On this occasion after some neat passing involving himself, Lennox and McBride, he picked up a square ball on the edge of the box, rounded left-back Jimmy Briggs and hammered home a glorious goal.

Half-time came with Celtic still well on top, and the remarkable thing was that they were not further ahead. United had had a few chances as well, but McNeill was clearly well on top of Dossing. Celtic fans noticed that Bobby Carroll, one of the many 'Kelly Kids' who had not made it at Celtic Park, was not having a good game for Dundee United either. Indeed the only Dundee United player to come out of the game with pass marks was the left-back Briggs whose tackling on Steve Chalmers was crisp and fair.

It being the end of August, darkness was now beginning to fall when the second half began and Celtic resumed where they left off. Joe McBRIDE scored his first goal of what would be a sparkling but sadly injury-bedevilled Celtic career, getting the better of Scandinavian Lennart Wing, as he picked up a Gallagher pass on the run and scored with his left foot high into the right-hand corner of the goal.

Celtic continued to sweep forward in a way that cowed the Dundee United fans and awed their own support as they passed mesmerisingly. This was all done at high speed and was a tribute the fitness of the team and the training methods worked out by Jock Stein and Neil Mochan in the pre-season period. 'We all enjoyed training under Jock,' Billy McNeill would say.

A penalty kick was awarded when Lennox was downed in the box by Tommy Millar. Following a little petulance and 'it couldn't have been me' in the Dundee United defence, the ball was given to the ever cool and much underrated Ian YOUNG to do the needful. Young had been with Celtic for a few seasons now with that curious hunch-backed run of his and his ability to tackle 'like a tank', as a veteran of the Desert Army put it.

There followed a sustained period of Celtic pressure with MacKay in inspired form to save a Lennox header, a Chalmers shot and a McBride header. Then the other full-back Tommy GEMMELL got in on the act. Tommy was now developing more and more confidence in the 'overlapping' technique which allowed the full-back to assume an attacking role, and he was well aware of the 'surprise' effect that such a technique could have on a defence. In the 66th minute he found himself on the edge of the box as the ball came to him from a corner kick on the other side. He simply belted it in past an astonished Donald Mackay to put Celtic 4-0 up.

That ended the scoring, although it was only heroic Dundee United defending that kept the score from double figures, so much on top were Celtic. But it was not the end of the action, for Frank Munro, a local Dundee boy but (like so many Dundonians) Celtic-daft, was booked for dissent. (He would eventually get his opportunity to play for Celtic in awful circumstances in the 1977/78 season when he was well past his best. He was a fine player but on this occasion the Celtic forwards were simply too good for him.) Then Orjan Persson (who would in later years play for Rangers) who had made nothing of Ian Young and was trying to see how he would do on the other wing against Tommy Gemmell, was pushed ever so slightly by the ebullient Thomas and took a wild kick at him. He actually failed to make contact with Gemmell, but the attempt had been so violent that the referee Mr Davidson invited him to take the long walk – and with the tunnel in the opposite corner of the park, it was indeed a very long walk at Tannadice that night.

Then the Dundee United fans joined in as well. Forever praised by the local press as being excellent examples of how football fans should behave (as distinct from the 'wild hooligans from Glasgow'), they now decided that they would dent their haloes bestowed upon them by the *Courier* and the *Evening Telegraph* by throwing coins at Tommy Gemmell, John Fallon and a few policemen as hate took over the Shed, while the Celtic fans refused to retaliate. (The *Celtic View* was continuing an anti-hooliganism campaign spearheaded by no less a person than Jock Stein himself.) Instead they looked on with pity and laughter at such pathetic behaviour.

The game finished 4-0, and it was a very good start to the league campaign – two points at Tannadice being traditionally difficult to get – which set Celtic in good stead for the rest of the season, even providing the springboard for them to become unlikely winners of their League Cup section. In that context, it was a very important victory indeed.

25 v **Rangers** 2-1
Scottish League Cup Final, Hampden
23 October 1965

CELTIC	RANGERS	REFEREE
Simpson	Ritchie	Mr H. Phillips, Wishaw
Young	Johansen	
Gemmell	Provan	
Murdoch	Wood	
McNeill	McKinnon	
Clark	Greig	
Johnstone	Henderson	
Gallagher	Willoughby	
McBride	Forrest	
Lennox	Wilson	
Hughes	Johnston	

IT IS one thing to reach the top. It is another to stay there. Celtic fans were learning the truth of these aphorisms in autumn 1965. The Scottish Cup had been won, of course, in glorious style in April, but could Stein's young team retain their ability to produce silver? The League Cup (held sensibly in the 1950s and 1960s in the autumn, before the start of winter) would prove an acid test of whether Celtic's success was transient and illusory or sustained and real.

On at least two occasions it had looked as if Celtic were going out of the League Cup well before the final. At the sectional stage they lost two of their first three games including one at home to Dundee, but then rallied and recovered, beating Dundee United, Motherwell and then qualifying in electrifying style at Dens Park, Dundee in a game forever remembered for a glorious individual goal of big John Hughes.

Then, after Raith Rovers presented few problems in the quarter-final, they came up against Hibs at Ibrox in the semi on a muddy pitch, and with minutes left were 2-1 down and looking as if they were going out. The supporters certainly thought so and were streaming homewards when Tommy Gemmell's piledriver was not adequately dealt with by the Hibs defence and Bobby Lennox squeezed in the rebound. Extra time then failed to produce a winner (although both teams came close), but in the replay everyone wondered what the fuss had been about as the spirited Celtic team won at a canter, 4-0.

This brought, for the second year in a row, a Celtic v Rangers League Cup Final. Around 12 months previously Rangers had won 2-1 (not without some good luck) and had plunged Celtic into the profound depression of that mid winter which had compelled chairman Bob Kelly to appoint Jock Stein as manager. Circumstances had thus changed in the last year at Parkhead, but at Ibrox too things had altered, this time for the worse, as Rangers had had a bad spell in early 1965 and had now decided that Jim Baxter was more trouble than he was worth and had sold him to Sunderland. Their fans were far from happy about that.

Yet for this game odds still tended to favour Rangers, if only because they had won the Ibrox league encounter between the two sides a month previously. On the other hand, we had seen much evidence of really great classic attacking football from Celtic – in the 4-0 defeats of Hibs and Dundee United, a 5-2 win over Hearts, a 7-1 beating of Aberdeen and an 8-1 tanking of the hapless Raith Rovers. This however would be different. It would be a grim struggle for hegemony, with a lot more than the League Cup at stake.

Celtic had beaten Hibs in the semi-final replay on the Monday before the final. Stein, far from congratulating his players on what they had achieved by beating Hibs, tore into his players (according to one barely credible story, slapping his own face vigorously before he went into the dressing room so that he would look red and angry), telling them that all would count for nothing if they did not beat Rangers on Saturday. On the other side of the coin things were different in public with everything all smiles and 'quiet confidence'. In the intervening four days they went onto the offensive in the propaganda stakes. Assistant manager Sean Fallon wrote a piece in the *Scottish Daily Express*, normally pro-Conservative and pro-Rangers, in which he stated quite blandly that he expected with a great deal of confidence that Celtic would win the League Cup. This naturally provoked the Rangers fans into howls of protests, but Celtic's supporters and players had a psychological advantage.

Rangers had already had their confidence undermined when Stein and Celtic had objected to the Ibrox floodlights for their semi-final against Hibs. By the standards of the time there was probably little wrong with them (and indeed the appeal was summarily thrown out by the Scottish League) but it was an excellent time to deal another blow at Rangers whose arrogant description of Ibrox as 'Glasgow's Football Palace' had annoyed many people.

It was a crisp autumn day, perfect for football, as both teams started off playing towards their own fans in the 107,609 crowd – a record for the League Cup which will now never be beaten. The Celtic end looked slightly fuller than the Rangers contingent, but both sides enjoyed the full-throated support of their fans. It was Rangers who had the better of the opening exchanges with Jim Forrest having a few half chances that he might well have put away on another occasion.

Controversy reigned from the first five minute after Celtic's full-back Ian Young scythed down Willie Johnston, cheerfully earning a booking for his troubles. It was a tackle which would trouble Young's conscience in later years, apparently, but it was a clear sign that this Celtic team, the Stein Celtic team, meant business, and that there would be 'no more Mr Nice Guy'. In the past, Celtic teams had been famed for their gentlemanly approach to the game, for chairman Bob Kelly was always determined to protect Celtic's reputation, even if this meant losing with dignity. To the Celtic end, it had often appeared like supine submission.

Tackling was tough with each side having strong men who tended not to be messed about – John Greig, Tommy Gemmell, Ron McKinnon, Bobby Murdoch – and the fear was expressed that this game might not see the best football that the teams had to offer. There were for example four excellent wingers on show. Rangers had Willie Henderson and Willie Johnston, while Celtic had Jimmy Johnstone and John Hughes. They might not be seen at their entertaining best.

Slightly over quarter of an hour had gone when a bizarre incident saw Celtic go ahead. A free kick taken by Bobby Murdoch seemed to be sailing harmlessly over everyone's heads when Ron McKinnon suddenly jumped up and handled it in the box. To this day, Ron doesn't know why he did it and it was apparently an instant reaction, but a penalty kick was awarded. Up stepped John Hughes to take the kick.

To many of us behind that goal, it did not seem that 'Yogi Bear' was the most temperamentally suited of men to take the kick. He was certainly powerful and strong and had had some great games in recent weeks, but was he the man to take a penalty kick in this pressure situation? HUGHES himself did not seem to have any doubts and slotted the ball home.

This early success immediately settled the Celtic defence. Billy McNeill, for example, who had had loads of trouble with Jim Forrest early on in the game and indeed in the past few years, now settled into his role and asserted aerial dominance, using, thankfully, his head rather than the hand used by his Rangers counterpart.

A short spell of Celtic dominance now followed, and ten minutes later, just on the half-hour mark, Celtic incredibly went two ahead, again through the penalty spot. This time it was a softish award when Rangers left-back Davie Provan brought down Jimmy Johnstone. TV replays tended to indicate that the award was indeed dubious, and Provan himself protested his innocence vigorously, but Mr Phillips was adamant. The award would possibly not have been made if it had not been in front of the screaming Celtic fans who were of course all convinced that it was a penalty, but a spot-kick it was. Rangers chairman John Lawrence allowed himself to be quoted in the following day's newspapers as saying, 'What I have to say about that decision could not be printed', and was duly hauled over the coals for that. But for the second time we held our breath as big John HUGHES lumbered up to do the needful. This time goalkeeper Billy Ritchie managed to get a hand on it, but Celtic were 2-0 up.

Yet was this not too early? Half an hour had barely elapsed. A long time remained, and just on half-time the anxious hearts behind the King's Park goal were indebted to a fine save from Ronnie Simpson as John Greig tried a long-range shot. We feared that there would be a lot more of this in the lengthy second half. Optimists kept talking about the 7-1 game of eight years ago at the same stage of the same tournament and the score then was also 2-0 at half-time, with the teams even playing in the same direction as in 1957, but we knew in our hearts that things would be very different.

Raymond Jacobs in the *Glasgow Herald* put it very well when he said that when Celtic meet Rangers 'the meek do not inherit the earth'. He possibly exaggerates when he talks about an 'Orgy of Crudeness' – other newspapers like the *Sunday Post* would call it the 'X Certificate Final' – but it was indeed a grim occasion with five players booked by Mr Phillips who, nevertheless, made sure that things never got totally out of hand.

Minutes passed – 60, 70, 80 – and Celtic seemed to have weathered the storm, when Rangers scored. It was an odd goal, following a Henderson free kick which floated into the box. John Greig and Ian Young went up for it together and the ball skidded into the net off YOUNG's face. It was a freak goal, but it allowed Rangers a late lifeline, and caused all sorts of palpitations to the green and white clad behind the goal.

It was at this moment that Ronnie Simpson proved his worth. Ronnie, now aged 35 and the proud possessor of two English Cup medals with Newcastle United in 1952 and 1955, had not been the most high profile of Celtic signings a year previously. In fact, Jock Stein, then manager of Hibs, had given every impression that he was glad to see him go, but now this son of a Rangers player (Jimmy Simpson of the 1930s) was the man who took over the Celtic defence, calming down the excitable McNeill, the harassed Young and the irascible Gemmell. He poured balm on the worried brows of the Celtic end by his repeated gesture of banging his fist into his left hand and telling everyone to keep concentrating. The minutes were now slipping away … and Simpson was in control.

For the second time in six months, Mr Phillips's final whistle brought joy to Celtic, but that was not the end of the matter. Some Rangers fans, disappointed, disillusioned, misguided and intellectually challenged, invaded the field as Celtic did their lap of honour. It was none too bright, but the Celtic players got off the field in the nick of time with the League Cup safely in hand and before they had the opportunity to inflict serious damage on the undernourished of Larkhall and Govan.

It would be one of these things that was talked about, like the rough nature of the game itself, and clichés like 'the cancer of modern society' and 'the failure of the Scottish educational system to integrate the…' were never far away, but the bottom line was that the Scottish League Cup had green and white ribbons on it and was in the possession of Celtic for only the third time in its 20-year history. Celtic's second penalty was maybe dodgy, and Rangers might have had one as well, but that mattered little. Celtic had won.

The real significance of this game was of course that everyone now knew that Celtic were here to stay. On the following Wednesday night they went to Dundee and won there as well in a league match where sheer professionalism saved the day after Dundee pulled a late goal back when Celtic had been 2-0 up. It was almost a rerun of the Saturday game, but it showed that Celtic now had the mettle to win league championships – and of course an awful lot more!

v Vojvodina Novi Sad 2-0
European Cup Quarter-Final, Celtic Park
8 March 1967

CELTIC	VOJVODINA	REFEREE
Simpson	Pantelic	Mr H. Carlsson,
Craig	Aleksic	Sweden
Gemmell	Radovic	
Murdoch	Sekeres	
McNeill	Brzic	
Clark	Nesticki	
Johnstone	Rakic	
Lennox	Dakic	
Chalmers	Radsosav	
Gallagher	Trivic	
Hughes	Pusibric	

THE THOUGHT that Celtic might actually win the European Cup was taken seriously by only a few fans in the winter of 1966/67. They were of course a good team, no-one denied that, but the thought that they were better than the likes of Inter Milan and Real Madrid took a little swallowing.

But there was no doubt that they would put up a good fight. They had already beaten Zurich and Nantes, and – of crucial relevance to the Scottish psyche – Liverpool, the representative of England, were out. Of equal relevance to the Scottish psyche (although possibly something that roused less enthusiasm at Celtic Park) was the fact that Rangers were doing equally well in the European Cup Winners' Cup.

A grim test however awaited in early March when Celtic were paired against Vojvodina Novi Sad in the country that was then called Yugoslavia, a strange place which was communist and repressive, but a wheen more westernised and civilised than the Soviet Union, from whom it repeatedly and pointedly distanced itself. Travelling to Yugoslavia in 1967 was unusual and when the Celtic party travelled from Belgrade up the country some 90 miles into Serbia, it would be a fair bet that very few Scottish people had ever been there before.

Celtic found themselves up against a strong team, full of correct, disciplined professionals. They didn't possess great flair players like Jimmy Johnstone or John Hughes of Celtic, but they were a team that could pass to each other, that could cover for each other and that would not allow themselves to be bullied. The atmosphere in Novi Sad was not particularly intimidating as European stadia could be in the mid 1960s, but it was not an easy ground either, and Celtic, bereft of their normally huge travelling support, and relying mainly for encouragement from the sometimes dubious support of the Scottish press, were content to play a low key game and hope for a 0-0 draw.

They would have achieved it but for a bad blunder involving Tommy Gemmell who was short on a pass back and John Clark who did not notice it in time, and Stanic scored the only goal of the game for the Yugoslavs. This was in the 70th minute and the remaining 20 minutes were spent with Celtic, backs to the wall, keeping out the Vojvodina attack, now inspired by the fanatical hooters, sirens and fireworks of their support. The game finished 1-0. 2-0 would have been a disaster, but 1-0, it was felt, would be manageable at Parkhead. It would be tight, though, and the defeat in Novi Sad means that for football historians, Vojvodina now join Dundee United as the only team to have beaten Celtic in the 1966/67 'annus mirabilis'.

If Celtic were disappointed on their return, they did not exactly show it, for they went to Love Street and beat St Mirren 5-0, as they braced themselves for the coming tussle. The 70,000 tickets had all been sold, and Glasgow was already seething with rumours of team selections. There was a problem with the centre-forward position. Willie Wallace, signed in December 1966, was still not eligible for this round in the European Cup (he was doing well on the domestic front), Joe McBride had been injured on Christmas Eve at Pittodrie and was ruled out – which left only Stevie Chalmers who himself was not 100 per cent fit.

Bertie Auld was rested in favour of Charlie Gallagher. There was in truth little to choose between the two of them in terms of footballing ability, but Stein possibly felt that Gallagher had a more equable temperament for a game of this magnitude and intensity. Bertie might easily be provoked by a Yugoslav defender into losing his concentration. In any case, almost as an afterthought, Stein reckoned that Charlie was a better kicker of a dead ball... He probably did not realise the importance of that decision at the time.

The crowd – in truth it looked more than 70,000 – was enthusiastic and noisy with the chants of 'CEL-TIC! CEL-TIC!' resounding round the ground, mingled with 'Sure, it's a grand old team to play for', 'We shall not be moved' (courtesy of The Seekers, Joan Baez and the anti-Vietnam protesters) and the new Irish rebel song that was making its debut in 1967 – 'The Merry Ploughboy':

Oh, I'm off the Dublin in the green, in the green
Where the helmets glisten in the sun
And the bayonets slash the Orange sash
To the echo of the Thomson gun!

It was meant to be frightening for the Yugoslavs who had never seen anything like this in their lives before, but if it was, it certainly did not affect their composure, for the first half was a bore with Celtic, applying the traditional, hysterical Scottish style of pressure, coming up against the technically correct Yugoslav defence, who were quite happy to waste time, concede free kicks in non-threatening parts of the field and pass the ball to each other with frustrating precision. They were rarely in the Celtic half, although Pusibric had missed an early chance to put the game beyond Celtic.

Half-time came with no let-up in the intensity of the emotions of the crowd, in spite of the seeming likelihood that Celtic were not going to break down Vojvodina. Yet everyone was aware that one goal would earn Celtic a play-off in neutral

Rotterdam (the 'away goals' rule had not yet been introduced and no-one had thought of the idea of a penalty shoot-out), and with men like Jimmy Johnstone and John Hughes, everything was possible. Even so, the consensus of opinion among the pessimists was that Celtic were not quite ready yet for the European game, that success in Scotland did not necessarily breed triumph in Europe, and that greater tactical awareness was necessary. It was even said by those who tried to rationalise everything that a defeat would be a good thing as it would allow Celtic more space to concentrate on the Scottish scene...

But Stein and his players kept trying. Players changed positions to disorientate the Vojvodina defence, long balls were tried, the short passing game was experimented with, and slowly, gradually, Celtic began to dominate as their opponents tired. Meanwhile (and crucially) the crowd kept up its relentless propaganda barrage, something which clearly strengthened the Celtic players. Celtic were playing in all green (as they had done on several occasions for the past two seasons) because it was believed by the authorities that Vojvodina's white with a diagonal strip (dare one mention the word 'sash'?) would clash with the hoops, or as they were still known in 1967, the green and white *stripes*.

And then just on the hour mark, the breakthrough came. Fittingly Tommy Gemmell, who had made the fatal mistake in Novi Sad, rectified matters at Parkhead. A long charge down the left, then a look up to see that there was no-one there who could head the ball in, so a fierce drive low down across the penalty area. Ilya Pantelic, the Yugoslav goalkeeper who had been having a great game, went down for it, but misjudged its speed and the ball hit his shoulder and rolled out to Steve CHALMERS who, like all good predators, was simply lying in wait to tap in from three yards.

So Celtic were back in the tie – but the players did not want a play-off in Rotterdam. More travel, a poor crowd and no atmosphere did not appeal. But the atmosphere tonight at Parkhead now went from red hot to white hot, as the crowd began to sense a famous victory. Murdoch and Gallagher now dominated the midfield, Hughes and Johnstone created mayhem down the flanks, the crowd were in perpetual uproar as pressure piled on the 'Rangers end' goal, but Pantelic was in inspired form, as corner kick followed corner kick with Ronnie Simpson now a lonely figure in the distant goal.

Everyone seemed reconciled to Rotterdam, a not too unpleasant prospect for the support, some of whom could have made it there, or for the press, who always enjoyed the idea of a 'freebie' in a civilised European country where there were quantities of alcohol to be consumed and the company of ladies to enjoy, when Celtic forced yet another corner, this occasion on the right in front of the Main Stand as time ebbed away. The weaker brethren had gone or were now going (this a besetting and perpetually annoying habit of Celtic supporters) to get an early bus or to avoid the quite horrendous traffic jams, convinced that although the team had played well and deserved to win, Rotterdam it was to be.

Charlie Gallagher trotted over. He then saw an instant playback of 1965's Scottish Cup Final as the other Celtic forwards went on decoy runs taking their markers with them. Out of the corner of his eye he saw captain Billy McNeill, surreptitiously and without making any fuss about it, coming forwards. Jimmy Johnstone ran towards him for a short corner alerting two men to the possibility of the wiles of Johnstone manufacturing a goal, but in the meantime McNeill had made ground. Charlie, unlike 1965, thought that a high drooping cross would give McNeill more time to get there, and then with the ball in flight, goalkeeper Ilya Pantelic made the big mistake of coming for it. McNEILL however got there first and the ball flashed off his head past the despairing figure of left-half Nesticki who tried to save it on the line with his hand.

Vojvodina made a few half-hearted appeals for a foul on the goalkeeper whom Chalmers had allegedly impeded, but this was totally drowned out in the cauldron of excitement that Parkhead had become. Scarcely had the ball been centred when Mr Carlsson blew for time up. 'Aye, Jock cut it fine the night,' said one of the journalists in the press box, but for Celtic supporters everywhere it was a great result, and one that allowed them to think that perhaps, just perhaps, this team had what it took to win the European Cup. It was a glorious night.

For Celtic fans unable to be at the game, there was no radio commentary in English (the parochial and pathetic BBC Scotland were reluctant to spend money on football on a Wednesday night), but those with some patience could find a Yugoslav station that did a commentary. It was then just a matter of going by the commentator's tone, or indeed his silence as distinct from the crowd's noise when the goal went in! STV did a highlights programme, and (laudably) Arthur Montford did not tell the score in advance other than to say that it was a 'cliffhanger'. Indeed it was.

Perhaps this was the night that Celtic supporters began to believe that a European Cup triumph, seemingly unbelievable even a few weeks ago, was now becoming possible. As for Vojvodina and their supporters, goodness only knows what happened to them in the awful genocidal civil wars of the 1990s, so incomprehensible to western eyes. One only hopes that some of them will recall that in 1967 they did come closer than anyone else to beating the eventual winners of the trophy.

v Aberdeen 2-0
Scottish Cup Final, Hampden
29 April 1967

CELTIC	ABERDEEN	REFEREE
Simpson	Clark	Mr W. Syme, Glasgow
Craig	Whyte	
Gemmell	Shewan	
Murdoch	Munro	
McNeill	McMillan	
Clark	Petersen	
Johnstone	Wilson	
Wallace	Smith	
Chalmers	Storrie	
Auld	Melrose	
Lennox	Johnston	

THE SCOTTISH Cup Final of 1967 was overshadowed by larger events. On the previous Tuesday night, Celtic had become the first ever British team (let alone Scottish team!) to reach the final of the European Cup. They had done so in Prague (in a strange stadium on the side of a hill where trees grew halfway up the terracing!) by drawing 0-0 with the Czechoslovakian Army side, Dukla. The victory had been achieved by abandoning Celtic's traditional attacking game in favour of a European style boring draw, but the victory had been justly hailed nevertheless.

They were back in Scotland by the early hours of Wednesday morning to prepare for the Scottish Cup Final, a fixture that does not normally take second place to any other. The opponents were Aberdeen, a team enjoying a welcome revival under manager Eddie Turnbull, an old foe of Jock Stein from his playing days. They would of course mobilise their massive support from the distant parts of Aberdeenshire and the Highlands, as they had done for their previous Scottish Cup finals of 1937, 1947, 1953, 1954 and 1959, and a great crowd was expected. The northern expectations were justified, for the Dons had beaten teams like Dundee, St Johnstone, Hibs and Dundee United en route to the final. But these, as some commentators pointed out, were all east coast teams. How could they cope with Celtic in the final in Glasgow?

But the question was now being asked of Celtic: 'could they win them all?' The Scottish League Cup and the Glasgow Cup were already there, they were ahead in the Scottish League with only a handful of games to go, they had now reached the European Cup Final to face Inter Milan in a month's time – and this game was now the final of what was often described as Celtic's favourite trophy, the Scottish Cup. They had won it 18 times; so too had Rangers. This was therefore another aspect to the game on 29 April 1967, in that Celtic could edge ahead of Rangers once again.

The 1967 Scottish Cup campaign had not yet seen Celtic at their best. They had easily disposed of Arbroath and Elgin City, but then Queen's Park had come to

Parkhead to put up a spirited performance before losing 3-5. More Glasgow opposition faced Celtic in the shape of Clyde in the semi-final. A truly dreadful 0-0 draw on April Fool's Day was forgotten about in the replay when Bertie Auld simply took command, scoring a brilliant goal and running the show to put Celtic into the final with a 2-0 victory. The Scottish Cup of 1967 is also famous, of course, for the greatest upset of all time when in late January Glasgow Rangers lost to the other Rangers, from Berwick.

But in the days between the return from Dukla and the Scottish Cup Final, doubts began to manifest themselves in the support, mainly caused by recent memories of the previous year at this time when Celtic had also been chasing a grand slam of trophies, but had gone down unluckily to Liverpool in a European Cup Winners' Cup semi, then equally unluckily to Rangers in the Scottish Cup Final. But that was 1966.

This was 1967, when a stronger, more streetwise, more professional Celtic had emerged. They were the bookmakers' favourites to win the Scottish Cup, but not overwhelmingly so, for Aberdeen were a fine team.

Their side centred on the talented inside-forward called Jimmy Smith. He shared the nickname 'Jinky' with Celtic's Jimmy Johnstone, and made no secret of the fact that he wanted to play for Celtic. Indeed Rangers, who had last summer signed another Smith called Dave from Aberdeen and yet another called Alec from Dunfermline, apparently made an enquiry about Jimmy but lost interest once they discovered that he had a major obstacle in that he was commonly know in Glasgow as a 'Tim' or a Roman Catholic.

Harry Melrose was now playing his third Scottish Cup Final against Celtic. He had appeared twice for Dunfermline in 1961 and 1965, winning one and losing one. Now arguably past his best, he was still a fine player and a doughty competitor. Aberdeen had also bought Jim Storrie from Leeds United, where he had never set the heather on fire, but he had made an impact on the Dons.

That Aberdeen were a team on the march was evidenced in their quarter-final replay against Hibs in March when in front of a huge Pittodrie attendance with serious overcrowding, they had put Hibs to the sword, winning 3-0. They had been luckier to get the better of a stuffy Dundee United side in the semi-final at Dens Park, but they had reason for optimism.

However the Dons suffered a major blow on the very morning of the final. Eddie Turnbull, who had been suffering from some time from hepatitis, simply could not leave the team's luxury headquarters at Gleneagles, and had to listen to the BBC Radio commentary from his hotel bedroom. This might have made a difference, for the presence of a manager can bring out the best in players, but on the other hand it is the players who really count, and in captain Harry Melrose they had a man who had been around for a long time. Managers can in any case do little once their men have crossed the touchline.

Celtic had had an illness problem as well. Jim Craig had come home from Prague suffering from flu. He was isolated on the plane coming home, and was sent to bed immediately on arrival in Glasgow, lest the infection spread, and recovered in time to play in the game. It had been well hushed up, the infection had not spread, and indeed Jim had an outstanding game.

Celtic's tactics for this game involved giving Jimmy Johnstone a 'roving commission'. This was not the first time that this had happened, for Johnstone, neurotic and insecure, needing tranquilisers before he could board a plane (such was his fear of flying), was often worried when his name was never mentioned in team talks. He would then ask in a timid voice of the mighty and physically overwhelming Stein, 'And what aboot me, Boss?' Stein would look at him and say 'You? Just you dae whit the hell ye want!'

The game began in pleasant spring sunshine in front of a crowd of 127,117 (some reports say it was only [!] 126,102) with Celtic playing towards the Mount Florida end into the breeze which was significant but not as all-pervasive as it sometimes could be at Hampden. The game was even during the first half with neither team looking as if they were going to dominate. Half chances came to both teams, but nothing was taken, and with half-time approaching, everyone looked happy to go in with the scores level. Jimmy Smith blotted his copybook however by getting himself booked for a rather unnecessary foul, thereby not doing much for his chances of persuading Jock Stein to sign him.

But then with the crowd already beginning to file up the huge terracings for the toilets and the refreshment stalls (some hope at the primitive Hampden of 1967!) Celtic struck. It was a simple enough goal, brought about by some good work down the left wing involving Lennox and Auld, with Lennox crossing low (when the Aberdeen defence were expecting a high one) from near the dead-ball line for Willie WALLACE, curiously unmarked, to score. Wallace had of course joined Celtic from Hearts the previous December, and by the end of this day would repay his transfer fee.

They often say that a goal before half-time has a devastating psychological effect. It certainly did on this occasion, for Aberdeen left the field with Hampden a sea of green and white, the noise at a barely tolerable level, their opponents cock-a-hoop, and the Dons did not have a manager to cheer them up. Hard though Harry Melrose and some of the backroom boys tried to gee them up, they must have felt that they were up against it now, 0-1 down to the European Cup finalists in rampant, confident mood and in front of a crowd that was about 70 per cent pro Celtic, singing things like 'We're off to Lisbon in the green' – a ditty that they had adapted from their favourite 1967 Irish rebel song!

Indeed Aberdeen's fate was sealed within three minutes of the restart. The hardworking Chalmers fed Jimmy Johnstone who ran to the dead-ball line on the left, beating one or two men and then sending across a perfect ball for Willie WALLACE who 'looked as if he were waiting for a bus' and sent the ball into the back of the net from about ten yards. The memory remains of the ball heading towards us near the bottom of the King's Park terracing, the net stopping it, and then about 50,000 ecstatic people landing on our backs!

But there was still a long time to go, and Aberdeen, now with little to lose, threw everything into the attack. Smith, Wilson and Storrie now began to get things together in midfield, and Ronnie Simpson (who two weeks previously had played for Scotland in the 3-2 win over England at Wembley) was called upon to make a few saves. On the other hand, Aberdeen's all-out attack opened a few doors for Celtic themselves, and Lennox, Chalmers and Wallace all might have added to Celtic's tally.

One can never be entirely sure in football, but the Celtic end was now engulfed in collective joy, as the minutes passed without Aberdeen ever putting serious pressure on the Celtic defence for whom McNeill was outstanding. Almost at the final whistle, with Dons fans already having sportingly shaken hands with their Celtic counterparts and gone home, Aberdeen might have scored a consolation goal had Ronnie Simpson not, for once caught off his line, appeared from nowhere to clear a ball which looked net-bound.

Seconds later, referee Willie Syme (a self-confessed Rangers supporter, incidentally, and even, allegedly, an Orangeman, although he had a good and impartial game that day) blew for full time, and Glasgow belonged to Celtic – even though Billy McNeill dropped the lid off the Scottish Cup as he lifted it. He would really have to get more practice in lifting silverware, for he would have a lot of it to do in the future!

Sometimes, when one does not really need any further good news, one gets it anyway, for it transpired that Dundee had done Celtic a great favour by drawing 1-1 with Rangers at Dens Park in the Scottish League that day, thus bringing the league championship a little closer to Celtic as well. And could this side now become the first British team to win the European Cup?

v Inter Milan 2-1
European Cup Final, Lisbon
25 May 1967

CELTIC	INTER MILAN	REFEREE
Simpson	Sarti	Herr K. Tschescher,
Craig	Burgnich	West Germany
Gemmell	Facchetti	
Murdoch	Bedin	
McNeill	Guarneri	
Clark	Picchi	
Johnstone	Domenghini	
Wallace	Cappellini	
Chalmers	Mazzola	
Auld	Bicicli	
Lennox	Corso	

THIS WAS of course no ordinary game. In some ways it defied analysis, and the outcome was one that only the most rabid of Celtic supporters could have predicted. It was indeed difficult to imagine that the team whose 60,000 supporters suddenly, as of one mind, turned their backs on them only four years previously in the Scottish Cup Final of 1963 and who were patronisingly dismissed even in the Scottish press as 'the poor team with the big support' were now competing for the right to call themselves the champions of Europe.

They had done this by beating Zurich, Nantes, Vojvodina and Dukla Prague – each of these encounters being classics in their own right and hard-fought victories – but they had also amazed the world by sweeping the boards in Scotland. They had lifted the Scottish League Cup in October, the Glasgow Cup in November, the Scottish Cup in April and the Scottish League on a rainy day in early May at Ibrox with a great 2-2 draw. All this was impressive, but could they beat Inter Milan?

Inter had won the European Cup in 1964 and 1965 and were generally looked upon as one of the best and the richest teams on earth. Managed by Helenio Herrera, that wily Argentinean, their style of play was not always pretty on the eye, certainly not to the Scottish eye with its love of open attacking football, but it was effective. Italian football in general was on a high in the mid 1960s. Or at least Italian club football was. Their national team had been humiliatingly defeated by North Korea in the World Cup in England the previous year! The hurt of that one remained deep.

This was the twelfth year of the European Cup, a tournament that had been won by teams from only three countries so far – Spain, Italy and Portugal. It had represented the peak of the aspirations of club football, and so far British teams had really done rather badly in it. In fact the fine Dundee team of 1963 had done as well as anyone in reaching the semi-final before losing to the eventual winners, Inter's city rivals, AC Milan. Celtic had been the first British team to reach the final – but those whose heads ruled their hearts and based life on the solid foundation of common sense, reckoned that although the world was impressed by Celtic's achievements, this was really as far as they could realistically be expected to go.

But Celtic received help of a sort from an unlikely source. This was Rangers, who were also having a good season in that they pressed Celtic hard in the Scottish League and Scottish League Cup, recovered from their disaster at Berwick in the Scottish Cup, and in a parallel campaign to that of Celtic, reached the final of the European Cup Winners' Cup, to be played some six days after the European Cup Final. It would not be a popular contention among Ibrox historians that 1967 was one of Rangers' better years, but in fact it was – for no other reason than that they lived with the Lisbon Lions and pressed them hard, thus ensuring that there were no easy games in Scotland. This was good training for Celtic in Lisbon.

Celtic's team for Lisbon had evolved over the 1966/67 season, having first played with each other against St Johnstone at Perth on 14 January. Those who felt that John Hughes, that mercurial but undependable genius, might have squeezed a place were to be disappointed, as were the many admirers of Charlie Gallagher, but there was no great argument about what the team formation should be, and Stein was distinctly lucky in that, apart from an injury to Joe McBride at Pittodrie on Christmas Eve, the squad remained intact. Bobby Murdoch had been out for a spell in March and April, but he had recovered and was able to play with his ankle strapped up. That was fortunate, for Murdoch was the great playmaker of that team, a role he shared in midfield with Bertie Auld.

Inter on the other had were struggling in Serie A, eventually losing the *scudetto* to Juventus on the last day of the season, and they were handicapped by an injury to their star man, Suarez (whom one of the Italians said was 'the equivalent of Bobby Murdoch') even though Stein was not prepared to believe Suarez's non-appearance until he saw it. He had already had a few propaganda jousts with Herrera and knew the Inter manager's capacity for gamesmanship and sometimes sheer mendacity and cheating. But there would be no Suarez.

About 30,000 Celtic fans travelled to Lisbon, but the game (unusually for 1967) was shown on TV on both BBC and STV. They were the only channels available in 1967, so there was no escape for the non-football minded. Walking the streets of any town in Scotland after the 5.30 pm kick-off that bright sunny May evening was like 'being the only survivor of a nuclear war', according to one person, for human beings were scarce and vehicles scarcer. Every house seemed to have its curtains drawn to get a better view of the black and white screen.

Celtic got off to an unfortunate start when in the 5th minute right-back Jim Craig collided with Cappellini just inside the penalty box. It was technically a penalty but by Scottish standards it was nothing at all, and one speculates what would have happened to a referee in the tough school of, say, Ayrshire Junior Football or even in the Scottish Football League if he had given such a piteous penalty kick. But this was a European Cup Final, and a spot kick it was, which MAZZOLA, after a few token Celtic protests, put away.

This reverse did, however, have some positives. One was that it happened early enough in the game, another was that Celtic now knew that the German referee did not like any bodily contact, and the third was that Celtic could now throw away any tactics such as 'containing them for the first half-hour' etc. Celtic had no choice now but to attack – the game that they felt they were the best in the world at. And they now had the opportunity to show it!

But it was not the hysterical Scottish aggression and pressure that had been the undoing of many Scottish teams in the past. It was well thought out, cerebral stuff all coming from the mighty engine room of Bobby Murdoch and Bertie Auld. In the first place, Jimmy Johnstone was to be given as much of the ball as possible. He had already been fed the ball in the first minute to win over the sympathies of the neutral. Red, curly hair is of course a rarity in both Italy and Portugal and indeed in most of Europe, as is the old-fashioned Scottish style of dribbling. It went down particularly well that night.

Fast runners Lennox and Chalmers were to be given the ball as often as possible. Lennox in particular, that super fit Saltcoats greyhound, might well have been in the Olympic 100 metres and the instructions were to put the ball ahead of him so that he could run on to it. Wallace was to bustle in midfield, and the defence was to remain solid, but Gemmell could go forward if he wanted. If that were to happen, Craig the other full-back needed to stay behind.

All this worked very well, but half-time came and no goal had been scored. Sarti in the Inter goal had had a few saves to make, and the Italian team had been forced back in face of the Scottish pressure, but still their defence had not been breached. The Celtic support in the ground remained loyal and optimistic; those of us back home who had seen this sort of thing before did not give up hope either, although we did say to each other that even if we lost, we had still shown the world what Scottish attacking football was like; and Stein remained calm and controlled, urging a few changes on the tactics, but expressing himself happy at what he had seen so far.

The second half saw more of the same with goalkeeping saves, near things, penalty claims and still Celtic kept pressing. It was clear that it was going to take something really unusual to win this game, and this was exactly what happened. Jim Craig had actually broken one of Stein's rules – for he was up in the attack when he should have been back defending, for Gemmell was also forward – but he could be excused, for it was Craig who picked up a ball from Murdoch, before sending it in to GEMMELL who belted the ball home from outside the box.

Watching the rerun of this goal can be an uncomfortable experience, for several Celtic players were technically in an offside position when Gemmell shot, but the ball was travelling so fast, they did not have time to be 'interfering with play'! In any case, the linesman would not have had time to notice this!

At this point we began to feel confident. Now that the breakthrough had come, it was hard to see anything other than a Celtic triumph – whether by extra time or a replay or even in the 90 minutes; but surely, victory must be ours. And indeed the green and white waves intensified after the equaliser as Inter, bereft of Suarez (although, in truth, it is doubtful what difference he would have made) had no attacking or creative option and simply had to try to soak up the overwhelming Scottish pressure which was engulfing them. To their credit, they did not stoop to dirty tactics as other teams might have done, and one got the impression that they were reconciled to their fate. Their only hope now was a replay and a chance to regroup.

Deliverance came for Celtic with five minutes to go. A dance over the ball, now this way now that, by Tommy Gemmell, a cut back to Murdoch, a shot at goal and a stab by Steve CHALMERS to put Celtic ahead. Steve Chalmers! One's mind went back four years to a game at Tannadice Park, Dundee where Steve was hideously out of place on the left wing and having a shocker. He was not helped by being subjected to the sort of abuse from some men masquerading as supporters that I would never want to hear delivered to any human being from another. I wonder if Stevie's detractors felt bad this glorious night?

There was now a long five minutes to wait. A veteran supporter who had seen Joe Cassidy, Tommy McInally and Patsy Gallacher had to go and hide in his garden shed until his bewildered wife, who wondered where he was and indeed feared for his health, came and told him that they had won. Others simply prayed. If they did, then the good Lord was listening, for Herr Tschescher's whistle eventually went, and life would never be the same again for so many people.

Once again, in the tradition of nearly 80 years, Celtic had shown their ability to make so many people happy... We walked on air for the rest of the summer. Nothing else seemed to matter.

Israel and the Arabs picked one of their periodic fights with one another a few days after the Lisbon occasion. Why? Why couldn't they just enjoy the Celtic?

v Rangers 3-1

Scottish League Cup, Celtic Park
30 August 1967

CELTIC	RANGERS	REFEREE
Simpson	Sorensen	Mr T. Wharton,
Craig	Johansen	Clarkston
Gemmell	Provan	
Murdoch	Jardine	
McNeill	McKinnon	
Clark	Greig	
Johnstone	Henderson	
Wallace	Penman	
Chalmers	Ferguson	
Auld	D. Smith	
Lennox	Johnston	

'UNEASY LIES the head that wears the crown', wrote William Shakespeare, and Celtic, crowned champions of Europe a few months previously, would discover how difficult it was to stay at the top. The start of the season saw them in a League Cup section that contained Rangers, Dundee United and Aberdeen. The games were all tough, and when Celtic had gone to Ibrox a fortnight previously, a 1-1 draw had been the result. But because Celtic had beaten Dundee United with a late Jimmy Johnstone goal on opening day while Rangers had had to settle for a draw at Pittodrie, a win for Celtic against their oldest rivals would effectively qualify them for the quarter-finals of the Scottish League Cup and eliminate Rangers.

Another dynamic was at work in Scotland that Wednesday night, however. It was the final night of *The Fugitive*, a long-running U.S. soap opera in which David Janssen repeatedly escaped from the police after the death of his wife for which he was wrongly accused, as he chased a one-armed man who was believed to have done it. It was gripping stuff, and quite a few fans would have been reluctant to leave their TVs that night, for it was long before the arrival of video recorders, iPlayers or DVDs. What they saw, however, was an escape every bit as gripping and compelling as David Janssen's.

It was a fine night as both teams started off playing towards their own fans. The game was in the charge of referee Tom Wharton, a huge bulk of a man who was called, by antiphrasis, 'Tiny'. He could play to the gallery on occasion, but he was a character in Scottish football. He was very fair and usually earned the grudging respect of both sets of fans. His performance that night would be crucial.

Summer 1967 had not been easy for Rangers supporters. To have your greatest rivals crowned champions of Europe was bad enough, but then six days after that glorious event, Rangers themselves lost in the final of what was then called the European Cup Winners' Cup. In truth they had been unlucky but had shot themselves in the foot by a crazy team selection (reminiscent of some of Celtic's blunders before the arrival of Jock Stein!) and the defeat had been hard to take, so hard in fact that some of their weaker brethren gave up and even jumped ship to join Celtic, as an air of depression settled over the 12 July celebrations that year.

But this made them even more determined to get back at Celtic, and the buying of players continued unabated as desperation replaced common sense. Andy Penman of Dundee for example had been a fine player when the Dens Parkers won the Scottish League in 1962, but now, five years down the line, was clearly past his best. And from Dunfermline came Alex Ferguson, a true Ranger by background and inclination but whose performances for St Johnstone and Dunfermline had been patchy and inconsistent.

Celtic's team was exactly the same as the one that had won in Lisbon, there having been no transfer activity of note over the summer months. In retrospect, it might have been better if there had been, for there were disturbing signs of heads swelling to an unacceptable level and a few new faces might well have added a little more competition for places. But this was not necessarily apparent at the time, and there still remained the aura about Parkhead with even the English BBC reluctantly, but nevertheless genuinely, admitting that they were the best team around.

Rangers had the better of the opening exchanges which were fast and furious, although lacking in finesse. In the 8th minute, Andy Penman slipped a ball through to Willie HENDERSON who put Rangers ahead. Celtic would claim long and vigorously that Henderson was offside at the time that the ball was played, but if he was it was marginal, and in any case he took the goal well. Celtic allowed themselves to be upset by this decision and their play suffered for a spell as Rangers now slowed the game down a little, wisely giving themselves time to regain composure.

Celtic's feelings of paranoia, the condition that affects fans, players and management alike, were by no means soothed when they themselves scored a goal on the half-hour mark through Bobby Lennox which was ruled offside. The decision was once again not clear cut, but Lennox often suffered from this in that linesmen could not believe how fast he was, and he was often flagged for offside when he had been onside as the ball was played.

Two marginal decisions against the team caused the normal mutterings in the Jungle about handshakes, goat molesting and flutes, but there was at least a moment of light relief and even laughter when Alex Ferguson found himself in a goalscoring position but fluffed his opportunity. What sort of future would there be for that fellow we asked ourselves?

Just before half-time Celtic began to rally, and Rangers began to concede fouls, always a sign that a team is under pressure, but the teams changed over with Rangers still that one goal ahead ... and back home (there was no radio or television coverage of the game), David Janssen was still apparently guilty of the murder of his wife. With no mobile phones in 1967, you could not even call home to tell your mother the score in return for finding out how *The Fugitive* was getting on.

The second half continued on the same pattern with Celtic exerting more pressure but Rangers still very dangerous on the break, the Jungle and Celtic ends in full voice, with the Rangers end revealing more than a little degree of anxiety. In this respect, one can trace an eerie parallel, except this time in reverse. In the early 1960s, no matter how well Celtic were playing, they always had the feeling, a death wish almost, that Rangers were destined to win. This feeling became a self-fulfilling prophecy. Rangers fans, for all their bravado and swagger, now had a similar feeling.

The game was punctuated with more than a few fouls – Gemmell was booked, Ferguson was booked – and a nana from the Rangers end ran on and grabbed a corner flag as if to attack a Celtic player with it, before Rangers' Davie Provan earned a ripple of reluctant applause from the Main Stand for putting in a brilliant rugby tackle followed by a half-nelson on him. But Celtic were still being denied by a stuffy Rangers defence. They were all too aware that one goal was really all that Celtic required, for they were, before the game started, a point ahead in the section.

But Rangers had their moments too. Willie Johnston hit the bar, Andy Penman came close too, and then with 15 minutes left to play they were awarded a penalty when Willie Henderson was brought down by John Clark. Henderson was of course a notorious diver and the award did not go down at all well at the Celtic end which had a good view of it, but referee Wharton was probably right. Celtic hearts now sank. If this penalty were converted, there would be no way back, and already some were thinking of an early exit to avoid the traffic and possibly see what happened to David Janssen.

Kaj Johansen was given the job of putting Celtic out of the League Cup. Poor Kaj! He was an ordinary, perhaps even a good full-back, but had been elevated to super hero status because of the goal he scored in the 1966 Scottish Cup Final replay. He was not quite as good as all that, and Jock Stein correctly and shrewdly twigged that he would always be expected by his fans to do the same again, when he wasn't really that type of player. He would never miss an opportunity to try again, and his departure from his position left lots of opportunities for Bobby Lennox in particular to exploit. Tonight, under pressure, Kaj wilted. His spot kick hit the underside of the bar, came down to the ground and rebounded without touching any other player. A few Rangers players were around and might have scored, but Kaj illegally headed the ball. Referee Tom Wharton immediately and correctly awarded an indirect free kick for Celtic because the penalty taker cannot touch the ball until it has been played by someone else.

A huge sigh of relief surged round Parkhead, and it was as if someone had pressed a switch. The reinvigorated Celts, correctly sensing that the Ibrox death wish was now in the ascendancy, charged forwards to the cries of their now animated support, and within a couple of minutes Willie WALLACE had equalised. It was a goalmouth scramble, but it was Wallace who applied the finishing touch and Celtic were level, or in the context of the League Cup section, ahead.

As mayhem prevailed on the terracings, Celtic now took a grip of the game and how fitting it was that the best player on the field, Bobby MURDOCH, should score the second goal some five minutes after Wallace's equaliser. Lennox beat a man and sent the ball across the penalty area for Murdoch who needed no second bidding to angle a shot past the stranded Sorensen from about 20 yards. The explosion of joy was unconfined, and Rangers were shattered. They were already deserted by their fans when Bobby LENNOX slipped between John Greig and Ron McKinnon to score a third goal virtually on the final whistle.

Thus ended one of the more remarkable Old Firm games. The players were cheered to the echo for such a stirring performance. Referee Tom Wharton left the field to a storm of boos from the unforgiving Celtic crowd, but smiled at them and looked with bemusement as if to say 'What's the problem? You won, didn't you?' And poor Kaj Johansen! In the same way as he had been built up to an unwarranted extent because of his goal in 1966 ('Kaj, Kaj Yippee, The Pope's a Hippy!' sang the Rangers fans), he was now pilloried as the villain of the piece, not so much because of missing the penalty as for his mistake in touching it again when someone else might well have scored. But then again, Rangers always need a scapegoat when things go wrong.

Celtic would go on and win the Scottish League Cup that autumn beating Dundee 5-3 in the final. Other things would go wrong in autumn 1967, drastically and dreadfully wrong, but Celtic recaptured the Scottish League Cup, thanks in part to that remarkable game at Celtic Park. Oh, and David Janssen was cleared of his wife's murder. It was the one armed man who did it, after all!

v Dundee United 5-0
Scottish League, Tannadice
30 March 1968

CELTIC	DUNDEE UNITED	REFEREE
Simpson	Davie	Mr E. Thomson,
Craig	Rolland	Edinburgh
Gemmell	Cameron	
Murdoch	Neilson	
McNeill	Smith	
Brogan	Wood	
Johnstone	Seeman	
Lennox	Millar	
Wallace	Mitchell	
Gallagher*	Gillespie	
Hughes	Wilson	
Sub: **Cattanach***		

FOR CELTIC, winter 1967/68 had been a long hard one. The European champions of 1967 had imploded, and looked as if they were to be dubbed 'the one season wonders'. The European Cup had been lost in the Ukraine as early as October, there had followed the South American fiasco from which recovery took a long time and then at the end of January, Dunfermline had beaten them in the Scottish Cup. Granted, the League Cup had been won, but one trophy would have been a poor return after such a momentous season as the previous one.

It was therefore incumbent to win the Scottish League. The problem was that after a nightmare game at Parkhead on 2 January, Rangers were frustratingly still two points ahead (two points being awarded for a win in 1968) and Celtic had no opportunity to play them again, for they had also lost the game at Ibrox in September. All they could do therefore was win their own games, and hope that other teams could do a job for them against Rangers. Frankly that did not look likely, as annoyingly Rangers kept beating the other teams.

Yet psychology came into it was well. Jock Stein realised that, although this season was a disappointing one, he still had a fine team. One does not win European Cups with bad teams. He also worked out that winning the league championship was more of an issue for Rangers, for four years would have passed by 1968 if they did not win it this year. Celtic would, after last season, be forgiven by their fans for at least one year.

There had been signs of panic at Ibrox. Astonishingly, Rangers had sacked long-term manager Scott Symon in early November at a time when they were at the top of the league! That had been bad enough, but then they replaced him by a tiro called David White, at that time manager of Clyde. He had indeed done well for that club, but the management of Rangers, Stein reckoned, would be beyond him. He also knew that Willie Waddell, by no means a close personal friend but certainly an acquaintance and associate, currently working with the *Scottish Daily Express*, possibly the most influential Scottish newspaper of the 1960s, coveted the Ibrox job and would do anything to undermine White. Stein would be a covert ally in Waddell's campaign by leaking stories and feeding Waddell information to portray White and Rangers in a bad light or, worse still, to keep Rangers off the back pages altogether.

But Rangers also scored a massive own goal. Still in Europe and the Scottish Cup (unlike Celtic) and therefore with far more fixtures to play, they decided to reduce their commitment by withdrawing from the Glasgow Cup. This was probably the death blow to that ancient and venerable competition, but more importantly it allowed Stein and Waddell, for all their different agendas, to state that Rangers were afraid of Celtic, whom they would have had to meet in this competition. Not all Rangers supporters agreed with this decision in any case, and words like 'cowards' and 'crappers' were freely bandied about Glasgow.

Stein remained convinced that Rangers would eventually crack, but they would only do so if Celtic made them crack. The way to do this was to win all their games, build up a great goal average (it still being goal *average* in 1968 rather than goal *difference* which determined the winner if points were level) and let the psychological pressure tell. After the middle of February, when Bertie Auld began to struggle with injury, Stein turned to a man whom he had used sparingly since the manager's arrival in 1965. This was Charlie Gallagher. Gallagher lacked the 'bite' and aggression of Auld, but was a silky footballer with tremendous passing ability, a cannonball shot, a turn of speed and the more than occasional ability to score. Stein reckoned that now that the weather was turning better and the pitches firmer, Charlie could yet be the darling of the Celtic crowds.

March saw loads of Celtic goals – six against Kilmarnock, four against Aberdeen, four against Airdrie, (only) three against Falkirk, five against Raith Rovers, and on the Monday night immediately before the visit to Tannadice, six against St Johnstone in a display described variously in the newspapers as 'breathtaking', 'thrilling' and 'awesome' with the *Courier* (the newspaper in Dundee, Angus and Tayside that enjoyed almost total circulation to every single house in the area) in particular being particularly wholesome in their praise of Celtic – and the *Courier* would be read by the supporters and players of Dundee United!

Perhaps there was something deliberate about this as well, and another example of how Stein could use the media, except in this case the journalist had the same agenda as Jock and was a more than willing accomplice. He was in fact Tommy Gallacher, the son of the great Patsy, whose attempts at neutrality were sometimes less than totally successful. He had been a great player with Dundee (and extremely unlucky not to win a Scottish cap) at the same time as Stein played for Celtic, and he knew Jock well.

Celtic's March offensive had had its effect on Rangers. They stuttered, stumbled and struggled in the Scottish Cup against Dundee. They then could only draw against Hearts at Ibrox in the quarter-final before going out to them at Tynecastle on the night of 13 March where the huge crowds caused a delayed kick-off. The game thus finished some time after Celtic's 4-0 league win over Airdrie – the news being obligingly relayed to them by the Tynecastle public address man – and Rangers went out of the Scottish Cup to a solitary Donald Ford goal.

So on 30 March, Celtic travelled to Tannadice to play Dundee United. United were as good as any team in Scotland at this time. They already had a good European pedigree, and were generally reckoned to be Celtic's most difficult opponents in the six games remaining. They would have a bearing on the Scottish League championship because Rangers would follow Celtic to Tannadice three days later, after the Ibrox men's trip to an equally dangerous ground at Airdrie. But 30 March was also Scottish Cup semi-final day – a rare occasion without either of the big Glasgow two – and both these games, Dunfermline v St Johnstone and Hearts v Morton, would end up in 1-1 draws.

It was a fine spring day and Celtic supporters arrived in town in strength, sensing that something was beginning to happen, and in any case eager to enjoy the good football that would undeniably be on offer from this fine Celtic team who were, of course, still the champions of Europe. They would not have long to wait for the action because in 13 minutes Jimmy JOHNSTONE had put them ahead after a great run.

The football was electrifying and men like Doug Smith and Andy Rolland, fine defenders both, were absolutely left standing by the sheer speed of it all. John Hughes was on the left wing that day and his runs down the left flank were a sight to behold as Dundee United struggled to string a few passes together. Before half-time Bobby LENNOX had cashed in on defensive uncertainty after a Hughes shot had been parried and Celtic went in at the interval a comfortable 2-0 ahead, when frankly, it should have been a great deal more. A few Dundee United season ticket holders (they sat in the Main Stand in those days where Celtic fans sit now) were seen to rise and clap Celtic off the park. Others simply shook their heads.

The second half brought more of the same with the massive Celtic support in constant uproar applauding the trickery of Johnstone, the speed of Lennox (who had himself scored four against St Johnstone on Monday night), the industry of Wallace and above all the control and mastery of football that came from Charlie Gallagher. Indeed a Freudian slip from a veteran supporter gave Charlie one of the greatest compliments of them all when a beautiful crossfield pass elicited the cry 'Well done, Patsy!' – an allusion to his near namesake Patsy Gallacher of a previous era.

Further goals were forthcoming when Jimmy Johnstone found Willie WALLACE who netted in the 70th minute. This came after Dundee United had briefly threatened to get back into the game and had forced Ronnie Simpson to make a save. Then Wallace himself fed Bobby LENNOX to score his seventh goal of the week (he had also scored against Raith Rovers the previous Saturday in addition to his four at Perth) a few minutes later.

And then just at the end came a great moment for one Celtic player. Charlie Gallagher had picked up a knock, and Stein, anxious to preserve him (for Hearts at Tynecastle were the next opponents) took him off and sent on David Cattanach, a player who had promised a huge amount in his early years with the club but had not quite made it. Indeed he was blamed by quite a few supporters for Celtic's exit from the Scottish Cup in January in one of his rare outings, for he had fluffed a pass which led to Dunfermline's only goal. On this occasion it was the same David

CATTANACH, almost on the full-time whistle, who, from a Craig pass, scored his one and only goal in his sadly underperforming career for the club.

Thus Celtic supporters left Tannadice in rare good humour, the only fly in the ointment being the news from Broomfield, Airdrie that Rangers had won 2-1. It was indeed a scrappy, lucky victory in total contrast to Celtic's great triumph at Tannadice. 'Lucky b******s!' was the cry as car radios and transistors (by now a common phenomenon at football grounds) gave the unwelcome news, but sooner or later, it was felt, Rangers would get their comeuppance.

Indeed they did, and some of it came at the same Tannadice Park on the following Tuesday night. Once again propaganda played a part. Not only was Celtic's great display emblazoned on the TV and the newspapers, but Dundee United were taken to task by Don John in the *Courier* for not doing a little better, even against such an obviously world class side, and manager Jerry Kerr also made it known that he (and the supporters) expected a little better, even against the big Glasgow teams and especially at home. Kerr, an honest man, said this to the *Courier* as well: 'I don't think any team could have lived with Celtic in that form. I know I shouldn't be saying this, but it was a pleasure to see the way they played.' This was an astonishing thing for a defeated manager to say, but he was only echoing what all the fans had said.

Celtic were due to play at Pittodrie in midweek, but a late frost and snow put that game off and diverted all attention to Tannadice. The Dundee United players dug deep and held Rangers to a 0-0 draw. By all accounts, they should even have won, but they had at least reduced the gap to one point, and more importantly had inflicted even more damage on the nervous psyche of the Rangers players who would now go on to lose in Europe to Leeds United as well as drawing in the league with Morton and finally collapsing to Aberdeen.

Celtic had no direct part in these games ... but then again perhaps they did! Their presence was everywhere, and the more that Rangers tried to pretend they didn't exist, the more Celtic asserted themselves, playing the football that deservedly won them the 1968 Scottish League championship.

v Hibernian 6-2
Scottish League Cup Final, Hampden
5 April 1969

CELTIC	HIBERNIAN	REFEREE
Fallon	Allan	Mr W. Syme, Glasgow
Craig	Shevlane	
Gemmell*	Davis	
Murdoch	Stanton	
McNeill	Madsen	
Brogan	Blackley	
Johnstone	Marinello	
Wallace	Quinn	
Chalmers	Cormack	
Auld	O'Rourke	
Lennox	Stevenson	
Sub: Clark*		

THERE ARE those who think that this was the best single game played by Celtic in the Jock Stein era. That is an ambitious claim but there are several reasons for this view. One is the sheer quality of the football and of the goals scored, another is that this game was in fact played against top quality opposition (Hibs were by no means a poor team in the 1960s as a glance at their team list might indicate), and other factors were the location, the fine weather and the crowd of over 74,000 who thoroughly enjoyed what can only be described as a great footballing occasion.

The game was played on 5 April 1969, by accident rather than design, for the League Cup Final was normally played in late October. It would have been 26 October, but a fire at Hampden the previous Monday damaged the centre stand and compelled a postponement. Things might have been different if the game had been played in October – one can never tell – but it was certain that playing the game in early April saw Celtic at their best, and the victory formed the first leg of a Scottish treble, all achieved in that glorious calendar month of April 1969.

A few weeks before the League Cup Final, however, Celtic had suffered a serious blow when they went out of the European Cup quarter-final by the narrowest of margins to the eventual winners, AC Milan. A goalless draw in Milan had been followed by a 0-1 defeat at Parkhead. A defensive error had been responsible, plunging the whole support into deep (but fortunately only temporary) depression, but it soon became clear from the demeanour of the players that they were determined to make up for the loss.

Already in the final of the Scottish Cup (which would be played three weeks after this game), Celtic were also well placed to win the Scottish League. On the Tuesday before the League Cup Final, Celtic had come back from the dead at Muirton Park, Perth to win 3-2 in the last minute of the game after having been (deservedly) 2-0 down to a good St Johnstone side at half-time. There was thus no lack of character in the team.

The League Cup campaign (which of course had begun the previous August) had seen two very good wins over Rangers in the sectional stage, then victories over Partick Thistle and Morton, an easy win over Hamilton Accies in the quarter-finals and some stuffy resistance from Clyde before substitute George Connelly had settled the issue.

Hibs were a team who often seemed to have better players than their results would indicate. They were well down the league table, but manager Bob Shankly (brother of Liverpool's Bill and himself the winner of the Scottish League in 1962 as manager of Dundee) had the ability to bring on good players. The talking point at the moment was young Peter Marinello, but there were also experienced players in the forward line like Pat Quinn and Peter Cormack, and at the back they had Pat Stanton whom many people thought to be the best defender in Scotland. Hibs had of course disappointed their fans and shot themselves in the foot by selling Colin Stein to Rangers for £100,000 – the first sale of a player between two Scottish clubs for a six figure sum. To replace Stein, they had brought in Joe McBride from Celtic, but Joe had already played for Celtic in the League Cup and was therefore ineligible for the final.

Celtic had two injuries. One was a dislocated shoulder to goalkeeper Ronnie Simpson in a Scottish Cup tie in February which would more or less finish his lengthy career (although he would come back for a few games the following season), and the other was a knock sustained the previous Tuesday night at Muirton Park by John Hughes. It would put John out for the rest of the season, but it gave Stein the opportunity to play his Lisbon forward line once again. As at Lisbon, the form displayed, often at high speed, was murderous to the opposition.

The two games between Celtic and Hibs in the league that year had been quite different. The Easter Road game at the end of November was remarkable. Hibs had gone 2-1 up within the last quarter of an hour when Joe Davis scored a penalty kick. It was as if someone had pressed a switch because Celtic, who had been none too impressive hitherto, suddenly turned it on and won 5-2 in a way which astonished even those of us who were accustomed to the power football that Celtic of that era produced.

The game at Parkhead on the other hand, played less than a fortnight previously on the Monday night after Celtic had beaten Morton in the Scottish Cup semi-final, saw Celtic playing well below their best, and with a bit of luck Hibs might well have pulled off a surprise victory. As it was, they had to settle for a draw (a bad result for Celtic who were striving for the league title) after Joe McBride equalised Willie Wallace's first half opener.

It was the first all-green Hampden cup final since the Coronation Cup of 1953, and Celtic started playing towards their traditional King's Park end of the ground. After a first 20 minutes or so in which all was equal, and during which time Eric Stevenson might have scored for Hibs, Celtic, described by Hugh Taylor in the *Daily Record* as 'Too fast. Too slick. Too confident', simply took command.

There were 25 minutes gone when a Bertie Auld free kick found McNeill, but he had centre-half Madsen with him, and the ball broke off the pair of them to the lurking Willie WALLACE who hit the ball through a mass of players into the net. Scarcely had the songs of triumph died down from the crowd when Celtic scored again, this time with a marvellously worked goal. Bertie Auld started it all, feeding Lennox who in turn gave the ball to Chalmers, then the ball returned to AULD who took his time, aimed for his spot and rifled the ball high into the corner of the net. And then with Hibs absolutely desperate to get to the sanctuary and relief of the half-time dressing room so that they could regroup, Celtic struck again with one of the craftiest goals of them all.

Bobby Lennox was famed for his speed, but less well known for his heading ability. So when Jimmy Johnstone took a corner kick on the right and Lennox peeled off from the mass of men in the centre of the penalty area, the Hibs defenders thought that it was little more than a decoy and concentrated on the more obvious threats of Wallace, Chalmers and McNeill. Thus LENNOX was virtually unchallenged as he glanced the ball into the net from about five yards. Clearly Lennox and Johnstone, great friends off the field, had worked this one out and Lennox immediately ran across to congratulate Jimmy as the Celtic end exploded with delirium.

Half-time came soon after, and although the joy of the Celtic supporters was tempered by the thought that Hibs, with their many fine players, might yet stage a second-half fightback, there was the appreciation that Celtic's performance had been nothing short of brilliant. The thought was expressed that if they had played like that against AC Milan in the European Cup quarter-final the previous month instead of approaching the game with too much caution, not only would they have won the European Cup again, they would even have revolutionised football. This was surely what the game was all about!

The second half saw a Celtic team still hungry for goals and still pressing forward, backed up by the roars of their huge adoring support who were enjoying the Hampden sunshine as well as the glorious football. Hibs deserve a great deal of credit for restricting Celtic to only another three goals in the second half, and even some of their own supporters were seen to be clapping the wiles of Johnstone, the trickery of Auld and the sheer power of Murdoch.

It was on the hour mark when Bertie Auld sent a marvellous, inch-perfect, defence-splitting pass to Bobby LENNOX to do the needful, then quarter of an hour later LENNOX did the same again, this time the spade work having been done by the ever willing Steve Chalmers. Lennox thus joined Billy McPhail in the exclusive club of those who have scored a hat-trick in a League Cup Final. Then Celtic's most unlikely goalscorer, Jim CRAIG, scored a sixth, a simple rebound after a cross had been blocked by a Hibs defender. Jim was normally the defending full-back while Tommy Gemmell was the attacking one, but Tommy had picked up a knock and had been replaced by John Clark.

This was clearly enough, although one felt that Celtic could have scored more. But the point had been proved and the foot was taken off the pedal – perhaps too much so, for Hibs, catching the goalscoring bug, scored a consolation goal through the hardworking Jim O'ROURKE – a goal that was given a loud cheer from the Celtic end as well as the Hibs supporters, but then we felt that Celtic were overdoing their generosity when Eric STEVENSON scored a second.

Hibs were deservedly given a round of applause as they collected their losers' medals, for they had played an honourable part in the afternoon's entertainment. But that was nothing to the sustained waves of cheering and applause that greeted Billy McNeill as he lifted the League Cup for Celtic. 'Laps of honour' were banned at Hampden in those days, so the Celtic team merely passed the cup back to each other to cheers that sounded like the 'Ole' of the Spanish bullfighting crowd or the 'Ave' of the Roman Colosseum.

And then, as if this was not enough to be going on with for the rapturous Celtic support, the transistor radios crackled out the joyous tidings of Dundee United 2 Rangers 1, soon to be translated into Glasgow dialect as 'The Huns goat bate two-wan', thus strengthening Celtic's position at the top of the Scottish League, and making a brilliant day perfect.

Jock Stein would later say, with tongue in cheek one suspects, 'I'm reasonably pleased'. Indeed he should have been. This was a fine performance, described by Rodger Baillie in his *Playing For Celtic* book as 'a memorable final, touched with the jewels of some great goals'. Even that is an understatement. This game was really what Celtic are, and should be, about. Bertie Auld would always say that both his Celtic managers Jimmy McGrory and Jock Stein emphasised the need to entertain. Especially since punters had paid a lot of money to see them. They certainly were entertained that day – and there was still more to come that sunny April.

v Rangers 4-0

Scottish Cup Final, Hampden
26 April 1969

CELTIC	RANGERS	REFEREE
Fallon	Martin	Mr J. Callaghan,
Craig	Johansen	Glasgow
Gemmell	Mathieson	
Murdoch	Greig	
McNeill	McKinnon	
Brogan*	D. Smith	
Connelly	Henderson	
Chalmers	Penman	
Wallace	Ferguson	
Lennox	Johnston	
Auld	Persson	
Sub: Clark*		

THE SCOTTISH Cup Final of 1969 was meant to be the occasion that Rangers struck back. They had in fact beaten Celtic twice in the league this season, but had still lost the title! This was because Celtic remembered better than Rangers that the two points that one got for beating Dundee, St Johnstone and Partick Thistle were just as valid as the points one got for winning Old Firm encounters, no matter how high profile they were. Rangers had far too often allowed themselves to slip up and lose or draw games that they should have won.

This did not alter the fact that they considered themselves to be a better team than Celtic and that they could beat them in a straight head to head, as the Scottish Cup Final now was. Rangers's 6-1 semi-final victory over Aberdeen at Parkhead had been highly impressive, and on their day it was felt that they could beat Celtic who had needed replays against both Partick Thistle and Clyde on their way to the final. There was however one fly in the Rangers' ointment, as it were. It concerned their own Stein – Colin, a centre-forward and no relation to Celtic's Jock. Colin Stein had been signed in the autumn from Hibs for over £100,000 and was seen as the solution to Rangers' goalscoring problems. Indeed he had been very impressive (mainly against poorer opposition, it would have to be said), but unfortunately he had a discipline problem.

On 15 March in a game against Clyde in the last minute with Rangers winning 6-0, Stein was sent off for kicking an opponent. He had indeed been provoked, but his rash retaliation at the end of a game which had been well won and in which he had starred, earned him a suspension which included 26 April, the day of the final.

The reaction to this astonished the football world, and, led by some mischief-makers in the press, notably the blatantly pro-Rangers *Scottish Daily Express*, a director of Morton FC (whose motives can only be guessed at) and countless letters of support from the more hysterical of their own support, Rangers started a campaign to try to get the suspension lifted or perhaps postponed, or even broken in the middle – so that Colin Stein could play in the final!

The Beatles had a song in the 1960s called 'You Can't Do That', the lyrics going along the lines of:

For, I've told you before
Ooh, you can't do that!

Indeed, you could not do what Rangers were attempting, for it would have made a mockery of Scottish football. Rangers themselves eventually saw the absurdity of it, and distanced themselves from this preposterous attempt not so much to rewrite the rule book as to make up the rules for themselves. In total contrast, in the very week of the cup final, Celtic's Jimmy Johnstone was also suspended, but the other Stein, big Jock, bit his considerable lip and accepted life's vicissitudes with dignity. This was the second blow to Celtic, for John Hughes had been out with an ankle injury for the whole month of April, and any slight, lingering hopes that he could make it for the final were soon dashed.

Colin Stein's suspension was good news for the likes of Alex Ferguson of Rangers who was now elevated to the centre-forward position and charged with the job of ending Rangers' three-year trophy famine. Similarly the unavailability of Hughes and Johnstone gave an opportunity to young George Connelly who had impressed for Celtic in his outings so far, although his experience was limited. Celtic had also been without Ronnie Simpson since February, and a great onus was therefore put on John Fallon, forever to be remembered for his howlers at Parkhead at New Year 1968.

All 134,000 tickets for the game were sold (although 'only' 132,870 made it through the turnstiles) and seldom has there been such a build-up to a Scottish Cup Final. It was clear however that all the pressure was on Rangers. Celtic had, after all, won the Scottish League and the Scottish League Cup and a defeat in the Scottish Cup Final, although disappointing, would not have shattered the fans in the way that it would Rangers supporters. The lads in blue were showing by their attitude and behaviour that they were struggling to cope with three years without a major honour, not helped by the fact that during this time Celtic had won the European Cup! Things had changed from the days of the early 1960s when Rangers won everything, everyone loved the Queen and went to church, and the Conservatives were in power.

But it would be all so different on the afternoon of 26 April. A victory parade had been scheduled for Ibrox that night, so that everyone could see the Scottish Cup in blue ribbons. This seems to have been a misguided attempt to spread propaganda on the grounds that confidence was high at Ibrox and that everyone would expect Rangers to win – and therefore they would! Such confidence however really has to be backed up by justified faith in the ability of your players.

Across the city no such plans were in force. An unfortunate defeat by AC Milan in the European Cup quarter-final had been taken on the chin and recovered from. Everything at Parkhead was more downbeat and more professional, while supporters wondered if Celtic could perform the unique feat of winning all three Scottish honours in the same calendar month. In addition, both teams had now won the Scottish Cup on 19 occasions. Who would be the first to 20?

Rangers were told by manager Davie White to 'watch McNeill at corner kicks!' Both full-backs were charged with the task of taking a post each (as one learned at primary school) and Alex Ferguson was given the job of going up with Billy if and when Celtic won corners. Therefore one could hardly believe what happened in the second minute. Celtic won a corner on the left at the King's Park end of the ground in front of their own supporters. Bobby Lennox took it and it was a high floater. Hampden watched in amazement as Billy McNEILL rose in splendid isolation to head the ball into the net at the vacant post to goalkeeper Martin's right.

It was the immediate aftermath of this goal that was revealing. It took a split second for the Celtic end to react and erupt, for there was a feeling of unreality about this goal, as if the referee's whistle must have gone to explain the lack of resistance to McNeill in the Rangers defence. Then as McNeill jumped in triumph, Alex Ferguson collapsed, head in hands, conscious of his failure to do what he had been told while John Greig was seen angrily gesticulating to Kaj Johansen and asking why he was unaccountably missing from his post. Had he been in the right place he would certainly have cleared the ball, but where was he? Poor Kaj; the hero of '66 was now the villain of '69.

The game then turned nasty. One particular charge on John Fallon as he saved the ball led to more than a few personal vendettas. Jim Brogan was the only player to be booked, but he can consider himself very unlucky, for there were one or two fierce tackles that bordered on assaults. It was noticeable that the men who kept their composure were also the best players; Bobby Lennox simply got on with it, George Connelly for all his inexperience kept distributing the ball with aplomb, and Bobby Murdoch, no shrinking violet when it came to the rough stuff, kept playing brilliantly and earned universal plaudits when he was blatantly headbutted by a man of now legendary reputation in managerial circles. Bobby did not go down and feign that it was worse than it was. Even more admirably he didn't retaliate, merely getting on with the job – and that probably hurt the offender more than anything.

The two minutes before half-time killed Rangers. Their left-winger Orjan Persson failed to control a ball on the left wing; George Connelly stepped in and with a fine pass found Bobby Lennox. LENNOX with his famous turn of speed, charged in on goal pursued by Willie Mathieson, and with Norrie Martin coming out to narrow the angle, slid the ball past him.

With the Celtic end now in fervour behind them, the Rangers defence incredibly collapsed again a minute later. This time it was John Greig who was slow on a short goal kick from Norrie Martin, and was robbed by the young George CONNELLY who stepped out of reserve team football to round the keeper and put Celtic 3-0 up. And it was not yet half-time!

This was unbelievable stuff. The half-time interval was spent with the occasional bottles coming out of the Rangers end and the subsequent diving in of the Glasgow police to drag out some pathetic specimen of humanity, and raw, raucous delirium at the other end who frankly could not believe what they were seeing. Three shocking elementary defensive errors from a Rangers team who were showing far too much aggression and far too little composure and common sense.

But common sense was still required from Celtic. Jock Stein's task was to keep his players' feet firmly on the floor. There were still 45 minutes remaining. It was hard to believe that Rangers would not mount some kind of a fightback. It would be truly awful to throw this game away. In truth Rangers did try but had far fewer chances in the second half than they did in the first, such was the stranglehold in midfield where George Connelly had moved back to strengthen McNeill, Brogan (who would be replaced by Clark) and Murdoch.

Speculation was more on who would be the first to be sent off, such was the ferocity of some of the tackling, rather than if there would be any more scoring. The arrests at the Mount Florida end were continuing, and then Steve CHALMERS ended any sort of doubt about where the cup was going when he ran, virtually unchallenged, about 40 yards to flick past Norrie Martin in front of the sullen, taciturn Rangers fans. There followed a rather predictable invasion from the Rangers end, but once again the Glasgow police put up a stronger defence than John Greig, Ron McKinnon and Dave Smith had done all day. Some Rangers fans were trying to get round the side of the terracing for an early exit. The sadistic policemen pushed them all back onto the terracing and made them watch the rest of this rout!

Such unpleasantness must not be allowed to disguise what was a fine victory for Celtic as they completed their second domestic treble in three years. Heroes were aplenty; young George Connelly, Bobby Murdoch, Billy McNeill, Bobby Lennox but above all else, goalkeeper John Fallon who had now shown the ability to come back from his own personal hell of 15 months previously and win all the honours, and more importantly the hearts and minds of the Celtic faithful.

v Leeds United 2-1

European Cup Semi-Final Second Leg, Hampden, 15 April 1970

CELTIC	LEEDS UNITED	REFEREE
Williams	Sprake*	Herr G. Schulenberg,
Hay	Madeley	West Germany
Gemmell	Cooper	
Murdoch	Bremner	
McNeill	Charlton	
Brogan	Hunter	
Johnstone	Lorimer	
Connelly	Clarke	
Hughes	Jones	
Auld	Giles	
Lennox	Gray	
	Sub: **Harvey***	

THIS GAME was in any sense of the word, huge. Inevitably it was dubbed 'The Battle of Britain'. As early as 1970 this was a meaningless, predictable and annoying cliché and indeed some even thought it an insult to Douglas Bader and those who had fought in the real Battle of Britain and, even more fatuously, likened to the tribal battles between Scotland and England of Wallace and Bruce, but that was, quite simply, not true.

In the first place, not all of Scotland wanted Celtic to win – a surprising amount of people did, however, even a few Rangers fans – and it was even less true that all of England wanted Leeds United to win. In fact, a straw poll in places like London, Bristol, Manchester and Newcastle would have revealed a huge spread of support for Celtic. There were several reasons for this.

Under manager Don Revie, Leeds United played a style of game that was 'robust'. Other people would have called it 'dirty' and Leeds United gloried in their reputation. Norman Hunter for example enjoyed the nickname of 'Bites Yer Legs', Jack Charlton's habit of standing in front of the opposition goalkeeper at a corner kick was a blatant attempt at obstruction, Billy Bremner knew exactly how to tackle in a way that looked innocent but in fact was brutal, and there were other less than complimentary things said about them as well. But there was more to Leeds than just fouling. They were 'professional' in the sense that they knew how to feign injury, to upset opponents by comments about the man's wife, to unsettle a referee, to waste time and so on.

But they were also good. They had some fine players in Jack Charlton, a World Cup winner with England in 1966, Alan Clark a predatory goalscorer, Johnnie Giles a great ball player, and a Scottish trio of Peter Lorimer, Eddie Gray and Billy Bremner (the last two being great Celtic supporters!). Revie, who had been a great player himself with Manchester City, was a superb motivator and in some ways his managerial career with the moribund Leeds United whom he joined in 1961 was not dissimilar to what Jock Stein had done with Dunfermline Athletic at the same time.

Another reason why they were not universally liked lay in the fact that they were 'parvenus' from Yorkshire. Yorkshire enjoys with the rest of England the same sort of relationship that Texas has with the rest of the United States. One is a Yorkshireman first before one is an Englishman and this was of course the time when Yorkshire cricket produced grim, dour, unlovable men like Boycott, Close and Illingworth – who seemed to wage an almost perpetual war against the rest of England (and in particular the moneyed South where the Establishment resided), let alone the Australians and the rest of the world.

There were also more positive reasons why Celtic were preferred to Leeds United in newspapers like the *Daily Telegraph* and *The Times*. Celtic, for one thing, played good attacking football and their performance in Lisbon three years earlier was recalled with a great deal of admiration. In addition, as loads of people in London loved to claim that they had a Scottish or Irish great-grandparent, it seemed sensible to support the flamboyant, charming Celts from Bonnie Scotland against the sometimes unpleasant Leeds United from the grim, industrial north of England.

The first leg a fortnight earlier on 1 April had raised a few eyebrows for it had resulted in a 1-0 Celtic victory. A goal scored early by George Connelly was the difference, although the same player seemed to score an equally valid goal early in the second half only to have it chalked off for offside. This result delighted the Celtic fans and meant that 136,505 attended Hampden Park for the second leg, a record for the European Cup and one that will never be broken. The crowd incidentally vindicated the decision of the Celtic board to shift the game from Parkhead to Hampden. A few diehards objected to this move on the grounds that Parkhead was Celtic's home, but their voices were silenced when the crowd was virtually doubled by the move. In any case, the Celtic board were able to bring forward some flimsy excuses about 'ground renovations' and 'public safety', although few people believed that. The reason for the shift was to a certain extent to 'play the Scottish card' and emphasise that this was a Scottish team at the national stadium, but the real reason was, to be frank about it, money.

Celtic had been at Hampden four days earlier – and it had not been a happy experience. Celtic, having won the Scottish League Cup in October and the league championship at a canter as early as 28 March, would have won their second consecutive Scottish domestic treble if they had won the Scottish Cup against Aberdeen. But they didn't, as Aberdeen had one of their rare moments of triumph in a 3-1 victory. Celtic, and Stein in particular, would blame Airdrie referee Bobby Davidson for it all. In truth, although there had been three indefensible decisions which had all gone against Celtic at key stages – a penalty awarded when the ball hit Bobby Murdoch on the chest, a disallowed penalty at the other end and a chalked off goal – there had also been a lack of conviction about some of Celtic's play that day, and the fear was expressed that this great side were either on the slide or suffering from a surfeit of over-confidence and had taken their eye off the ball for the Scottish Cup Final while concentrating on the Leeds match.

Leeds had fared little better, although they were still in the FA Cup Final, for they had drawn with Chelsea at Wembley the same day as Celtic had lost to Aberdeen. The league championship had been conceded to Everton, Leeds' cause not being helped by prolonged, self-piteous whingeing about 'fixture congestion', a problem which did not elicit much sympathy from the English FA. But there seemed little doubt that the trophy which really mattered to Leeds United was the European Cup.

It would be interesting to see the first half-hour, as roles were reversed. Normally one would have expected to see Celtic charging forward with all guns blazing to satisfy the demands of their huge support while Leeds would be the defenders, killing the game and striking with deadly force on the break. But because of the 1-0 score-line at Elland Road, Leeds would have to attack, while knowing that a goal for Celtic would more or less kill the tie.

Leeds in fact had the better of the early exchanges, although the menace of Jimmy Johnstone was causing them concern as poor Terry Cooper, who had struggled against Jimmy at Elland Road, was finding him even more difficult at Hampden. But it was Leeds who scored the first goal through Billy BREMNER. Not everyone liked Bremner for his terrier approach to the game, but even his detractors had to admit that this was a great goal. He picked up a pass from Johnny Giles, was given far too much room by the Celtic midfield, and crashed home a fierce shot from about 30 yards high into the corner of the net which goalkeeper Evan Williams hardly saw.

This reduced the vast Hampden crowd, already swaying dangerously at some points of the King's Park end of the ground, to momentary silence. There was even a ripple of applause for what was a good goal from a Scotsman who supported Celtic, but within a few minutes the encouragement and the cheering began again, growing in momentum, with everyone very aware that if Celtic did not win this one, it would effectively be the end of the season, with every other competition either lost or won.

Half-time was reached with the teams level on aggregate. As both teams left the field, Stein confided to his friend Don Revie that he was worried about the crowd, for the ground was overcrowded to an alarming degree. Don looked around, agreed curtly and then shrugged his shoulders as if to say 'What can we do about it?'

Celtic came out for the second half with additional determination. Billy McNeill, struggling with an ankle injury sustained in the Scottish Cup Final, clapped his hands in inspiring fashion as he led them out. The players, still hurting from Saturday's loss, followed him out. Auld was engaged in conversation with Murdoch, the two 'likely lads' Johnstone and Lennox came out together and Tommy Gemmell came out with that thunderous look on his face. He had never stopped telling everyone about his goal in Lisbon three years ago. He would like to do something similar tonight.

It all happened in the opening ten minutes of the second half. Celtic were now attacking the King's Park end, so Johnstone was operating in front of the main stand. In conjunction with Davie Hay, one of the real finds of the season, Johnstone forced a corner. He took it himself and played the ball into Auld who had been curiously overlooked by the Leeds defence who seemed to have underestimated him. Bertie sent a low ball into the penalty box and John HUGHES dived forward to head home the equaliser on the night and to put Celtic 2-1 up on aggregate.

John Hughes had not always been the hero of the Celtic fans, and he was destined to fall out in a big way with Jock Stein very soon, but this was one of his many fine nights for the club. A minute later he almost scored again but was thwarted by a brave dive from goalkeeper Gary Sprake who was injured in the process and had to be replaced by David Harvey, a local goalkeeper from Leeds who would later win 16 caps for Scotland because his father was Scottish. Poor Harvey's first act was to pick the ball out of the net!

Once again it was Jimmy Johnstone in front of the main stand who did it, making space for himself by leaving defenders trailing in his wake as he crossed for Bobby MURDOCH to score with a hard shot to the back of the net. Celtic were now 3-1 up on aggregate, and frankly never looked like conceding that lead, as the noise of the crowd grew and grew in intensity until the referee's whistle signalled the end of the game and the start of a huge Celtic party.

There was of course a sad postscript to this game in that Celtic then suffered from over-confidence and complacency and lost the final to Feyenoord of Rotterdam – a good team to be sure but well within the compass of the Celtic side that played against Leeds. It would have been a great deal better if the Leeds United game had been the final...

v **Dundee** 8-1

Scottish League, Dens Park
16 January 1971

CELTIC	DUNDEE	REFEREE
Williams	Donaldson	Mr A. McKenzie,
Craig	Wilson*	Larbert
Gemmell	Soutar	
Murdoch	Steele	
McNeill	Philip	
Brogan	Houston	
Johnstone	Duncan	
Wallace	Gilroy	
Hood	Wallace	
Callaghan	Scott	
Auld	Kinninmonth	
	Sub: Johnston*	

CELTIC WERE in a funny position in January 1971. It would appear that their crown was slipping. They had been league champions for the past five years, and the historically minded were aware that they needed only one more to equal the record set by Jimmy Quinn and Jimmy McMenemy's great team from 1905-1910, but they were under pressure this year from a different source than normal. This was the Aberdeen team of Eddie Turnbull who had of course beaten Celtic in the previous year's Scottish Cup Final and had more recently beaten them at Parkhead in mid-December.

In fact, in the calendar year of 1970 Celtic had lost three Cup finals: the Scottish Cup to Aberdeen, the European Cup on that dreadful night in Milan to Feyenoord, and to Rangers in the Scottish League Cup Final of October. In addition rumours persisted about Jock Stein. He was apparently off to Manchester United at the end of the season, having felt, not without cause, that he had done enough with Celtic and that a fresh challenge offered other opportunities. Johnstone, Gemmell and Auld were all, apparently, less than happy at Parkhead as well...

But all this, important though it was, had been engulfed in the terrible events of two weeks previously. At the end of the Rangers v Celtic game at Ibrox, 66 Rangers fans had been crushed to death on Scottish football's most tragic day. It was not easy 'to shrug one's shoulders and get on with it' after that, and even though it affected Rangers primarily, Celtic and their supporters could not escape their involvement in this horrible event. It was very noticeable that for a long time afterwards, Celtic fans refrained from nasty chants and songs about Rangers, and there was a total absence of the usual kind of sick jokes that one often hears in the wake of tragedies. Rangers were, for the time being at least, to be treated with respect. Players and supporters of both teams had happily attended religious services in Roman Catholic and Church of Scotland places of worship when memorial services were being held, and the hope was being expressed that perhaps the penny might drop about religious intolerance in Glasgow.

That very day at Ibrox, Rangers were playing their first home game since the disaster against Dundee United and a very impressive two minutes' silence was heard. It was therefore all the more distressing to arrive at Dens Park and find oneself assailed with cries of 'Fenians' and 'Pope lovers' from a minority of the Dundee support. This had been an element which had been conspicuously lacking a decade earlier when Dundee, with Ure and Gilzean on board, were the best team in Scotland, winning as they did the Scottish League in 1962 and enjoying a good run in Europe in 1963.

But as Dundee's team declined, so too did the quality of their support. Decent Dundee supporters, sickened by the repeated selling off of star players – Ian Ure, Alan Gilzean, Charlie Cooke – when they didn't really need to and in what seemed to many a canny Dundonian as making a fast buck, were alienated. They stopped going and were replaced by long-haired, foul-mouthed louts whose vocabulary was as limited as their intelligence. A young student teacher doing his training in that city in 1971 despaired at the magnitude of the task ahead of him!

It was a fine Scottish winter's day, and of course in 1971 Great Britain was in the middle of an experiment with the hours of the day so that in Scotland it was darker in the morning but lighter at night. There was sunshine – 'a weary winter sun' as Robert Burns would have put it – but it was cold and it was fairly obvious that a frost would come down at sunset. Yet it was a healthy day for a football match.

Celtic's team selection that year had lacked consistency, particularly in the forward line where it was felt that they had too many players. To an extent this bred healthy competition for places but it also meant that every Saturday saw a few disappointed players who might on occasion feel inclined to cause trouble. The five 'Lisbon Lion' forwards were still there, as was John Hughes, although becoming less and less happy with Stein and the set-up, but in the late 1960s Stein had also brought in Tommy Callaghan (an attack-minded midfielder) from Dunfermline and Harry Hood from Clyde. In addition, youngsters like Macari, Dalglish and Davidson were knocking on the door.

Today was Bertie Auld's day. Bertie, now approaching his 33rd birthday, had had a remarkable career. He had been with the club as early as the mid 1950s, had almost played in the 7-1 win over Rangers in 1957, had been transferred to Birmingham City for reasons other than footballing ability in 1961, and had been brought back in 1965 to coincide, more or less, with the arrival of Jock Stein. From then on, he had been Celtic's playmaker and had led them to unbelievable good fortune and success. Today, very much in the twilight of his Celtic career, he had been brought back in place of the injured Bobby Lennox. Indeed this was to be his first start of the whole season so far, his first in fact since Celtic's last visit to Dens Park the previous May.

Dundee were managed by John Prentice, a doughty veteran of Rangers and Falkirk. He had been manager of Scotland for a short spell in the mid 1960s but had departed for reasons never adequately explained. He was now doing a good job for Dundee, albeit hamstrung by a board of directors who found it hard to see football in terms other than making money, and as a result were now gradually beginning to lose the battle of the city as the pendulum was ever so slowly beginning to veer towards Tannadice Park.

But they still had good players – Ian Phillip, Doug Houston, Gordon Wallace – and their results were respectable most of the time, even though they had had a bad New Year, losing 0-3 to great rivals Aberdeen on New Year's Day at Pittodrie. Clashes between Dundee and Celtic at Dens Park had invariably been good ones, often described as the 'highlight of the season' in the local press. Dundee usually won by the odd goal between 1960 and 1965, then with the arrival of Jock Stein, Celtic reversed that process and edged it over the home side.

But today was different. Prentice, feeling that Celtic were vulnerable, gave his men orders to attack. So did Stein – but then Celtic fans never expected anything else from their team – and the result was some fine football in the tradition of these two teams. But it was Celtic who went in at half-time two goals to the good, one from Harry HOOD after quarter of an hour who 'turned on a sixpence to score' as Jim Blair of the *Evening Times* put it, and the other, the one which probably sealed Dundee's fate, just on the stroke of half-time from Willie WALLACE. Yet fair-minded Celtic fans thought that this was hard on Dundee, for they had turned on some fine football with some good crossfield passing, and it was felt that they were bound to come back in the second half. Sympathy for Dundee, however, was tempered by the behaviour of the supporters and their inane and provocative chants. After eight minutes of the second half, some of these pathetic specimens tried an invasion of the field which was greeted more with laughter than anger as the Dundee police did their job of clearing them off.

The second half was a lesson in the art of football. Much discussion on tactics had focussed on the use of wingers, and how they were redundant in the modern game. That this was rubbish was proved conclusively by the form of Celtic's Jimmy Johnstone and Bertie Auld. Bertie came inside quite a lot and bossed the midfield, although he created all sorts of damage down the left as well and Jimmy Johnstone was simply Jimmy Johnstone. One of his opponents, Iain Phillip, would recall years later: 'I will never forget that one, it was the Jimmy Johnstone show. He just ran amok and in that form the wee man was virtually unstoppable.'

Unstoppable was the word. Shots, drives and headers rained down on Dundee's goal and Ally Donaldson, Dundee's veteran keeper, deserves a great deal of credit for keeping the final score down to 8-1. After Willie WALLACE scored in the 60th minute, shortly after Dundee seemed to be mounting some kind of a fightback, Celtic simply went berserk with goals from CALLAGHAN, two from JOHNSTONE himself, an OWN GOAL and one from Harry HOOD right at the death. Even the goal that Dundee scored from John DUNCAN got a cheer from the triumphant Celtic fans (the Dundee supporters who had been provoking Celtic's with their chants about King Billy had long since gone home, realising that they were being laughed at), and there was even a sigh of disappointment at the end when Hood scored the eighth, because Celtic supporters do like that score of 7-1.

Dens Park was actually a really beautiful sight that afternoon. The low winter sun was setting in the west over the Provost Road end of the ground, and there was something rather symbolic in that as regards Bertie Auld, the maestro who had done the entertaining that afternoon and on many previous occasions. The glorious sunset seemed to mirror the end to the career of Bertie Auld who played only a few more games for the club before being given his free transfer in April. Now in his senior years, Bertie Auld will always be willing to talk to those who idolised him. A frequent attender at supporters' functions, he will always stress that both 'Mr McGrory' and 'Jock' (revealingly, that is how he refers to both of them) told them to 'entertain', on the grounds that the punters had worked hard all week, had spent good money to come and watch Celtic, and they deserved to be entertained. Seldom did Bertie entertain them better than at Dens Park that day.

The managers' comments at the end were revealing. Prentice paid tribute to Celtic, but then ranted and fumed at his own team's performance: 'It was humiliating. No professional team should ever lose by seven goals.' Maybe not, but very seldom did anyone come up against Celtic in this form. Jock Stein on the other hand, having heard this and with no desire to say anything that might further humiliate Dundee, ignored questions that were put to him and asked 'What was the score with Dunfermline?' He was told they had beaten St Mirren 1-0, smiled and then smiled even more when the reporter added that Hibs had beaten Aberdeen 2-1 and that Celtic had therefore regained control at the top of the league.

Celtic would have a few bad games that season but they never really lost the initiative again, and were on their way to a league and cup double. In some ways it was Stein's best season, for he came back following the disasters of summer 1970 and with a partially rebuilt team, emerged yet again as top dog. And this game at Dens Park was as good a game as any...

v Hibernian 6-1
Scottish Cup Final, Hampden
6 May 1972

CELTIC	HIBERNIAN	REFEREE
Williams	Herriot	Mr A. McKenzie,
Craig	Brownlie	Larbert
Brogan	Schaedler	
Murdoch	Stanton	
McNeill	Black	
Connelly	Blackley	
Johnstone	Edwards	
Deans	Hazel	
Macari	Gordon	
Dalglish	O'Rourke	
Callaghan	Duncan*	
	Sub: Auld*	

GOING TO a Hampden cup final was no new experience for Celtic supporters in 1972. Since 1965 they had missed only one Scottish Cup Final and they were ever present in the Scottish League Cup finals since 1964. Not that they had all been triumphant occasions, of course. Indeed this very season they had lost the League Cup Final in October 1971 to Partick Thistle in a way which had mystified and distressed their supporters, and had hurt Stein to such an extent that he amazed the Scottish footballing world by signing a man called John 'Dixie' Deans from Motherwell in the immediate aftermath of the game.

It was a distinctly odd signing. Deans could indeed score goals, but he was a wild boy. On the day of Willie Wallace's debut for Celtic in 1966 against Motherwell, Deans, playing for Motherwell, had been sent off, and that was by no means his only offence. Indeed, when he actually joined Celtic, he was in the middle of a suspension (for this reason, perhaps, Stein got him cheaper at £17,500 than he might have done) and his Celtic debut had therefore to be necessarily delayed! Yet Stein did have an almost unerring ability to spot a good striker.

Deans had scored 19 goals in the league that season from November onwards, and there was every sign that Stein was turning round a hitherto rather disappointing career. But it was one famous mistake of Deans' that everyone talked about.

It was a penalty kick in the shoot-out at the end of the European Cup semi-final against Inter Milan at Parkhead, and poor Dixie had been the only man of the ten penalty takers on both sides to miss! It had been a wretched night for Celtic and for Deans himself, one imagines, but some 17 days later he had a chance to redeem himself as Celtic, league champions for the seventh year in a row and having broken their own record for consecutive championships set in 1910, could win the Scottish Cup for the 22nd time.

Their opponents would be Hibs. In contrast to Celtic's proud Scottish Cup record, Hibs were rare visitors to Glasgow on cup final day. They had last been at Hampden in a Scottish Cup Final in 1958, there to lose to Clyde, and they had won the trophy on only two occasions, in 1887 and 1902. The 1887 victory was the first time that a team from the east of Scotland had won the cup, and it had had an indirect effect in that some Glaswegian Irishmen noticed how well the Edinburgh Irishmen had done and started moves to found their own club. It was indeed that very club that Hibs had beaten in their next Scottish Cup Final in 1902 when McGeachen had scored with a back-heeler to allow Bobby Atherton to bring the cup home.

Everyone at Easter Road was painfully aware that this was a long time ago, and although cruel jokes were made about how the men who were building the Edinburgh Castle got a half-day off to celebrate because Mary Queen of Scots insisted, or how Bonnie Prince Charlie was distinctly miffed about not getting his portrait taken with the cup, the humour was wearing thin. They had lost finals to Celtic in 1914 and 1923, to Airdrie in 1924, to Aberdeen in 1947 and to Clyde in 1958 – some of them unlucky losses – and the time had surely come to put that right. Efforts were made by the Edinburgh-based newspapers and by the club themselves to dig up survivors who had been there in 1902 (70 years ago) and they did indeed find a few, but the majority would indeed have had to have been 'dug up'.

Hibs (now under the management of Eddie Turnbull) were no bad side. They finished third equal in the league and had beaten Rangers 2-0 in the semi-final, having also disposed of Aberdeen. They also had some fine players like Pat Stanton, John Brownlie, Alex Edwards and Arthur Duncan. Eddie Turnbull (who had recent experience of beating Celtic in the Scottish Cup Final of 1970 when manager of Aberdeen) described himself as 'quietly confident' and sure that 'my boys will do well'. Edinburgh braced itself for a celebration, a fatal thing to do, especially in Edinburgh where it had been almost a decade since either team had last won anything (in that case Hearts winning the League Cup of 1962/63).

Turnbull himself tells the story of how on Scottish Cup Final day in 1972, by sheer chance both teams met at the same hotel for lunch. While Hibs were nervous and uptight, Celtic were buoyant and exuberant. One can imagine the scene with Johnstone and Lennox telling jokes, Craig and Brogan in conversation, McNeill relaxed and smiling and watching over them all, Stein, without in any way losing any of his dignity and gravity, being the perfect soulmate, talking about holidays and who was likely to win the English Cup and so on. Hibs, on the other hand, most of whose players could hardly imagine what a six-figure crowd would be like, were 'psyched out' by the upbeat Celts.

The crowd was 106,102 – an eloquent testimony to the pulling power of two good football teams at a time when gates were meant to be falling. It was estimated that Hibs made up about 30,000 of that crowd (where were they every Saturday?), there would be about 10,000 neutrals and dignitaries and the rest would be Celtic fans (again, one could ask a similar question about their whereabouts on a November Saturday), desperate to see their side win a back-to-back league and cup double and needing something to cheer them up after their gnawingly disappointing European exit.

Celtic fans were pleased to see Dixie Deans in the team – his place had not in any way been guaranteed – for he had surely proved himself by his goalscoring, but they were disappointed to see Bobby Lennox not in the starting XI. Bobby was also tried and tested, but it was comforting to know that if things were going badly, 'little Lennoxie', the substitute, could be deployed. Indeed, Lennox was now a frequent substitute, so much so that jokes began to go round Glasgow that he should be called the 'judge' or the 'magistrate' – because he was always on the bench!

Celtic started off playing towards the Mount Florida end and before the nervous Hibs side had time to settle, McNEILL had scored. McNeill was of course famous for scoring goals from free kicks and corners, and this time Alan Gordon was detailed to mark him. Gordon, a highly intelligent man, was once famously told by Eddie Turnbull, 'The trouble with you, Alan, is that all your brains are in your head!', but on this occasion he failed to carry out his instructions and McNeill put Celtic ahead from a Tommy Callaghan free kick, thus scoring his first ever cup final goal with his foot, the others being headers.

Any rocket that Alan GORDON was going to get from Eddie Turnbull at half-time was stayed in its tracks as he equalised ten minutes later, getting a boot to a cross from Arthur Duncan and allowing the Edinburgh greens their one and only chance to celebrate. For a short while after that Hibs took command, and began to pass the ball to each other with confidence.

It would only last a short time though, for halfway through this eventful first half, Dixie DEANS vindicated Jock Stein's judgement in picking him by putting Celtic in front again. Johnstone had been fouled about 35 yards from goal and to the right. Bobby Murdoch took the free kick and picked out Dixie who headed home brilliantly an almost archetypal Celtic goal. Dixie, by no means the tallest player on Celtic's books, with his squat, almost fat physique, not looking like a natural jumper, surprised them all, and Celtic were back in the lead, a lead they held until the interval.

It was ten minutes after half-time that DEANS scored what might be reckoned to be the greatest cup final goal of them all. Fortunately, it is fairly readily available on DVD and video to watch, for words scarcely do it justice. Alan Herron in the *Sunday Mail* does his best: 'Lou Macari set it up with a long cross field pass which Brownlie only nudged with his head towards Deans, running at his back into the Hibs box. Deans collected the ball, beat the diving Herriot on the line, took it round him and beat Brownlie on the line. All the time the goal was getting nearer and all the time it looked as though Deans had lost his chance. Again he evaded Herriot before eventually thumping the ball into the net. A great goal – taken with incredible confidence.' As famous as anything else, however, was his somersault after he scored, the grin splitting his face from ear to ear as the Celtic end erupted in the face of such brilliance.

And he wasn't finished yet! DEANS scored his third and Celtic's fourth when he picked up a crisp Callaghan through-pass and got to the ball before Herriot did. No-one quite appreciated it at the time, but this hat-trick was only the second ever scored in a Scottish Cup Final, the other coming from Jimmy Quinn in 1904. Thus Deans, whose season had sagged alarmingly in the autumn when he was suspended while playing for Motherwell, had been picked up by Stein, then had hit what seemed like an all-time low of unhappiness with his missed penalty, was now linked with Jimmy Quinn!

It was now 4-1 in the 75th minute and we had the rare sight of hooliganism from Hibs fans. Thuggery was a besetting sin of the Scottish footballing scene in the early 1970s, but it was strange to see it coming from that source as some of their fans spilled over from the terracing in a particularly pathetic attempt to stop the game. Maybe they wanted a blade of grass as a souvenir from their one and only visit to Hampden, said an unkind Celtic fan.

The idiots having been banished, the game continued. By this time, Hibs had brought on the old Celtic favourite Bertie Auld to replace Arthur Duncan, who was injured in a clash of heads. Bertie never really looked like adding to his tally of three Scottish Cup winners' medals, but was given a great reception by the Parkhead fans who still clearly classed him as one of theirs. Celtic now ran through a panic-stricken and shattered Hibs defence who were looking with desperation for the final whistle and an end to their agony. Lou MACARI scored another two goals – one a glorious shot to complete a great Celtic move, and the other a tap-in after good work from Craig and Connelly.

To describe this as a rout is perhaps unfair on Hibs. They had their moments and might have had another goal. They were by no means a bad side as they would prove in the next season or two, but on this occasion they had no answer to Celtic. And it was a shame that Dixie Deans missed that penalty in the European Cup semi-final. It would have been interesting to see Celtic playing like this in the European final; 1967 might well have been replicated.

v Hibernian 6-3
Scottish League Cup Final, Hampden
26 October 1974

CELTIC	HIBERNIAN	REFEREE
Hunter	McArthur	Mr J.R.P. Gordon,
McGrain	Brownlie*	Tayport
Brogan	Bremner	
Murray	Stanton	
McNeill	Spalding	
McCluskey	Blackley	
Johnstone	Edwards	
Dalglish	Cropley	
Deans	Harper	
Hood	Munro	
Wilson	Duncan**	
	Subs: Smith*	
	Murray**	

NOT FOR the first time was it said that Celtic were in decline. If you win the league for nine years in a row, as Celtic had done, there comes a time when you fade and when someone else really has to take over. Rangers, Aberdeen and Hibs had all come close to doing that, but had all for various reasons lacked the perseverance, stamina and self-belief to keep pace with the extraordinary standard that Celtic had set.

But now in autumn 1974, it was felt that there really might be a decline. In the wake of a successful World Cup, Davie Hay had gone to Chelsea. He had been unhappy with his terms and conditions for some time, but his move to Chelsea was no success. He would be back to Parkhead as manager in ten years' time, and in sundry other guises in later years. Another man in and out of Parkhead, albeit on a shorter-term basis, was George Connelly, a hugely talented but unstable player who could never make up his mind whether to retire from the game or not. His inability to either stay or go was another thing which did no-one any good, but those who saw him play wondered what on earth the problem was! On his game he was a superb player.

Celtic had started the season well enough, recovering from an unusual defeat at Somerset Park, Ayr to win their League Cup section while Rangers lost out in theirs to Hibs. But there were causes for concern. A defeat to Rangers at Parkhead in the Scottish League was not, in itself, any great cause for alarm, but the real disaster came in the exit in Europe to a team of incredulous Greeks called Olympiakos whom more spirited Celtic teams of a few years back would not have seen in their way. It was simply that Celtic did not create enough from midfield – a clear testimony to the folly of allowing the departure of Bobby Murdoch and Davie Hay – while other players like Tommy Callaghan, Jimmy Johnstone and Kenny Dalglish struggled to find consistent form.

Dalglish seemed to divide the support. He was still young, of course, and clearly had talent, and therein lay the reason for his occasional unpopularity with the Celtic support. Celtic fans find it difficult to tolerate a good player going through a bad spell. They have been conditioned to the best, and will accept nothing less than that. In addition, what was Dalglish's best position? Was it as an out and out striker? Or was he better just slightly behind the forwards as a purveyor of the ball? The boy was able, little doubt about that, but in October 1974 questions were being asked of him, particularly in the wake of that hard-to-accept European defeat.

And what about Dixie Deans? He seemed to be out of favour with both Stein and the supporters at the start of the season but was now clawing his way back as Celtic beat Hamilton Accies and Airdrie (none too convincingly) to reach their 11th successive League Cup Final. This competition was one with which Celtic had a love-hate relationship. There were five glorious wins from 1965/66 until 1969/70 but then four successive final defeats (all of them annoying in their different ways) and the suspicion among their fans that they did not always take this tournament as seriously as they might have, preferring to concentrate on the riches of Europe. But this year would have to be different, for there were no European fish to fry!

Their opponents were to be Hibs, a team under Eddie Turnbull who promised more than they delivered. Man for man, they were a match for most teams, including Celtic, but traditionally they were a 'trophy-shy' club. Hibs far too often let their fans down. An exception had been the League Cup Final two years previously in 1972/73, where Hibs deservedly won in a good game against Celtic, but apart from that their supporters were driven pathetically to boast about how well they had done in the Dryburgh Cup, a pre-season tournament with little to offer anyone other than its advertising of inferior beer. It would soon be abandoned and relegated to its deserved obscurity.

For the past two seasons the League Cup had been the victim of foolish and fruitless tinkering in an attempt to produce better and more entertaining football. An experimental Law stated that a player could only be offside within his opponents' penalty box or 'its lateral extension', and lines were drawn from the edge of the penalty area to the touchline. This experiment proved unpopular as defenders and attackers had to adjust their thinking when playing in other competitions, and it did not, in any case, noticeably produce any more goals than before. It was quietly dropped at the end of the 1974/75 League Cup competition, and nobody was too upset at its departure.

What was more than a little alarming however was the attendance of 53,848, more or less half the number who had attended the Scottish Cup Final between the same two sides some two and a half years previously in May 1972. Gates were generally falling, and Celtic's more than anyone's, as the support had grown sated with success over the past decade and lacked the hunger that they once had. There were of course other factors like hooliganism (that curse of the 1970s) and the primitive and grossly inadequate facilities at most grounds, but wise Celtic supporters would agree with fans of other teams that the sharing around of honours might be no bad thing.

The outside world was confusing. Inflation was rampant with Western govern-ments clearly unable to put any sort of a stop to it. There had been two general elec-tions in 1974 which had removed the Conservative government of Edward Heath. Harold Wilson was now back in power but already struggling with economic and industrial problems including strikes being threatened by Glasgow dustmen and Scottish teachers – neither group of people particularly being known for militancy! In Scotland the SNP had gained strength in both general elections.

The week before the League Cup Final, Celtic and Hibs met at Parkhead on league business. It ended up 5-0 for Celtic with a hat-trick from Dixie Deans. This seemed to betoken good news for Celtic before the upcoming League Cup Final, but Stein was well aware of the possibility of an 'ambush' whereby Celtic would be yet again affected by the 'serpent of complacency', as they had been on too many occa-sions in the early 1970s when they had underestimated the opposition. In any case Hibs had possibly taken their eye off the ball in the league game, for they were due to play Juventus in the UEFA Cup in midweek at Easter Road. Unfortunately for them they lost that one as well, so Stein was able to tell his men how dispirited Hibs would be – but also how determined to fight back!

It was a fine, mellow autumnal day with leaves falling from the trees outside the Mount Florida station as supporters made their way to the ground. It was sunny and pleasant in total contrast to the last two League Cup finals which had been played in the month of December for reasons that defied any sort of logic.

Celtic started off playing towards the Mount Florida end of the ground. From early on, it was clear that this was going to be a fast open game with both teams trying to make it up with their supporters for previous poor performances – Hibs for the previous week's shocker at Parkhead and their midweek disappointment, and Celtic for their European exit. Jimmy Johnstone decided to play one of his better games (he had had one or two dreadful performances of late) and it was JOHNSTONE who opened the scoring in the fifth minute as he picked up a through-ball from Kenny Dalglish and slotted it past McArthur in the Hibs goal.

Celtic now stayed on top for a spell with Dalglish's passing a delight to behold. On the half-hour mark Celtic went two ahead when DEANS, who had hustled and bustled all the first half, causing all sorts of problems for the Hibs defence, scored from a Pat McCluskey pass. But with half-time approaching Celtic relaxed, and Joe HARPER for once got the better of McNeill and scored to keep the Edinburgh side in it. It was generally agreed by all at half-time that if Scottish football was in decline, the answer was surely to give them more of this.

More of this was indeed forthcoming in the second half; first Paul WILSON, that grossly underestimated player, scored from close range and then HARPER took advantage of a moment's hesitation in the Celtic defence when McNeill and Hunter seemed to leave the ball to each other. The score was 3-2 with still half an hour of the game to play. With the crowd in permanent fervour and David Francey, the BBC Radio commentator, in overdrive, the outside world seemed of no concern to the crowd inside the ground or the millions listening throughout Scotland and the world.

Two goals within a couple of minutes of each other killed Hibs, and they were both scored by Dixie DEANS. His first was a crisp low drive, and then with Hampden still in uproar in appreciation of that goal, there came another which has a claim to be one of the most remarkable ever seen in the long history of Hampden Park. Celtic forced a corner on the left, and it was taken by Harry Hood. It was a long, high one which eluded all defenders and came to Jimmy Johnstone at the other edge of the penalty area. Jimmy fired for goal, but the ball cannoned off a Hibs defender and rebounded to Dixie Deans, who dived forward to head the ball home – all at full speed. As often happened, the Celtic end took a split second to digest the enormity of what had happened, but then exploded into raptures of delight with the song of 'Dixie, Dixie, Dixie, Dixie Deans' reverberating all round the ground more or less until full-time.

The scoring did not even finish there for Steve MURRAY scored for Celtic, and then, late in the game, Joe HARPER scored yet again for Hibs, so that the game finished 6-3 in a feast of football entertainment that was second to none, and restored any faith that had been lost in Scottish football. It was a remarkable game for many reasons. Dixie became the third Celtic player to score a hat-trick in a League Cup Final alongside Billy McPhail and Bobby Lennox, and he also became the only player to score a hat-trick in a League Cup Final and a Scottish Cup Final (and against the same opposition), and he performed the unlikely feat of scoring hat-tricks on successive Saturdays against the same opposition.

Aye, the Hammer of the Hibs right enough! He said that 'he didn't like the green jersey!' – in fact that was maybe true, for he had started off life as a Rangers supporter! And even the hardest-hearted of Celtic fans had to give a wee cheer to their old enemy Joe Harper who performed what is possibly a world record for a national final of scoring a hat-trick and ending up on the losing side!

But Celtic fans would have been well advised to make the most of that triumph – for the next few years would not be so good…

v Rangers 4-2
Scottish League, Celtic Park
21 May 1979

CELTIC	RANGERS	REFEREE
Latchford	McCloy	Mr E. Pringle,
McGrain	Jardine	Edinburgh
Lynch	Dawson	
Aitken	Johnstone	
McAdam	Jackson	
Edvaldsson	MacDonald	
Provan	McLean*	
Conroy*	Russell	
McCluskey	Parlane	
MacLeod	Smith	
Doyle	Cooper	
Sub: Lennox*	Sub: Miller*	

NEITHER CELTIC nor Rangers could really claim that 1979 was a vintage year for them. By sheer chance, it was the first year as manager for both Billy McNeill and John Greig, once adversaries on the field and now in the dugout. Scottish football was going through a major credibility problem in 1979 as well, it would have to be said, for it was the first season played in the wake of the Argentina fiasco whose reverberations kept on running in the shape of general disillusion and cynicism, with drastically reduced attendances and a consequent lack of finance.

It was also one of the worst winters on record for the loss of fixtures. The game in question really should have been played at the New Year, but snow and ice made a mockery of the fixture lists in January and February. Celtic, for example, did not play a single league match between 23 December 1978 and 2 March 1979. Undersoil heating was simply an experimental concept in 1979 and had not reached Scotland.

There were advantages to be had from this state of affairs. In Celtic's case, it gave the players, whose form had been inconsistent and mediocre until Christmas, a chance to have the famous 'long hard look at themselves', and in particular it allowed the recovery from injury, a mysterious foot problem which no-one understood, of Danny McGrain, by some distance Scotland's best player at the time and who would undeniably have made a vast difference in Argentina, had he been there.

Celtic's team was young and enthusiastic, but not yet of the Lisbon Lions quality. One of the Lions, Bobby Lennox, was still there, but he was used sparingly by his old colleague Billy McNeill. McNeill had made two very sound investments in the purchase of two quality players from the lower reaches of the Scottish League – Murdo MacLeod, a doughty midfielder from Dumbarton, and Davie Provan, a fast and impressive winger from Kilmarnock.

So when spring reached Scotland in March 1979, no clear pattern was emerging in the Scottish League as all teams were 'much of a muchness' as the saying went. Dundee United were doing well, as were St Mirren, with the usual suspects of Hibs, Hearts and Aberdeen challenging as well. Such is the nature of Scottish football, however, that the 'also rans' gradually dropped out, although Dundee United lasted longer than most, and the stage was left for the big two to fight it out.

Rangers were, on the face of it, in better shape than Celtic. Already possessors of the League Cup, and still in the Scottish Cup (Celtic had exited miserably to Aberdeen at Parkhead in mid March), they had also had a good run in Europe, beating teams like Juventus and PSV Eindhoven before losing out narrowly to Cologne. Two games between Rangers and Celtic were scheduled in May – one at Hampden (Ibrox was being redeveloped) on Saturday 5 May and the other at Celtic Park on Monday 21 May.

The impetus seemed to have passed to Rangers when they beat Celtic at Hampden, some two days after the historic and baleful appearance of Mrs Thatcher in Downing Street for the first time. It was only 1-0, but Celtic had been tame, and Rangers now had the lead. But Celtic rolled up their sleeves and won the next three games, albeit none too impressively, against Partick Thistle on the May Holiday Monday, St Mirren at Ibrox (held there because Love Street was being redeveloped and Ibrox, also being renovated, and which could not safely hold a Rangers v Celtic crowd, was adjudged capable of holding the St Mirren v Celtic crowd!) on Friday 11 May, and then against the now relegated Hearts at Parkhead on Monday 14 May in a 1-0 stagger to victory in which the referee was given the biggest cheer of the night for blowing the final whistle!

All this meant that Celtic had 46 points to Rangers' 43, but Rangers had two games in hand, against Partick Thistle and Hibs, games that they would have expected to win. Two points only were awarded for a win in 1979, so a win or even a draw for Rangers would be very much to their advantage. It was Celtic's last game of the season, and a win would guarantee them the championship by giving them 48 points, leaving Rangers with a maximum of 47.

Celtic's form may have left a little to be desired, but Rangers too were struggling. They were involved in the Scottish Cup Final against Hibs, which had now gone to two games without producing a result. The first game on Saturday 12 May had been shown live on BBC, and Celtic fans had seen how ineffective Rangers were in a game that Hibs really should have won. The first replay, on the night after Celtic's win over Hearts, was a similar story of Rangers failing to win a game that they really needed to, and thus the second replay had to be scheduled for the Monday after the Celtic v Rangers game. It couldn't be any earlier for Scotland internationals were now getting in the way!

Thus the 52,000 fans who had kept their tickets from January made their way to Parkhead that night. It would be the only opportunity for seeing the game, as STV, who were scheduled to show the highlights and might just, in a move unusual for the times, have made a bid for live rights, were hamstrung by a strike, the curse of the 1970s and the reason for the recent triumph of Margaret Thatcher and the Conservatives. BBC might also have made a move for the game, but they were similarly hamstrung, not by a strike, but by managerial fecklessness. They didn't even provide a radio commentary! Thus no good visual or audio record of the game exists, although the Celtic Cine Club made a brave effort.

The game turned out not to be a classic – for it was far too scrappy for that – but a thriller in which the tides of fortune turned frequently, and eventually decisively in Celtic's favour. Rangers, attacking the Celtic end of the ground, scored first within minutes. It was a good goal too, made by Davie Cooper and scored by Alex MacDONALD to reduce the Celtic fans to silence. Rangers then held onto their lead until half-time comfortably enough, but not without a few scares.

Celtic fans were disappointed, but not completely downcast. They were very aware that they needed to score twice, for even a draw was of little use to them. A major effort was required and Celtic's fans were now willing to play their part. Spurred on by the singing, chanting, scarf-waving support, they attacked the Rangers goal with frenzy and passion, but ten minutes into the second half occurred the incident which in some ways defines this game, but which seemed at the time to have killed Celtic off.

Near the Rangers penalty area, Alex MacDonald went down after a foul. Referee Eddie Pringle, who was the only calm man in the whole cauldron that was Parkhead, correctly awarded a free kick, but some Celtic players seemed to think that MacDonald was making too much of it in an attempt to waste time. While several players gathered round to remonstrate with MacDonald who was still on the ground, Johnny Doyle was seen to aim a kick at him, not with any viciousness, but rather by frustration at the break in play when Celtic were in the ascendancy. Mr Pringle had no option and Doyle had to be sent off, after the referee consulted the brave linesman in front of the Jungle who told him what he had seen. What was harder to endure, however, was the smirks of the Rangers players and the pattings on the back of MacDonald who somewhat predictably recovered after Doyle departed.

Celtic now seemed dead and buried, but still the songs and the encouragement continued in what seemed more like defiance than a genuine feeling that the cause could be saved. As if in response to the barrage of noise, Celtic surged forward – McGrain and Lynch were both attacking full-backs that night – with Aitken immense in midfield and the two McNeill signings Provan and MacLeod now showed their value. An equaliser came in the 67th minute after a goalmouth scramble when Roy AITKEN was able to prod the ball home.

The score 1-1, the crowd in bedlam, and McNeill now decided to replace the defence-minded Mike Conroy with the sprightly veteran Bobby Lennox, still regarded as one of the fastest men in the game, even at the age of 35. Aitken's goal brought Celtic back into the game, but it was still not enough. Attack was now the order of the day, and with renewed vigour the ten men pressed forward, playing with all the determination of the Celts of old in a cause which seemed lost.

Just 15 minutes remained when George McCLUSKEY put Celtic in front, hooking in a ball after an Aitken drive had been blocked by the Rangers defence. This had followed a sustained period of Celtic attack, but then Celtic forgot one of the oldest dictums in the game – that you are always at your most vulnerable after you have scored a goal. Almost immediately Rangers forced what was then a rare corner, and the ball came to the hitherto anonymous Robert RUSSELL who drilled the ball through a mass of legs and bodies past Peter Latchford, to tilt the game and the title once again in the direction of Ibrox.

The score was 2-2 and ten minutes remained as encouragement and support simply poured from the terraces. The Rangers end, triumphant for a minute or two, now held its collective breath once again as Celtic poured forward. Such occasions often produce a tragic figure. For example, there was Alan Craig of Motherwell in the 1931 Scottish Cup Final, Dixie Deans of Celtic who missed the penalty against Inter Milan in 1972; tonight it was Colin Jackson of Rangers. He had had a great game up to this point, but had been booked for one or two robust tackles a few seconds previously. Perhaps this affected his judgement.

George McCluskey made ground on the right, crossed and Peter McCloy parried the ball towards Jackson. JACKSON, with a few Celtic attackers closing in on him, attempted to head the ball clear or even out for a corner kick, but all he could do was divert the ball past the bewildered McCloy for an OWN GOAL to put Celtic 3-2 up! A lucky goal, perhaps, but not undeserved on the run of play.

There were now only five minutes left. The league championship was tantalisingly close. 'Wiser' teams might have shut up shop for the remaining five minutes, put the ball out of play, conceded free kicks in non-threatening places, feigned injuries, argued pointlessly with the referee – all to use up the time. But Celtic were never wise in that sense. With the crowd still jumping over one another in ecstasy, they surged forward, reckoning that if they kept the ball in the Rangers half, they would find it hard to equalise.

Time was almost up when the ball came to Murdo MacLEOD about 25 yards out. He could hold onto the ball, find a colleague to pass to, even allow it to go out for a throw in. But he reckoned that he should try to score. It was unlikely from that angle, but as long as McCloy didn't save it, the ball would go into the Celtic end from where it would take a while to come out and the whistle would go for full time. So he belted it as hard as he could – and the ball flew straight into the corner of the net!

Pandemonium once again, and almost immediately the full-time whistle came from Mr Pringle. Parkhead had seldom seen anything like it! The immediate celebrations seemed to go on forever, with poor Johnny Doyle, skulking in the dressing room to avoid Billy McNeill's wrath, being summoned by Billy and ordered to join the celebrations! And very soon in the following season, Celtic supporters had made up their own song in honour of this game. It went: 'Ten Men Won The League – Na-ne-na-ne-na-ne-na!' and was repeated *ad infinitum*.

38 v St Mirren 7-0
Scottish League, Celtic Park
14 March 1981

CELTIC	ST MIRREN	REFEREE
Bonner	Thomson	Mr H. Alexander, Irvine
McGrain	Beckett*	
Aitken	Young	
McAdam	Fulton	
Reid	McCormack	
Sullivan	Stark	
Conroy*	Abercrombie	
Burns	Weir	
Provan	Bone	
McGarvey	McDougall**	
Nicholas**	Spiers	
Subs: MacLeod*	Subs: McAveety*	
McCluskey**	Logan*	

1981 WAS a good year for Celtic. It all started at the New Year. Form in the latter part of 1980 had been far from satisfactory with defeats at the hands of Rangers, Aberdeen and St Mirren in November, and then another beating from Aberdeen at Pittodrie in the week between Christmas and the New Year in which the only words of comfort that the *Sunday Post* could find to say for Celtic fans was that they outshouted their Aberdeen counterparts.

In fact, with the exception of the Scottish Cup (and even that was tarnished by the riot of our less well educated fans against their bone-headed counterparts at Rangers), 1980 had been a bad year. The league had been criminally thrown away with some appallingly unprofessional performances (Celtic managed to lose 1-5 to Dundee – and Dundee were subsequently relegated!) and even after the start of the 1980/81 season, although we saw the emergence of Charlie Nicholas and a good goalkeeper in Packie Bonner, we disappeared out of Europe (to a side called Politechnica Timosaura who have singularly failed to join Europe's elite since their win that day) and the Scottish League Cup in what was now a pitiful, predictable and annual occurrence. The defeat at Pittodrie in the last game of 1980 seemed to sum it all up.

Rangers were little better, but that was of no consolation. The fact of the matter was that Scottish football was in a new situation with the emergence of what became known as the New Firm of Aberdeen and Dundee United. Both these teams were blessed with good managers in Alex Ferguson and Jim McLean and were beginning to win silverware. Aberdeen had been the league champions in 1980, and Dundee United had now won the Scottish League Cup for the past two years. Celtic were in the unusual position in 1980 of looking at the north-east of Scotland in envy.

But then with the New Year it was as if someone had pressed a switch, or something was put into the New Year drinks, or (more probably) Billy McNeill's tactics began to pay off. Frank McGarvey began to score goals (two each against Kilmarnock and Morton), Nicholas kept on improving, and, as is always the case when a team puts on a good run of form, as if by some cosmic power as yet beyond our comprehension Celtic's rivals sensed what was happening and begin to stumble.

On 31 January when Celtic very competently beat Hearts at Tynecastle 3-0, Rangers beat Aberdeen 1-0 at Ibrox – funnily enough a good result for Celtic, because Alex Ferguson's Dons were the title holders and the main threat, and then on 7 February when bad weather knocked out Celtic's game, both Aberdeen and Rangers blew up, Rangers losing at Dundee United and Aberdeen before their own angry fans against Morton, who indeed would prove to be a bit of a bogey team for the Dons.

Celtic then beat Rangers 3-1 at Parkhead, and Morton 3-0 at Cappielow with McGarvey once again among the goals. McGarvey in fact seemed to be coming good. He had not always been popular with the fans, for he was prone to miss chances, didn't seem to be incisive enough and had an annoying habit of arguing too much with referees and his own colleagues instead of scoring more goals. He had started life at St Mirren with Alex Ferguson, then was transferred to Liverpool in 1979 but was unable to break into that team, and returned to Scotland, to the team that he loved, Celtic, in March 1980. He had not yet totally convinced the fans, but he soon would.

But arguments about McGarvey paled into insignificance in comparison with what was said about Charlie Nicholas. Comments varied from: 'the best in the world', 'tremendous prospect', 'better than Dalglish ever was' (and one veteran fan even compared him sacrilegiously with Patsy Gallacher!) to 'chancer', 'lucky' and 'one season wonder'. He clearly divided the fans. But, not yet under the baleful influence of agents, and still refusing to do what the wicked journalists told him, preferring instead the wise guidance of Billy McNeill, Charlie was a great personality player and one that the Celtic support, particularly the matronly middle-class ladies, were beginning to love.

The 18,100 – a disappointing crowd but perhaps typical of the times – who turned up for the St Mirren game in 1981 expected to see Celtic administer the traditional beating to the Buddies when they appeared at Parkhead. St Mirren had a reputation for eccentricity. The previous year against all odds and precedents, they had won at Parkhead – and shortly afterwards dismissed their manager Jim Clunie for, apparently, using bad language in front of some directors' wives! They were now in the hands of Rikki McFarlane, and were a capable side, currently more than holding their own in the top flight.

Celtic Park was a huge, empty, echoing place that day. The supporters who were there were enthusiastic enough, but there were quite simply not enough of them to justify the huge stadium. The stand was fairly full, as was the enclosure in front of the stand. The Jungle across from the main stand was where all the fanatics went and was its usual hotbed of humour, arguments, bad language and committed (although by no means uncritical) support for the cause. The song of the moment was 'The Boys of the Old Brigade', a song commemorating the Easter Rising of 1916:

Where are the lads who stood with me
When history was made?
Oh glory be, I want to see
The Boys of the Old Brigade!

Behind the Celtic end (the west terracing) there were a few pockets of support, but the 'Rangers' end was virtually empty. It was possible to 'walk round' so as to be behind the goal that Celtic were attacking in each half, but one phenomenon, previously very obvious, was now missing, and that was alcohol on the terracings, now banned after the infamous riot at the previous year's Scottish Cup Final.

Celtic came out in their lime green tops and white shorts to a huge cheer from a crowd who sensed that this team could win the league championship and indeed perhaps the Scottish Cup this year, but feared the sort of slips that had occurred last April when the championship was all but won. This rankled all over the summer of 1980 as was indicated in the true story of how one old Celtic supporter met another months after the championship was lost. One was in his garden and was about to ask his friend Alec (whom he had not seen for some time) if he liked the roses, or make a comment about how England were doing in the Test Matches against the West Indies, or the coming struggles between Sebastian Coe and Steve Ovett in the Moscow Olympics ... but Alec did not even say 'Hello', instead merely barking: 'Thae f***ers threw awa that league!' and storming on up the road to leave his friend to nod sagely and remark on what 1980 had done to the supporters. The hurt had been seething inside old Alec for months.

The pitch was not one of Parkhead's finest. It was a bit bare in places, had suffered badly from the winter and had been played on too often in an age when the technology which produces the verdant sward that Celtic Park is now, was in its infancy. From an early stage it was clear that Celtic were on song. Aitken was immense, stamping his authority all over the field, and flair players like Provan and Burns were beginning to play some marvellous football, passing to each other at speed and creating all sorts of opportunities. Mark Reid, Mike Conroy and Dom Sullivan are among the lesser known old Celts, but they all had their moments for the club, and 'Dom the Bomb' in particular, never exactly a hero with the fans, began to show the world what he could do.

Roy AITKEN scored the first with a header in the tenth minute, then Frank McGARVEY picked up a fine through-ball to make it two on the half-hour mark. But it was McGARVEY's second and Celtic's third on the stroke of half-time which will be remembered. He picked up the ball about 30 yards from goal (Celtic were still attacking the 'Rangers' end of the ground), shrugged off tackles from Fulton and McCormack, charged at goal, evaded another tackle and from the edge of the box hit a shot with such venom that the ball was coming back out of the goal whilst goalkeeper Billy Thomson (one of the better goalkeepers in Scotland at that time) was still in mid air. 'Well, that might be the goal of the season,' said TV commentator Jock Brown without a hint of exaggeration.

McGarvey himself in his book *Totally Frank* (a good read, incidentally, in which he does not always paint the best picture of himself, is devastatingly honest, and portrays a graphic warning to all gamblers) tells a tale about that goal. So overwhelmed was he by the greeting and welcome that it received from the Parkhead faithful that he was physically sick in the dressing room at half-time! Billy McNeill, as was his wont, was about to say something to him about 'keeping your feet on the floor' or 'don't let it go to your head' when he realised that Frank was nowhere to be seen. But he could be heard vomiting in the toilet!

Thankfully Frank recovered and Celtic resumed where they left off, scoring another four in the second half. NICHOLAS got in on the act but injured himself in the process and had to be replaced by George McCluskey, then McGARVEY completed his hat-trick before 'supersub' George McCLUSKEY scored another two more or less on the final whistle. Celtic's best player that day did not score, but it was Davie Provan on the right wing who, his socks round about his ankles, twisted and turned the St Mirren defence all afternoon and delivered some breathtaking balls for the other forwards. St Mirren, in fact, were lucky to get off with only seven goals. It might have been a lot more.

It was a good day for the Celtic supporters and it was soon to get even better. The players on the field would have been aware of cheering, clapping and general animation at times which seemed inappropriate to what was happening on the field. This was of course caused by the radio transistors, sometimes listened to by people with headphones, who were telling their audiences that both Aberdeen and Rangers were doing badly. Indeed they were. Aberdeen lost at Kilmarnock that day and Rangers at Hearts, thus strengthening Celtic's position at the top, and showing yet again that if you win your games, your rivals will inevitably stumble, particularly if you play with such aplomb as Celtic did that day.

Celtic duly won the league that year, doing so at Tannadice Park with a couple of games to spare. It was a shame that as spring was the time of year when European tournaments were resurrecting themselves again after their winter shutdown that there was no Celtic to grace these competitions. On this form they would have been unstoppable and Europe would have seen, yet again, how football should be played. As it was, European games continued to be won by teams who could 'soak up pressure', 'keep it tight at the back', and win games 1-0. As a result, things were so much the poorer.

v Dundee United 2-1
Scottish Cup Final, Hampden
18 May 1985

CELTIC	DUNDEE UNITED	REFEREE
Bonner	McAlpine	Mr B. McGinlay,
W. McStay	Malpas	Balfron
McGrain	Beedie*	
Aitken	Gough	
McAdam	Hegarty	
MacLeod	Narey	
Provan	Bannon	
P. McStay*	Milne	
Johnston	Kirkwood	
Burns**	Sturrock	
McGarvey	Dodds	
Subs: O'Leary*	Sub: Holt*	
McClair**		

THE MID 1980s were difficult years for Celtic supporters. In addition to the increasing signs of incompetence at the top – both Charlie Nicholas and Billy McNeill had been allowed to go in 1983, blows from which Celtic were still reeling – the team seemed to lack belief in themselves, often tending to lose games that they had to win.

In 1984, for example, both domestic cup finals had been lost to a team that was not as good as Celtic on the day, and in the 1985 league season, although they had twice beaten champions Aberdeen at Parkhead, they had let themselves down badly on other occasions, notably in a dismal 0-1 defeat to Hibs in March at a time when they had seemed to be challenging for the championship. Questions were now being asked of manager Davie Hay.

But there had also been a major kick in the teeth to Celtic delivered by the powers that be in Europe. It has been called the Rapid Vienna affair, and was an excellent example of how cheats can get away with it, if they have the right contacts. Celtic had of course walked right into it, when a fool had thrown a bottle. It landed harmlessly, yards away from the player it was aimed at, but he collapsed, and after a long wrangle, UEFA deprived Celtic of their victory and ordered a replay. The angry and over-motivated Celtic lost that one.

That was of course desperately bad luck, and Celtic's sense of grievance was justified, but they now needed to bounce back. The Scottish League had gone to Aberdeen by some distance and the Scottish Cup, as often in the past, represented Celtic's best bet. Hamilton Accies and Inverness Thistle provided few problems, but then replays were needed to get the better of Dundee and Motherwell, both of whom might well have won the first games. But Celtic eventually got the better of Motherwell in a replayed semi-final at Hampden on the same night as Dundee United beat Aberdeen at Tynecastle to do likewise.

Dundee United were probably the most technically capable team in Scotland in 1985. A rigorously drilled defence, well disciplined by Jim McLean, they were a team who, once they went ahead, were notoriously difficult to break down. They had done consistently well in Europe – far better than Celtic over the equivalent time – and last year had been distinctly unlucky not to get the better of AS Roma in the European Cup semi-final. Players like Paul Hegarty, David Narey, Paul Sturrock and Davie Dodds were as good as one would find anywhere in Europe.

There was, however, one chink in their armour, and that was a chronic inability to play well in Glasgow, with Hampden Park in particular being a bogey ground. The three trophies that they had won (the Scottish League Cup in 1979/80 and 1980/81, and the league championship of 1983) had all, amazingly, been won at Dens Park, home of their city rivals, Dundee, and only a hundred yards up the road from their own ground of Tannadice Park! But Hampden was a different matter. They had already lost two Scottish Cup finals (1974 and 1981) at Hampden and the calendar year of 1981 had also seen them lose the Scottish League Cup Final there as well. The current 1984/85 season had been an excellent example of how they 'froze' at Hampden. In the League Cup they had done well, beating Celtic narrowly after extra time at Tannadice, then Hearts over two legs in the semi-final, before, as if in deference to some immutable law of the Gods, succumbing to a vastly inferior Rangers at Hampden in the final.

So where were Celtic? The fans, though loyal, had given up on them as far as the Scottish League was concerned, with home games against Dumbarton and Dundee registering attendances of less than 10,000, as a hollow Parkhead echoed to the cries of the players and the managers' comments from the bench! At the game against Dundee on 4 May (a dismal 0-1 defeat) a Dundee player was given a warning by the referee about a bad tackle, and such were the acoustics of the half-empty Jungle, one heard every word! 'Just you mind that, then!' was the cry from one Celtic fan!

Yet, it was not that Celtic lacked good players. Paul McStay, Tommy Burns, Davie Provan and Murdo MacLeod were excellent midfielders; Roy Aitken, although prone to lapses in defence, was wholehearted and inspirational, and up front Frank McGarvey could take a goal, as indeed could Brian McClair and Maurice Johnston, that somewhat charismatic yet controversial figure who kept telling everyone how great it was to play for 'the only team I ever wanted to play for'. One really felt that the team could do better, and there were many who felt that on the Scottish Cup Final of 18 May 1985 hung a few careers, not least that of manager Davie Hay.

The day was overcast and dull as Brian McGinlay started the game before 62,346 fans. After 45 minutes he brought it to a close for half-time with very little of note having happened. Both sides were playing cat and mouse, Dundee United because that was the way they were and Celtic because they feared that if Dundee United did score, they would be very difficult to break down. In addition, Celtic's flair players like Paul McStay and Tommy Burns were as yet failing to make any impact. The BBC TV team which consisted of Billy McNeill found it difficult to say very much in favour of this mediocre Scottish Cup Final, with quite a lot of attention being paid to the FA Cup Final between Everton and Manchester United instead.

Roy Aitken, who was to play a pivotal role in this final, was treading very carefully. He was aware that he had let the team down badly in last year's Scottish Cup Final, when he had been sent off before half-time. Admittedly, it had been a harsh decision, with the referee influenced by the despicable antics of Gordon Strachan. The player concerned, Mark McGhee, showed astonishing powers of recovery, but it had been a silly and unnecessary foul, and Celtic had lost the final as a result. This must not be allowed to happen again.

Perhaps that influenced him in his reluctance to tackle as Dundee United went ahead in front of their own fans at the Mount Florida end of the ground. It was indeed a fine piece of work as Dodds beat Aitken and slipped the ball to BEEDIE to put Dundee United ahead. This was after only ten minutes of the second half, and Celtic's worst nightmare now loomed: 0-1 down to the technically correct Dundee United defence which contained Paul Hegarty, Davie Narey and Maurice Malpas (who had earned the nickname of Maurice Backpass for his defensive capabilities) and seemed unlikely to be breached.

Apart from the rainbow of tangerine at the Mount Florida end, Hampden was plunged into depression. Normally in such circumstances, Celtic fans rouse their team. It was far more difficult to do so today, for introverted gloom was taking over the hearts of each and every fan at the ground and those watching at home and listening all over the world. Celtic tried but found it difficult to get going as Dundee United began to feel that this was the day that their Hampden hoodoo was to be ended.

The beleaguered Davie Hay was seen in his dugout, head in hands, as the minutes slipped away. He took off Tommy Burns, who had not been having the best of days, and replaced him with Brian McClair. A few half-chances came Celtic's way – even Danny McGrain had a wild shot at goal – but Dundee United looked well in command.

In the 75th minute, Hay threw everything on a hunch, bringing off Paul McStay. Paul was far from happy and apparently made a remark along the lines of 'couldn't manage a supermarket' about Mr Hay. Boos were heard, but Billy McNeill in the commentary box backed up his successor: 'There are times when a manager just has to be unpopular,' he said. It was indeed a bad moment for the McStay family, as brother Willie was being booked at precisely the same time.

It was replacement Pierce O'Leary that really nonplussed everyone. A little-known, underperforming defender, this charming Irishman (named, one assumed, after another Irishman who gave the British a wee bit of bother at that Post Office in 1916) did not really look as if he was the man to save the day. There were enough defenders on the park, as Dundee United already had 11! But the decision to bring O'Leary on was to allow Roy Aitken to move forward. In the commentary box, Billy twigged the plan: 'He's gambling now with 15 minutes to go!'

The effect was immediate; Aitken grabbed the game by the scruff of the neck. Gone were any pretences about plans and tactics, it was to be all about cavalry charges and attack. The crowd and the other Celtic players detected a change in mood. Everything became more animated, and within a minute of the change, Eamonn Bannon, for reasons best known to himself, decided to foul Murdo MacLeod on the edge of the box when Murdo was running across goal. Davie PROVAN stepped up to take the kick and scored direct.

Celtic were born again. From now on, waves and waves of sound cascaded from the terracings. There is no finer sight and sound in football, and Dundee United buckled, showing the clear symptom of a team under pressure – arguing among themselves and snarling at each other. It was Aitken who was the inspiration for the winning goal. After a prolonged period of head tennis from some Dundee United defenders (something that they would never have done if they had been more composed and in control), Aitken charged up the right wing. McGARVEY realised what was going to happen and ran into the middle to be there for the cross, and headed home a glorious typically Celtic goal, as Hampden and the world's living rooms exploded once again.

Five minutes remained and Dundee United rallied, with Tom McAdam and Pierce O'Leary earning plaudits for they way they dealt with the tremendous Dundee United pressure. At the other end Celtic missed a sitter and pressed as well, but the full-time whistle came with Celtic 2-1 winners of one of the more emotional cup finals of them all. Frank McGarvey said: 'I nearly cried.' *Nearly?* He must have had much greater control over his feelings than most of the support then! The veteran supporter, for example, who had cried in 1925 when Patsy Gallacher and Jimmy McGrory produced the goods, was happy to admit that he was similarly lachrymose 60 years later when Davie Provan and Frank McGarvey scored at the same stage of the same trophy at the same ground, into the same goal against a team from the same city!

The game bought Davie Hay some time. More importantly, it gave the Celtic support something to cheer about, and in the traumatic times of the mid 1980s, they certainly needed that!

v St Mirren 5-0
Scottish League, Love Street
3 May 1986

CELTIC	ST MIRREN	Referee
Bonner	Stewart	Mr A. Waddell,
McGrain*	Wilson	Edinburgh
Whyte	D. Hamilton	
Aitken	B. Hamilton	
McGugan	Godfrey	
MacLeod	Cooper	
McClair	Fitzpatrick	
McStay	Abercrombie	
Johnston	McGarvey	
Burns	Gallagher*	
Archdeacon	Mackie	
Sub: Grant*	Sub: Speirs*	

IT WAS a dull, slightly depressing day at Love Street. It was now into May, and the weather really should have been better, as it was the last day of the league season. Only 17,557 went to the St Mirren v Celtic game that day, and those who did went out of a feeling of loyalty and commitment to the cause and a realisation that it would be a few months before they could see their team again. There was no great feeling that history was about to be made in breathtaking style.

The season had, in fact, been a disappointment. Out in both domestic trophies at the quarter-final stage to Hibs (of all people!) at Easter Road, a miserable flop once again in Europe – only partly to be excused by the fact that Celtic had to play their home leg behind closed doors at Parkhead for their part in the Rapid Vienna fiasco of the previous year – and the Scottish League...? Well, they were still in it, the victory at Motherwell on Wednesday night having assured that, but the title would surely go to Hearts today, for as long as the Jam Tarts did not lose at Dens Park (a difficult fixture, admittedly) and Celtic did not beat St Mirren 4-0, the title would be heading to Tynecastle for the first time since 1960.

It had been a strange championship, with Celtic, Rangers, Hearts, Aberdeen and Dundee United all in with a shout at various points of the season. It had been odd as well in that there had been a fight with the authorities against the BBC and STV, and no televised football was available, even in highlight form! Was this much of a loss, we asked ourselves, given the mediocre nature of the fare on offer? Still, they had kissed and made up – or rather, the TV companies had offered more money and made up – and football was now back, with even the occasional live game scheduled for future seasons. In fact, a vital live match had already been shown – Hearts drawing with Aberdeen at Tynecastle on 20 April, with the draw helping Hearts and effectively killing off the Pittodrie challenge.

Hats had to be raised, reluctantly, to Hearts. Chairman Wallace Mercer had provided some much-needed cash, and manager Alec MacDonald albeit 'an odious wee Hun' as the Celtic fanzines called him, had made something of the team; a quaint mixture of goldie oldies rejected from other clubs, including John Colquhoun from Celtic, a few youngsters, and of course the prodigious goalscorer John Robertson, the Hibee who grew up and became a legend at Hearts and was mentioned in the same breath as Willie Bauld! They were now on the cusp of winning the Scottish League and were in the following week's Scottish Cup Final as well.

But in the last few games, Hearts had not looked all that impressive. In their penultimate game, 'looking like a man about to be mugged', they had scraped home 1-0 against relegated Clydebank, and it was clear that nerves were beginning to get the better of them, even though Edinburgh sports retailers and the Hearts Shop itself reported a huge boom in Hearts scarves and favours as the Johnny-come-latelies jumped on board. Hearts had, four years earlier, exited the Scottish Cup to Forfar Athletic at a virtually deserted Tynecastle. Where were they all then?

It would be fair to say that, although most people other than Celtic or Hibs fans wanted Hearts to win the league, little affection was extended to their supporters. In the early 1980s when Hearts were members of the First Division, innocent civilians of towns like Kirkcaldy, Dunfermline and Perth used to await their visit with dread, for hooliganism, theft and vandalism were prevalent.

Sympathy for what happened to them on this day would be tempered by such recollections. It was from this day, too, that the Jambo hatred of Celtic (always strong and evidenced by their singing of Rangers songs) now reached irrational and even unmanageable proportions. And yet, even the hardest-hearted of Celtic fans would have to show a little compassion for the decent Hearts fans. Hadn't Celtic been there before? Wouldn't they be there again?

Hearts had last won the league in 1960, a year after they had managed to lose to a half-hearted Celtic at Parkhead on the bizarre last day of the 1959 season, thus giving the league to Rangers, who had themselves lost to Aberdeen that day! Then in 1965, on the very day of the birth of the new Celtic in the Scottish Cup Final against Dunfermline, Hearts had entertained Kilmarnock at Tynecastle, knowing that they would win the league if they did not lose 2-0... They proceeded to do just that. There was therefore nothing new about Hearts throwing away a league championship on the last day of a season!

At Love Street, Celtic manager Davie Hay put a brave face on things and sent out his best team, including a few youngsters who had progressed well that year – Paul McGugan, Owen Archdeacon and Peter Grant, who would be on the subs' bench. There was a certain feeling that this might well be Hay's last game in charge, because Celtic fans, since the Jock Stein days, have found it hard to accept second place, even though this year second place was considerably better than Rangers, who had now been panicked into bringing in Graeme Souness as their manager. Would Celtic also go for a big name in the summer?

Celtic appeared in their lime green strip. Rain of course is seldom far away from Paisley and there were intermittent showers for some of the game. Celtic often play well in wet conditions, and today was no exception. The home support was meagre, for they had given up for the season and clearly preferred staying in the pub to attending what seemed a meaningless game. In any case, St Mirren's supporters possibly preferred Celtic to Hearts. Their proximity to Ibrox meant that they did not like Rangers, and Paisley had been one of the Scottish towns which had regularly been on the wrong end of a few pastings when the Hearts louts came to call. Celtic were possibly the least of the evils!

And what were the thoughts of Frank McGarvey? Far from the only Celtic supporter in the St Mirren team, Frank had been the hero of the hour the previous year for his contribution to the Scottish Cup Final, but had taken umbrage at being offered only a one-year contract by Davie Hay, and had left for St Mirren. He felt he had a point to prove to those in command at Celtic, yet his heart still lay with the club.

Celtic started brightly and a corner kick inside the first five minutes brought a goal from Brian McCLAIR who headed it home sweetly. Continuing to press, Celtic then went further ahead on the half-hour mark with Maurice JOHNSTON scoring after a fine through-ball from Paul McStay. Just a minute later came a goal, fortunately preserved on video, which had 'Celtic' written all over it. It was 'the best developed goal of the day,' said commentator Jock Brown, and it certainly was good. The move involved Danny McGrain, twice, and Paul McStay, Roy Aitken and Brian McClair once before the ball came to Maurice JOHNSTON to score his second. Then five minutes later came the best dummy that one is ever likely to see as Murdo MacLeod jumped over an Owen Archdeacon cross for Paul McSTAY to drill home.

This was vintage Celtic stuff, and had they played like this all season the league would have been won comfortably. As it was, it was now 4-0 at half-time, and this raised the possibility that if Dundee were to score, and if St Mirren were not to pull one back, then ... but, no it wasn't really likely. But at Dens Park, hard though the Hearts management team tried to spread 'disinformation' (i.e. deliberate lies) to their team about the Love Street score, everyone was uncomfortably aware that Celtic were winning 4-0. Dundee had played well (for they had their own agenda of trying to qualify for the next season's UEFA Cup), but had lacked any penetration up front where it mattered.

The second halves started at more or less the same time, and very soon the Love Street game died as a contest. McCLAIR scored a fifth after MacLeod had miskicked in front of goal, thereby more or less guaranteeing that Celtic would win the game by the requisite four goals, even in the unlikely event of the feckless St Mirren attack pulling one back. The rest of that game became an irrelevance with the crowd lapsing into silence apart from the odd bit of applause for a particularly good piece of football.

At Dens Park, Hearts were a little off colour (they would claim, unconvincingly, later that some of their players had a 'virus') and after John Robertson missed a couple of reasonable chances, and then Colquhoun took the ball wide when he should have shot, they seemed to have decided to settle for a draw – a result that would, of course, suit them. Their fans remained anxious, but conventional wisdom was that the Hearts defence would be good enough to hold out Dundee. Henry Smith, their ever popular goalkeeper, had already made a few good saves and looked in top form.

But then in desperation to score a goal, Dundee's manager Archie Knox turned to one of his substitutes called Albert Kidd. This fellow was little known even to the

Dundee supporters and had been, not to put too fine a point on it, a failure. He would possibly be disposed of to some other club in the close season. He was a local boy, and like many Dundonians was a Celtic supporter. With his 1970s-style long hair and bandit moustache, he looked more like a decadent musician than the Angel of Destruction to the Hearts fans, who were now more and more anxious for the final whistle which they relished with pleasurable anticipation.

Seven minutes remained at both Dens Park and Love Street. Some of the Celtic fans had gone home, having seen some good football by their team who had, on this showing at least, deserved to win the league. "Hoo could we no' hae played like that aw season?" was the cry of the embittered. But on the other side of the country, Dundee had a corner on the right in front of the Hearts fans at the packed Tannadice end of the ground. Across it came, John Brown rose and couldn't quite get enough on it, but the ball came to substitute KIDD, and he scored for Dundee!

The crackling transistors ensured that this goal was registered instantly throughout Scotland. Joy greeted that goal at Love Street with St Mirren goalkeeper Jim Stewart not realising that his picking up of the ball was as good as all that! The rest of Scotland reacted tribally. At Ibrox, the news that Kidd had scored meant to the Rangers fans that *Walter* Kidd had scored for Hearts and they cheered accordingly, not knowing that *Albert* Kidd played for Dundee! At Easter Road, Joe Tortolano took a throw in for Hibs – a good throw in, it has to be said, but hardly worthy of the ecstacy that was revealed on the thinly populated terraces!

Anxiety now took over at all the Scottish grounds with most ears glued to transistors. Then KIDD scored again for Dundee! This time it was an excellent goal, as he ripped through the Hearts defence, played a one-two with a colleague, and fired home! There followed a pitch invasion at Dens, as some of Gorgie's finest specimens of under-educated humanity tried to get the game stopped, but were shoved back none too gently by the Dundee police, some of them, clearly lovers of Celtic, with grins on their faces!

Love Street had never seen anything like it. The Dens Park game finished first, for there had been an injury or two to a St Mirren player, but when referee Andrew Waddell blew for time up, confirming Celtic as champions, the scenes among what Padraig Pearse would have called 'the risen people' were not unlike those of a war film when prisoners of war are released. Long pent-up emotion was released, and once again, we saw that Celtic are not an ordinary club...

v Dundee 3-0
Scottish League, Celtic Park
23 April 1988

CELTIC	DUNDEE	REFEREE
Bonner	Carson	Mr A.N. Huett,
Morris	Forsyth	Edinburgh
Rogan	Angus	
Aitken	Shannon**	
McCarthy	Smith	
Whyte	Saunders	
Miller*	Lawrence*	
McStay	Rafferty	
McAvennie**	Wright	
Walker	Coyne	
Burns	Campbell	
Subs: Stark*	Subs: Frail*	
McGhee**	Harvey**	

THE OFFICIAL attendance given for this game was 60,800. In fact there were a lot more than that with Parkhead looking as full as at any time in its existence, even surpassing Rangers games and the European tussles of the 1960s. It was not a little dangerous at several parts of the ground, with even the section reserved for the away support being taken over by eager Celts. It was somehow appropriate that such a huge crowd would have the opportunity of seeing Celtic on such a significant day in their history.

This was Celtic's Centenary Year. Some claim (and they are technically correct) that the Centenary Year should have been 1987, for it was on 6 November of that year that the famous meeting took place and the decision to found the club was made, but as 1888 was the first game, then 1988 has a case as well. It would be nice, it was reckoned, if they could win the league championship to celebrate the event. They had certainly spectacularly failed to do so in 1987.

It was also the end of the first season of the second coming as manager of one of Celtic's greatest ever men. Billy McNeill had been manager between 1978 and 1983, and had done well with some fine successes, winning one domestic honour per season, but then had parted company with the club because they refused to offer him a contract. He had gone to Manchester City and then Aston Villa, but like Tommy McInally of old, had pined for home. His absence from Celtic had done no good for anyone, and when he was offered his old job back again one day in May 1987 in a Clydebank car park, as legend has it, he jumped at the chance. His predecessor, Davie Hay, had been betrayed by the despicable antics of some of his squad who spent all 1986/87 complaining about wanting away to some other club. The players were more than adequate but the attitude was totally wrong, and as a result the Scottish League had been thrown away in a disgraceful fashion. McNeill therefore more or less had to rebuild the squad – a task he set about with a will with the able help of his assistant, Tommy Craig, who had had a great playing career with Aberdeen and Newcastle United.

Mick McCarthy had been bought by Davie Hay a few days before his sacking, but McNeill brought in men like Andy Walker, a not particularly well known striker from Motherwell, Billy Stark, a utility man who had done so well for St Mirren and Aberdeen in the past, Chris Morris, an unknown from Sheffield Wednesday who became a brilliant full-back, Joe Miller, a winger from Aberdeen, and Frank McAvennie, a striker from West Ham United who had cut his teeth with St Mirren.

Therefore it was virtually a totally different team, although the old hands of Roy Aitken, Packie Bonner and Paul McStay were still there. There was one early success at the end of August at Parkhead when Celtic beat Rangers in a game in which Rangers player-manager Graeme Souness was sent off for a tackle on Billy Stark when Stark did not even have a boot on!

Things took a while to gel, and there were the customary and predictable exits from the League Cup and Europe in the autumn (possibly blessings in disguise this season), but by the start of winter a credible team was beginning to develop. On 17 October there was the infamous game at Ibrox where McAvennie and two Rangers players ended up in court thanks to something of a knee-jerk reaction by the Scottish judiciary system, then the team lost a shocker to Dundee United at home the following week – but they didn't lose again in the league until the championship was all but won.

Crucial victories were registered against Rangers at the New Year (2-0 at Parkhead) and in March in a televised Sunday match at Ibrox (2-1), and other challengers were disposed of adequately. A strike by Andy Walker was enough to get the better of Aberdeen at Pittodrie at the end of March, and then a few days later a 2-0 win at Easter Road put them within striking distance of the championship. A feature of the team's performances was their ability to win by scoring late goals – Joe Miller's late strike at Tannadice Park on Boxing Day being a case in point, as indeed was McStay's wonder goal at Falkirk a day or two before Christmas. As McNeill would himself say later: 'This team doesn't know how to lose. They never give up.' Rangers meanwhile collapsed, as happens when Celtic are playing well.

As winter gave way to spring, the form of the team continued to impress (most of the time – there were a couple of extremely lucky victories over Stranraer in the Scottish Cup and Morton in the Scottish League!) as indeed did the preparations for the festivities for the celebration of the Centenary. A musical play had been written for the occasion. It was called *The Celtic Story*, performed by the Wild Cat Theatre Company and opened in April to appreciative houses at the Pavilion in Glasgow. Various other events like dinners were also held. It was as well that the team were going strong, otherwise things might have fallen flat.

The title might well have been won on Saturday 16 April at Tynecastle, but Hearts had one of their rare good days against Celtic and won 2-1. The previous Saturday in the Scottish Cup semi-final, Celtic had been a goal down very late in the game, but had produced two goals out of thin air to dump the Edinburgh men out. The 16 April league game was a grudge match in which Hearts got a little revenge, but it did not matter all that much to Celtic, for they still had another three games in which to win the league.

And so it was Jocky Scott's Dundee who were the guests at Parkhead on 23 April. In some ways that was fitting for it had been against Dundee in the middle of November when Celtic beat them 5-0 that eyebrows began to be raised, that this might indeed be a special team, and it had been against Dundee at Dens Park in the middle of February, after another late win, that Celtic fans had begun the countdown of games to the championship. Dundee would put up a good fight, and were destined to finish a respectable 7th in the 12-team league.

From very early on, crowds began to assemble at Parkhead. It was not an all-ticket game (perhaps it should have been) and the Main Stand, the only seating accommodation in 1988, was closed at 1.30 pm, a full hour and a half before the start of the game. By about quarter of an hour before the start of the game, the Jungle and the Celtic end were clearly full, and some supporters were redirected into the bit of the 'Rangers' end normally designated for away supporters. There were, in any case, precious few Dundee supporters who had made the trip.

But even this did not succeed in containing the shoals of Celtic fans, and the police had to make the decision to allow them to sit round the track. In normal circumstances this would not have been allowed, but the alternative might have been a lot nastier. As it was, this did have one unfortunate side effect in that it made the inevitable pitch invasion at the end a great deal more difficult to stop.

The game started in a frenzied atmosphere on this dull and muggy sort of day, and Celtic, playing towards the 'Rangers' end of the ground, went ahead in two minutes. The goal was made by McAvennie and, after a goalmouth scramble, was scored by full-back Chris MORRIS, the fair-haired right-back who had been a great hit with the Celtic fans, being as he was in the fairly unusual position of being a Cornishman who played for the Republic of Ireland!

Parkhead exploded at this early goal, and for a long time after that it looked as if Celtic were destined to score an awful lot more as they peppered the Dundee goal with shots. But Dundee held out, rallied a little and even took the game to Celtic for a spell, without however managing to break through the Celtic defence.

Half-time came with Celtic still 1-0 ahead, and the Celtic fans in party mood. It would have been a terrible anti-climax if Dundee had equalised, but that didn't happen. Instead with 15 minutes remaining after some good play from the midfield and a fine pass from McAvennie, Andy WALKER scored. This meant that the league was won, and just to make sure, a minute later, 'Handy Andy' WALKER scored again. A glance at the Celtic end just as these goals went in reminded supporters of the opening of a Venetian blind, with green and white scarves appearing simultaneously, and remaining aloft for the rest of the game as everyone sang 'Happy Birthday, Dear Celtic'.

Just before full time the sun appeared, proving, as if there were any doubt about it, that God is a Celtic supporter, and wanted to join in the fun. Once the pitch invasion was cleared, the players reappeared wearing specially printed white t-shirts for the occasion. From the Main Stand, one could see the radio commentators. One of them was Murdo MacLeod, one of the men who had left Celtic last summer and was now plying his trade with Borussia Dortmund. It might have been felt that

Murdo would be jealous of this team, which was of course radically different from the one that he had left. Not a bit of it. With the crowd singing 'Sure it's a Grand Old Team to Play For', Murdo, no longer on air one presumes, joined in!

He then joined the team in the dressing room for their celebration, and told the *Daily Record* that: 'We worked very hard under Davie Hay, but the hunger in this team for success is something totally different. Billy McNeill and Tommy Craig have put that into them and made them a team of winners. Before I left here, one trophy was enough for a season – but that's not enough now. They want more.'

They did indeed, Murdo, and more was forthcoming in the Scottish Cup Final ...but the real hero of the hour was Billy McNeill. Billy had never lost his popularity in the eyes of the Celtic fans from the day of his debut in 1958 through the bad days of the early 1960s, the good days of the late 1960s and the early '70s until his retirement as a player in 1975. He had been manager of Clyde and Aberdeen until 1978 when he returned to Celtic Park to work for a board that were even then showing the first signs of the dysfunctionality that was almost to kill the club in the early 1990s. His triumph in 1988 was carried out almost in spite of the board, and in the years to come, how we needed that triumph to sustain us!

v Dundee United 2-1
Scottish Cup Final, Hampden
14 May 1988

CELTIC	DUNDEE UNITED	REFEREE
McKnight	Thomson	Mr G. Smith,
Morris	Bowman	Edinburgh
Rogan	Malpas	
Aitken	McInally	
McCarthy	Hegarty	
Whyte*	Narey	
Miller	Bannon	
McStay	Gallacher	
McAvennie	Paatelainen*	
Walker**	Ferguson	
Burns	McKinlay	
Subs: Stark*	Sub: Clark*	
McGhee**		

1988 WAS of course Celtic's Centenary year. Three weeks previously, Celtic had celebrated this event in style by winning the league championship at a packed Parkhead, and the intervening three weeks had seen an almost unprecedented scramble for the 74,000 tickets for the Scottish Cup Final at Hampden Park to see them play, once again in a Scottish Cup Final, against Dundee United.

Ah, Dundee United from 'the city of laughter and tears', as a Tayside chronicler put it. Three years ago Celtic had pipped them at the post in the Scottish Cup Final, thereby intensifying their feelings about a Hampden hoodoo. Since then they had lost in the 1987 Scottish Cup Final as well, this time to Frank McGarvey's St Mirren ... and the feeling was that sooner or later, the Hampden hoodoo had to be broken, for they had now lost four Scottish Cup finals since 1974. Their luck had to change, one felt.

There was something about Dundee United and their supporters that one couldn't help admiring. Their dour manager, Jim McLean, was not exactly everybody's favourite uncle but he did command respect for his consistently good performances in both Scotland and Europe, albeit with a style of play that was hardly scintillating. They had quite a few Celtic supporters in their team, and they even had a great deal of Celtic supporters in their own support, i.e. supporters who would gladly admit that they would rather Celtic won the league than anyone else if they themselves were not directly involved.

Dundee United had of course been the 'Irish' team of Dundee when they were founded in 1909 as Dundee Hibs. This no longer applied of course – even to the extent of Dundee United having changed their colours in the early 1970s from black and white to tangerine (or orange!) in a rather too obvious attempt to get rid of the

'Irish' connection. But their support still contained a large amount of Roman Catholics – so of course the less well educated of their rivals at Dens Park sang Rangers songs at them! Such was life in that crazy yet somehow loveable city of Dundee.

Much interest centred on Kevin Gallacher. Kevin had appeared on the scene in the last few years and had impressed everyone as a fast running, free scoring forward. For Celtic fans, it often seemed that he should have been playing for Celtic, for his grandfather was none other than the great Patsy Gallacher of the 1910s and 1920s. Kevin, it was widely believed, would one day sign for Celtic, but it was perhaps as well that he didn't, for he would always have been compared to his illustrious grandfather – and that would have taken a lot of living up to!

Celtic had reached the final of the Scottish Cup, not without a few wobbles on the way. They had struggled to beat Stranraer, then in a televised game on a Sunday against Hibs, they had horrified their fans by playing real rubbish in a 0-0 draw and compelling the Jungle to sing the praises of Dunfermline Athletic instead, for the Pars had put Rangers out of the cup the previous day! They then won the replay at Easter Road at the last gasp, and a similar phrase could also be used for their victory over Hearts in the semi-final with two very late goals over a Hearts team who still suffered from a 'Celtic death wish', caused by the events of 1986.

In one of the games between Celtic's winning of the Scottish League and the Scottish Cup Final, Roy Aitken, in many ways the hero of the hour who epitomised Celtic in 1988, was not playing. This was not because of injury, nor because he was dropped for not playing well enough, instead it was because he was on the threshold of a suspension. Roy did of course have 'form' as far as referees were concerned, and Billy McNeill felt that, given Roy's hard and committed (perhaps overcommitted) style of play, he should give Roy a rest, lest he pick up a booking and therefore get himself suspended for the Scottish Cup Final!

The SFA made the strange decision to invite the Prime Minister of Great Britain to present the trophy. In other circumstances and in other years, this would have been a good idea to invite the current leader to do the honours, but the Prime Minister in 1988 was none other than Mrs Margaret Thatcher, seen (not without cause in Scotland) as being responsible for the dreadful unemployment statistics and the deliberate running down of educational and health provision, let alone what was happening in Northern Ireland. The fans of both clubs came in with red cards and showed them to her, as a clear sign that she was not wanted!

Of more immediate concern to Billy McNeill was a series of injuries to goal-keeper Pat Bonner. These had been apparent for some time, but had intensified in the week before the game.

McNeill had done well to keep most of this from the press, but on the morning of the game he had to make the decision to drop the luckless and ever-popular Pat and replace him with the less well known Allen McKnight. McKnight had had two short spells in the side earlier this season when Bonner was out, and had already played for Northern Ireland, so he was not exactly a tyro, but it must nevertheless have been a big ask for him suddenly to be pitched into a cup final.

Hampden was bathed in sunshine for the final and presented a marvellous sight that day, as thousands of Celtic supporters made their way to the ground (all armed with red cards for Mrs Thatcher!), the lucky ones with tickets to actually get into the ground, the less lucky ones to watch the game in one or other of the many pubs in the vicinity. Either way, it was destined to be a great experience as Celtic pursued their 28th Scottish Cup in 100 years, and Dundee United chased their first.

As often happens in cup finals the first half was poor, with both teams playing cat and mouse and reluctant to commit themselves. Celtic in fact came closer with Joe Miller mistiming his jump to a cross, but apart from that there was little to enthuse about. 'You get the feeling that the powder keg is about to explode, but the fuse has not yet been lit,' was the way that one commentator put it.

It all started early in the second half. Roy Aitken, a crucial and central character in any Celtic drama of the 1980s, was booked for a foul on Kevin Gallacher. Soon after that, a poorish clearance from McKnight found Gallacher who charged in on goal with Aitken running alongside him. It went through the heads of all Celtic fans, and thankfully through the head of Aitken himself, that he could not tackle Gallacher, for the slightest mistiming would have seen a second booking and therefore a red card – and everyone was well aware of what happened in the Scottish Cup Final of 1984 when Roy's red card gave the cup to Aberdeen.

The result of all this was that GALLACHER was allowed to run on and score, with McKnight, possibly failing to read the nuances of the situation vis-a-vis Aitken and possible disciplinary action, not coming out to narrow the angle. The result was that Celtic were, like three years ago and at a similar stage of the game, a goal behind to Dundee United, the world's experts at shutting up shop, and by some distance Scotland's finest at playing a containing, European type of game.

But this was a confident Celtic team and Celtic support. It was also Centenary Year. This was Hampden in the sun, and a comeback was positively demanded by the massive Celtic support and the feeling of history that had seen previous glorious Scottish Cup final comebacks in 1904, 1925, 1931, 1965 and 1985. No club on earth has a greater consciousness of their own history. Celtic were just about to add a little more.

It was also a team which contained an incredible amount of team spirit. Mark McGhee would claim years later that they all 'loved' one another. What he meant by that is of course open to interpretation, but it was certain that there was a total absence of cliques and cabals in the squad. Moreover, there were no unsettled 'I want more money' kind of players who felt they were too good to play for this Celtic side, and who had, in the past, caused all sorts of trouble for the team. Manager McNeill was right to compare them to the team that had won the European Cup in Lisbon 20 years previously in this respect at least. Possibly they were a little short of the ability of that great team ... but they did all have the correct attitude.

Attacking the King's Park end (as in 1985) where were housed most of their support, Celtic charged forward. Manager McNeill, wearing an inappropriate rain coat for superstitious reasons, waved them forward, making two clever substitutions in Billy Stark and Mark McGhee – Stark to give extra drive to the midfield, and McGhee to pep up the forward line and unsettle the Tannadice defence who had hitherto coped very well with Andy Walker.

The equaliser came in the 75th minute (round about the same time as the equaliser had come in 1985 as well!) when Anton Rogan, the fast running Irish left-back, made ground on the left, sent over a harmless looking cross which Billy Thomson in the Dundee United goal failed to deal with, and Frank McAVENNIE headed home as the terracing behind him exploded, and the Dundee United fans would have been forgiven for thinking *here we go again*!

Once again we must not underestimate the power of the Celtic fans. 'Roaring their team to victory' was in danger of becoming a cliché, but that was exactly what happened, as Celtic forced corner after corner. Almost on the final whistle, as if it had all been 'meant' by some benevolent deity (and wasn't it?), Chris Morris won a corner on the right. Jim Craig, the Lisbon Lion, would later be very kind in the BBC studio when he said that it was 'not the best corner in the world' by Joe Miller which landed fortuitously at the feet of Billy Stark, who miskicked and the ball broke to Frank McAVENNIE who banged the ball home to win the Scottish Cup for Celtic in scenes of almost indescribable joy.

The final whistle went almost immediately afterwards, and then Mrs Thatcher (she had apparently enjoyed the game, according to SFA secretary Ernie Walker who had been 'privileged' to sit beside her), did the only good thing she ever did in her life by presenting the Scottish Cup to Roy Aitken. She then disappeared immediately afterwards for security reasons, but no-one noticed her going ... or even cared. The celebrations were the important thing.

v Airdrieonians 1-0
Scottish Cup Final, Hampden
27 May 1995

CELTIC	AIRDRIEONIANS	REFEREE
Bonner	Martin	Mr L. Mottram,
Boyd	Stewart	Wilsontown
McKinlay	Jack	
Vata	Sandison	
McNally	Hay*	
Grant	Black	
McLaughlin	Boyle	
McStay	Smith	
van Hooijdonk*	Cooper	
Donnelly**	Harvey**	
Collins	Lawrence	
Subs: Falconer*	Subs: McIntyre*	
O'Donnell **	T. Smith**	

THE WORD 'desperate' is frequently overused in footballing circles, but no Celtic supporter making his way to the Scottish Cup Final on 27 May 1995 would say that he was anything other than 'desperate' for success. Six years had passed since Celtic's last trophy – six long, painful years in which the very heart and soul of the club had come close to being ripped out by incompetent management and a shameful betrayal of all the club and its supporters stood for.

One would have to agree that Rangers were good in those days, but that is only half the story. A team is only as good as its opponents allow it to be, and Celtic had, frankly, allowed them to get away with murder in Scotland, so comprehensive had been the Parkhead collapse. Other teams had occasionally won a trophy during these dreadful years – Aberdeen, Hibs, Dundee United, Motherwell – but no sustained challenge had come from Celtic, whose board seemed, like a rabbit dazzled in a car's headlights, unable to do anything other than watch Rangers win the Scottish League year after year.

'Poverty' was the cry. This, frankly, was rubbish, because Celtic, with as large a support in Scotland and, in world terms, a far larger potential support than Rangers, would surely be able to do what Rangers did ... if the board were prepared to make an effort.

But the problem was that the board would neither do that, nor would they allow anyone else in with money who might be able to help them do it, for control of the club lay inexorably and exclusively in the hands of family dynasties whose current members were surely shaming the memory of their forefathers. Players were bought – but cheap ones, a front man called Terry Cassidy was appointed whose role seemed to be nothing other than to act as a shield for the board who were increasingly afraid to face their public, ludicrous appointments were made, incredible decisions were taken about moving to a new stadium – and the whole first five years of the early 1990s is an era which one cannot recall, even now, without a frisson of horror rolling down one's spine. Words sometimes fail the chronicler.

Gradually, however, the rebellion grew. From moanings and groanings (something that Celtic fans have always excelled at even when the team is doing well!), a few rebel fanzines began to appear, meetings were held, attendances slumped, slogans like 'Save Our Celts' began to be heard, and eventually the edifice cracked. In early March 1994, in scenes reminiscent of a coup in South America, the board collapsed, and Celtic were reborn.

Things had thus taken a decided turn for the better as Fergus McCann, a tough Scottish-Canadian but at least a genuine Celtic supporter, took over. Tommy Burns was appointed as manager, a fans' share issue was put into place, and the decision was taken not to move from Parkhead but to redevelop the existing ground. All this meant that season 1994/95 was never going to be an easy one. For the first time since 1892, Celtic did not play their home games at Celtic Park, for it was flattened for redevelopment – and the club had to move for a season to Hampden. And although money was now available for Tommy Burns to buy new players, so much damage had been done in the previous seasons that recovery was difficult.

Celtic limped to the Scottish League Cup Final on 27 November 1994 to play First Division Raith Rovers at Ibrox. Here, at last, was a chance to win a trophy, to show the supporters that Celtic were back and to light up a few faces with unaccustomed joy. Sadly, Celtic's enemies could not have written the script for this one any better if they had wanted to twist the knife even further into the heart of Celtic fans. 2-1 up with minutes to go, then an equaliser for the Kirkcaldy men from ex-Ranger Gordon Dalziel, then the agony of a penalty shoot-out which went to sudden death, and Paul McStay, Celtic's best player by some distance over the past ten years or more, missing the decisive penalty.

This was painful, and 'a defeat too far' (as the *Scotsman* put it) for Celtic's legions of fans, some of whom now suffered from a depression from which there seemed to be no escape. Indeed as Celtic made progress in the Scottish Cup in spring 1995, there were those in the support who actually did not want them to get to the final, fearing a repetition of the horrible events of the previous November. Indeed the progress was unimpressive, with home (Hampden) wins over St Mirren, Meadowbank and Kilmarnock, then an awful display against Hibs in the semi-final in which Jim Leighton brought back the dreadful memories of Raith Rovers by saving a penalty in the same goal at Ibrox as Scott Thomson had saved Paul McStay's. This meant a 0-0 scoreline, but Celtic were considerably better in the replay and won 3-1.

Their final opponents were to be Airdrieonians, like Raith Rovers, of the First Division. As with Celtic, they were also homeless, for they were in the throes of moving ground. They were managed by the doughty old Rangers player, Alex McDonald, who had also managed Hearts in the past. He was a tough and occasionally unscrupulous character, not much loved of the Celtic support.

The Scottish Cup Final was to be a funny one that year. In the first place it was played at Hampden. This was odd for two reasons. The first was that Hampden itself was being redeveloped and the crowd would therefore be reduced to 36,915 – and the other was that Hampden had been Celtic's home ground that season. Ibrox seemed a better bet (it had already hosted the League Cup Final), or even Murrayfield in Edinburgh – but Hampden it was, and royalty would be present in the shape of the Duchess of Kent, a charming lady who looked well in place at Wimbledon – but in the rough, tough, muscular world of Scottish football, seeing a match where the supporters of one team quite blatantly did not recognise the British royal family, was she a good choice?

Celtic had problems in the run-up to this game, played on the astonishingly late date of 27 May 1995. There was a morale boost in the shape of a victory over Rangers in a meaningless game in early May but Tony Mowbray, that most wholehearted of Celts, was suspended for the cup final, and another wholehearted Celt Peter Grant was injured. This had happened two weeks previously at Tannadice Park on a day that was sad for other reasons in that it relegated Dundee United, Celtic having to pull the reluctant trigger to send down a fine team with whom they had had many great tussles in the past and indeed a certain historical affinity.

Peter now looked distinctly doubtful for a game that now assumed mammoth proportions in the general well-being of the support. But Peter had one great ally, and that was his determination to play through pain for his beloved club. 'Playing for the jersey' and 'wearing his heart on his sleeve' were some of the many cliches turned out by the scribes in the approach to the final. Peter would turn out to be a great hero for Celtic that day.

Grant may have played for the 'jersey', but it was a funny jersey that day. It was green and white stripes, or 'hoops' as they became known, and for that we had to be thankful, but the stripes were of different size and thickness! The sponsor's logo was prominent (always something to be deprecated as well – but that is the name of the game, these days!). We traditionalists sighed but shrugged our shoulders. They were at least wearing the green and white!

No Celtic historian will point to 1995 and say that this was a vintage team. There were one or two fine players like Tom Boyd, Paul McStay and John Collins, but there were also very many men who could be called honest journeymen – Rudi Vata, the first Albanian to play for the club, Mark McNally, Brian McLaughlin, Simon Donnelly, who promised more than he delivered, and a few others. But there was also the massive presence of Dutchman Pierre van Hooijdonk, signed early in the New Year in the wake of the Raith Rovers fiasco, a man who was said to be not particularly easy to manage but ... he was scoring the goals.

Following the presentation of the teams to the royal party – the Airdrie team actually broke all sorts of rules about royal protocol by kissing the beautiful Duchess of Kent (and one or two of them said they wouldn't have minded a little more!) while the Celtic players contented themselves with a polite shake of the hand, the game itself began its tension-ridden course. Celtic began attacking the King's Park end and after McNally had missed a good chance with a header, took the lead with less than ten minutes on the clock.

A ball was not properly cleared by the Airdrie defence and came to midfielder Tosh McKinlay. McKinlay, now playing for Celtic after a not always totally successful career with Dundee and Hearts, sent a high ball into the penalty area and Pierre VAN HOOIJDONK rose spectacularly to head home – a goal much enjoyed throughout the land and indeed throughout the world where the game was being watched on TV by Celtic's far-flung followers.

And that was about it as far as highlights of the game were concerned, for there was no further scoring. The closest that anyone came was John Collins in the early stages of the second half when he headed wide. The rest of the game was turgid and uneventful, and if it had not mattered so much to the Celtic family, would have been switched off the television. But it did matter such a great deal, and the whole of the second half was one long anxious looking at watches and willing the clock to go round. Man of the match was without doubt Peter Grant who shrugged off injury and a few attempts to make the injury worse by cynical opponents. Several of Peter's tackles were brilliant, one on Lawrence in the penalty box where the slightest misjudgement would have meant a penalty kick and possibly a red card. But this was Peter's day and he emerged triumphant, tears in his eyes at the end.

He was not the only one. The Duchess said 'Paul, well done!' as she handed over the trophy to Paul McStay, the man who had suffered most of all in the aftermath of the Ibrox nightmare. You could possibly say that of Celtic's 30 Scottish Cup victories up to that point, this one was possibly the poorest in terms of entertainment and playing performance, but in terms of spectator satisfaction and relief, it scored very highly indeed. That night for the first night in six years, we slept the sleep of the just. Celtic had been born again.

v Rangers 2-0
Scottish League, Celtic Park
2 January 1998

CELTIC	RANGERS	REFEREE
Gould	Goram	Mr H. Dallas, Bonkle
Boyd	McCall	
Annoni	Cleland	
McNamara	Gough	
Rieper	Porrini	
Stubbs	Albertz*	
Larsson	Thern	
Burley	Ferguson	
Brattbakk*	Negri	
Lambert	Gattuso**	
Wieghorst	Laudrup	
Sub: Jackson*	Subs: Gascoigne*	
	Durie**	

I T IS true that most games against Rangers are 'must win' games, otherwise the Celtic-supporting part of the city, the country and the world slips into depression while the other half rejoice. This one however as the year turned from 1997 to 1998 was more important than most. It was an absolute imperative that Celtic should win the league that year, otherwise the unthinkable was going to happen and Rangers were going to win ten titles in a row, thereby beating what had been achieved by Jock Stein's side from 1966 until 1974. This simply could not be allowed to happen.

The recent past had of course been particularly painful for those who loved the green and white. The sacking of Tommy Burns in 1997 (like Billy McNeill, too much of a supporter to be a manager) had seen the appointment of a little known fuzzy-haired character called Wim Jansen, who had actually played for Feyenoord against Celtic in the 1970 European Cup Final! The Dutchman (with Murdo MacLeod as his assistant) had gone on a spending spree, bringing so many players to the club that the squad list was virtually unrecognisable from what it had been a year ago.

Some of the new players were simply 'names' when they arrived. Not many Celtic supporters would have heard of Henrik Larsson or Harald Brattbakk, although Craig Burley and Paul Lambert would have been more familiar from their Scotland connections. It took time, of course, for them all to bed in, and the first few games of the season had been far from happy ones with defeats to Hibs and Dunfermline in the first two games, for example.

An extraneous factor entered the equation at the end of August when Princess Diana was killed in Paris. This meant the postponement of the game against Rangers at Parkhead, for Celtic fans would never have observed any minute's silence for a member of the royal family! Indeed the song at the moment was the 'Field of Athenry', with its unequivocal message:

Against the famine and the crown
I rebelled, they brought me down.

The postponement may well have been a good thing for gradually form had improved. A flying header from Henrik Larsson at McDiarmid Park, Perth in August had set things going and by the end of October, a league challenge was credible. A few stumbles in November at Ibrox, and a particular shocker against Motherwell at Parkhead in which Regi Blinker had shown his immaturity by being sent off for something really stupid, had seen the team at a particularly low point in mid November. However when Rangers came calling to Parkhead for the postponed game the following Wednesday, a last-gasp header by Alan Stubbs had rescued a point and possibly the league challenge as well, and then the month of November had finished on a very high note when a piece of silverware came our way in the annexing of the Scottish League Cup in a rather brilliant 3-0 win over Dundee United at Ibrox.

Those who argue that the Scottish League Cup is insignificant are wrong. On this occasion, the boost given to Celtic was incalculable. It was something tangible, and (incredibly) was only the second time in the 1990s that Celtic had won a trophy. Such had been the price to be paid for incompetent management and stewardship of the club, the return of green and white ribbons to a piece of silverware was a positive sign of the club's return to respectability, if not yet glory. In addition the game had been on terrestrial TV and had been a massive propaganda boost.

Moreover, Celtic had given Liverpool a run for their money in Europe. They had eventually gone out on away goals, but it had been close, and the feeling was that Celtic were 'going places'. Everything however boiled down to the fact that the league championship was the vital thing. This tournament simply had to be won, for the consequences of Rangers winning 'ten in a row' (that nightmare phrase) would be dire and permanent.

There was however another dynamic at work in Scottish football this year and that was Hearts, who were giving both Rangers and Celtic some competition. Amazingly, some Celtic fans, for reasons that in other circumstances would have been barely credible but were totally understandable in the context of 1997/98, would say that they would settle for Hearts winning the championship that year! That at least would stop the 'ten in a row' nonsense. Nine was bad enough, but as a Celtic t-shirt said: 'Nine in a Row? What's the big deal? We did it first!' Ten would be a different matter altogether.

Celtic finished 1997 on a low with a defeat at Perth on 27 December. Significantly, in this game, Henrik Larsson was out injured and Celtic were simply unable to batter a way through a packed St Johnstone defence. Both Rangers and Hearts won that day, and the result of this was that Rangers finished 1997 four points ahead of Celtic with Hearts wedged in between the two of them.

The significance of the 2 January fixture at Parkhead was thus that if Rangers won, they would be a massive seven points ahead of Celtic. A draw would suit Rangers, but Celtic really had to win if they were to narrow the gap. There was also a certain complex beginning to develop about Celtic's apparent inability to beat Rangers. All four league games last season had been lost, this season had seen a defeat and a draw and the last win on league business had been in May 1995 when Celtic were playing their home games at Hampden, when there had been no significant league challenge at all and the result meant very little.

Celtic Park was of course still incomplete in January 1998. The North Stand had been built as indeed had the Lisbon Lions Stand, but what is now the Jock Stein Stand was still temporary accommodation, unroofed and open to the elements. Celtic started off defending that goal which had a funny, unnerving look about it. Some grounds that were in the throes of redevelopment had nothing at all behind them. This one had something, but it was bizarre and ugly. It would stay until the end of the season.

The game was played at a frenetic pace, fast even by Old Firm standards, but nothing of any great importance happened until half-time. Rangers had an early penalty claim denied them by referee Hugh Dallas within the first ten minutes, but it looked like an innocent clash of bodies between Alan Stubbs and Brian Laudrup. If anything Rangers played slightly more composed football in the early stages, and their one real star man of that decade Brian Laudrup looked as if he could cause all sorts of damage down the right flank until Enrico Annoni, Celtic's very popular Italian left-back, gradually got the better of him. Yet one always feared about Laudrup. He was intelligent (off the field as well as on it) cultured and responded well to a slow and more thoughtful pace of football, and he was certainly a match-winner. We often wondered how a man like that ever managed to fit in at Ibrox!

Tommy Boyd was having a particularly good game. Tommy's career of course had coincided with most of the bad days, and he had come through it all with dignity. A very reliable defender, he now seemed more and more to be developing as an attacking full-back, and on this occasion began to create a great deal of moves for Celtic. Larsson, one suspected, may not have been totally fit, not quite having recovered from his recent injury. Certainly his impact in the first half had been minimal.

In the second half, Celtic gradually took control, and those of us who are delighted to see Scottish players doing well would notice that it was the Scottish trio of Lambert, Burley and McNamara who were controlling the game, with McNamara in particular doing a great deal of ball distribution, as the Rangers midfield slowly began to disappear from the picture. The Celtic fans, sensing their ascendancy, responded as well and very soon they would have their reward.

Halfway through the second half, Celtic struck. A clearance from Lambert found McNamara who made a little space and then angled a good backward pass to find Craig BURLEY, who was able to slot the ball past Andy Goram in the Rangers goal. Goram, a man who sometimes seemed to go out of his way to court controversy, had been notorious for his luck in previous games at Celtic Park. Not this time, though, and Celtic were on top.

With quarter of the game left, this was now the crucial test for Celtic. Previous Celtic teams with less backbone than this one had blown it on such occasions and allowed the opposition back into the game. But as well as commitment and pride, there was also a high degree of professionalism in this side, and it was the Celtic midfield that continued its domination of the game, even allowing defenders like

Boyd and Stubbs to come forward now and again as well. Yet, everyone knew that midfield domination counted for nothing if the opposition sneaked a late equaliser, or earned a lucky penalty. Rangers had now brought on Paul Gascoigne, and, say what you want about the guy (and everybody did!) he was not without talent and could change the game.

But as time was running out and Celtic remained on top, it was Paul Lambert who made the difference. Paul had played for St Mirren and Motherwell, and had then won the European Cup with Borussia Dortmund in Germany before deciding to return to Scotland when Celtic showed an interest. It was a great move on Celtic's part, never more obvious than today when LAMBERT picked up a ball from Jackie McNamara and, curiously unmarked by a now tired Rangers team, hammered home a shot into the roof of the net from over 20 yards, as the temporary bleachers behind that goal gave every sign of collapsing under the strain of exultant, dancing supporters.

Rangers had no time left to come back at Celtic, and they finished the game a well beaten side, Walter Smith conceding with quiet dignity that Celtic were the better team. Indeed they were, but there was, as everyone was well aware, a long, long way to go. Another 16 games remained. No-one ever wins the league at New Year, and indeed Rangers were still top of the league. But the marker had been laid down. Celtic had proved to their supporters that they could beat Rangers, and they could look forward to the next few crucial months with increasing optimism.

Jim Traynor (well known, even notorious, for his trenchant views expressed in print and on his radio phone-in, and by no means the greatest Celtic supporter in the world) wrote in the *Daily Record* the following day that 'A mighty second half display from Celtic dispersed the gloom which had gathered over their East Glasgow domain. Where there was despair, there is now vibrant hope.' For once, it was generally agreed by Celtic fans that Traynor had got it right.

v St Johnstone 2-0
Scottish League, Celtic Park
9 May 1998

CELTIC	ST JOHNSTONE	REFEREE
Gould	Main	Mr K. Clark, Paisley
Boyd	McQuillan	
Annoni	Preston	
McNamara	Sekerlioglu**	
Rieper	McCluskey***	
Stubbs	Whiteford	
Larsson**	O'Halloran*	
Burley	O'Neil	
Donnelly*	Grant	
Lambert***	O'Boyle	
O'Donnell	Jenkinson	
Subs: Brattbakk*	Subs: McMahon*	
Blinker**	Griffin**	
Wieghorst***	Connolly***	

IT WAS all set up by the combined efforts of Ally Mitchell and Craig Faulconbridge the week before. These otherwise obscure characters, hardworking and good professionals no doubt, made the run-up to the game of 9 May 1998 the tensest, probably, of any in Celtic's history. Ally Mitchell was the man who scored for Kilmarnock at Ibrox with the last kick of the ball on Saturday 2 May – something which meant that Celtic could win the league at Dunfermline on Sunday 3 May. They looked like doing this until late in the game, Faulconbridge beat Jonathan Gould with a looping header to deny Celtic three points. A draw was not enough.

Celtic's salvation still lay in their own hands. A win over St Johnstone at Parkhead would be enough. This didn't sound too difficult, for St Johnstone, a team whose supporters come from a rural part of Scotland and who (they say) vote Conservative, were by no means the best in the land. Yet they had consistently caused Celtic problems, not least this season when they won at McDiarmid Park in the last game of 1997. Managed by Paul Sturrock (who had learned all he knew from the grim Jim McLean of Tannadice Park) the Saints could be relied upon to put up a good fight, and they had good players like Roddie Grant and George O'Boyle.

Rangers were at Tannadice Park. All they could do was beat Dundee United and hope for the best. The focus was certainly on Celtic. Celtic could lose the title if they lost or drew and if Rangers beat Dundee United. It was a frightening scenario, for Celtic would take a long time to recover from a record-breaking ten in a row league titles for their rivals. It could go on to be 11 or 12 or....

Any supporter of any team in any given year can always say the meaningless rubbish of 'We should have had it won by...' or 'We threw it all away'. These statements are the reverse of helpful to a team who is struggling and who need the backing of their support more than ever. The Celtic support, however querulous and critical of their team's performances in the run-in, remained loyal.

There had been two terrible games at Parkhead against the two Edinburgh teams, for example, 0-0 in both cases, which had raised the question of whether Celtic were good enough to win the championship, and on two successive April Sundays, defeats from Rangers in the Scottish Cup and the Scottish League had seemed to pass the initiative back to Ibrox – only for them to subsequently lose to Aberdeen at Pittodrie. For a spell, Hearts had kept pace with the big Glasgow two – a welcome development for those who worried about the future of the game in Scotland – but they had stuttered towards the end and had finally blown up rather spectacularly in a 3-0 defeat at Tynecastle against Rangers in the third last week. The Edinburgh men would however have their recompense in the Scottish Cup.

Celtic had not really played brilliantly that season. There were two great players in Craig Burley and the dreadlocked Henrik Larsson, a fine acquisition in Paul Lambert, and one or two others who had all played their parts on occasion. The whole thing had not been helped by the ill-disguised 'fall out' between manager Wim Jansen, the 'first-team coach', and Jock Brown, 'general manager'.

Part of this piece of childishness seems to have lain in the undeniable fact that neither of them were all that aware of the boundaries of each other's job, but both are culpable in that their disagreement was allowed to become public – in fact it was made public by each of them in turn – and the form of the team inevitably faltered. Men who earn huge salaries and are in positions where a lot depends on them, really must develop the skills to get on with each other. No-one says that they must be bosom buddies, or even that they should go out for a pint together, but they really must learn to co-operate! Thus it was that Celtic faced one of the most important games in their history without any clear knowledge of what their management team would be next year.

Celtic Park not yet being completed at what is now the Jock Stein Stand end of the ground, tickets were limited to 49,701. Thus it was that the area around the ground saw thousands of Celtic fans begging for tickets, being prepared to pay outrageous prices for them and when they couldn't get one, settling for listening to the radio commentary – a far more gut-wrenching way of following a game than actually being in the ground. There was no live television broadcast, so the streets round Celtic Park after 3.00 pm were thronged with people in green and white scarves clustered round radios, or with headphones on, or even in the 1960s style, with the old-fashioned 'tranny' cocked to one's ear.

Celtic were more or less at full strength, but St Johnstone, whose manager Paul Sturrock claimed that he had had death threats from both Celtic and Rangers supporters in the course of the week, had a side weakened with injury and suspension. They could neither make Europe, nor were they going to be relegated, so there was nothing at stake for them. Their season had been respectable and their supporters had been happy with their performances. They were here to enjoy themselves.

It was a fine day, with a gentle breeze and loads of sunshine. Celtic started off playing to the Lisbon Lions end of the ground, and in the second minute they went ahead with an excellent piece of work from Henrik LARSSON. He picked up a ball from Paul Lambert on the left, cut across the field and then, without giving any great indication that that was his intention, turned and beat goalkeeper Alan Main with a tremendous shot.

This gave Celtic's support in the ground, outside the ground and all over the world a tremendous boost, and for a while after that, as Celtic kept pressing, it seemed that the result was going to be a formality and that Celtic would win easily. But after a few chances were missed, nervousness came into play, and the crackling transistors told us that Rangers were ahead at Tannadice, St Johnstone came more into it with that doughty character George O'Boyle, who had given Celtic loads of bother when he was with Dunfermline, coming close, and it was probably true to say that we were all glad to enjoy the temporary relief of half-time.

The second half saw attempts to raise the team with singing, but the chants were tension-ridden and sporadic. Soon after half-time Rangers went two ahead at Tannadice, something that made us all the more aware that one slip-up, one goal-keeping error, one refereeing decision, could plunge Celtic into the sort of Stygian melancholy that would be unimaginable in its ferocity, intensity and permanence.

The second half crawled on. Simon Donnelly, a wholehearted and permanently 'promising' kid who looked not unlike Leonardo di Caprio, the leading actor in the film *Titanic*, and had suffered from being compared to Kenny Dalglish, was withdrawn in favour of the scholarly Harald Brattbakk, another fellow whose potential had so far exceeded his performances. One goal at either end, we knew, would finish it. A goal for St Johnstone would lose it for us, a goal for Celtic would win it. The standard of football was uninspiring with neither team showing any great ambition to score – Celtic because they were terrified of committing men forward, and St Johnstone clearly intending to keep it at 1-0 until the final stages when they would win the hearts of all Rangers fans with a late equaliser. Someone might do an Albert Kidd in reverse ... but we tried not to think of that.

Meanwhile some fans unashamedly left their seats and hid in the toilets. Prayers were said by lifelong atheists, and the transistor-carrying brigade outside the ground eased tension by pacing back and forward through car parks and streets, their faces gaunt and pinched with tension. Those at home went for walks in the garden, trying to pretend to be interested in roses and daffodils as the minutes ever so slowly ticked away.

Momentary relief came when the crowd started saying 'Zetterlund' after a few cheers. This was the name of the Dundee United player who had scored at Tannadice, making it 2-1. Now if only he could score again... Jonathan Gould in the Celtic goal looked confident as he dealt with the odd St Johnstone attack. But was he? Certainly some other members of the defence were seen to shout at one another – a clear sign that things were far from rosy...

But then suddenly in the 72nd minute the bubble burst, and we all not so much cheered the team to the echo, as heaved a massive sigh of relief. Jackie McNamara did well on the right, and sent over a ball into the centre. Harald BRATTBAKK ran onto it, amidst the tension and gasps of 'This time!' and 'Now', before Harald, cool as a cucumber, scored this most crucial of goals for the club.

There was a very interesting vignette caught by the BBC TV cameras of the aftermath. As Harald ran to the fans in the Main Stand, in a lovely show of Scandinavian solidarity, Henrik Larsson ran to him, jumped on his back, looked at the crowd and pointed downwards toward Harald as if to say 'I told you he would do it'. The crowd laughed and cheered all the more.

Even at this point, there were still some fans, inured to the heartbreak of the past ten years, who remained pessimistic. In truth it had been a long, long time and we were all aware that there were some young fans who had never seen Celtic win the championship, and that, conversely, other supporters who had been around in 1988 were no longer here to see this one. All these confused thoughts whirled around our heads in the maelstrom of emotions that engulfed us – the main one being *Please, don't let St Johnstone score twice!* – until the glorious moment when referee Kenny Clark picked up the ball, turned to the Main Stand and blew his whistle.

v Rangers 6-2

Scottish League, Celtic Park
27 August 2000

CELTIC	RANGERS	REFEREE
Gould	Klos	Mr S. Dougal, Glasgow
Valgaeren	Ricksen*	
Mahe	Amoruso	
McNamara	Konterman	
Stubbs*	Vidmar**	
Petta	Reyna	
Petrov	Ferguson	
Lambert**	van Bronckhorst	
Moravcik***	McCann***	
Larsson	Dodds	
Sutton	Wallace	
Subs: Mjallby*	Subs: Tugay*	
Boyd**	Kanchelskis**	
Burchill***	Lovenkrands***	

CELTIC HAD taken the plunge in summer 2000 by appointing Martin O'Neill as their manager. The previous few years, as Celtic staggered towards the end of the millennium, had been unsatisfactory, many of the poor performances caused by the appointment to managerial positions of men who simply were not suited to the job. The 1998 league triumph had been marred in its immediate aftermath by a managerial fall out and resignation, 1999 had seen Jo Venglos, a lovely man with a great European pedigree but no longer a young man and manifestly unsuited to Scotland ... and the less said about the Barnes/Dalglish fiasco the better. Inverness, a place hitherto much enjoyed on holidays and indeed a very beautiful city, could not now even be contemplated without vivid flashbacks to the awful night of 8 February 2000.

But the corner had been turned – or had it? O'Neill had been a great manager for Leicester City, but Celtic would be a different matter. The support had taken him to their hearts, for indeed he had been born and bred a Celtic supporter, but how would he cope with Glasgow? He had been a good player for Nottingham Forest where he had learned a few things about management from the quixotic, quirky but undeniably successful Brian Clough, and he had also played international football for Northern Ireland under men like Billy Bingham. He looked studious and gentlemanly, but it was immediately apparent that he was choleric and excitable. He was a man who enjoyed his football – and who became very emotionally involved in it.

First impressions of the 2000/01 season had been favourable – indeed he had won his first four league games in a steady, but unspectacular way – but everyone was well aware that the first game against Rangers is often the one that defines the season. It does not in itself win anything, or even prove very much, but it very quickly sets the tone for future performances. 'One cannot win the league in August, but one can sure as hell lose it,' said one veteran supporter. A beating must be avoided. Most Celtic supporters recalled the awful day in 1988 when Celtic, league and cup double winners of a few months ago, surrendered pitifully at Ibrox, and did not recover from the 1-5 drubbing for many years.

O'Neill had already invested heavily in the transfer market. On 11 July, he had broken the Scottish record by paying a colossal £6 million for Chris Sutton from Chelsea, while Joos Valgaeren, a little known Belgian, had been bought to bolster the defence, and as important as anything else, he now had Henrik Larsson back to full fitness, following Larsson's leg break the previous autumn which had caused so much misery to Celtic. Bobby Petta, whose contribution to Celtic hitherto had been anything but impressive, was also given a run, and seemed to thrive under O'Neill. In addition, O'Neill began to rid Celtic of those who had let the club down – Mark Viduka, for example, was on his way, Eyal Berkovic would soon become a peripheral character, and gradually, this would become O'Neill's team. It would all need time, and this is why most Celtic supporters would have happily settled for a 0-0 draw against Rangers on that momentous Sunday lunchtime of 27 August 2000.

Rangers had had a very easy life in the years 1999 and 2000. It is a sad fact (and becoming more and more true as every year passes) that if Celtic collapse, then no-one else in Scottish football will take up the baton to fight against Rangers. Aberdeen, Hearts, Hibs, Dundee United, those of whom a challenge might reasonably be expected, lamentably fail to do so. The SPL championships in 1999 and 2000 were won by Rangers with embarrassing ease, and in the Scottish Cup Final of 2000 they had been opposed by a third-rate Aberdeen team who had embarrassed the traditions of the Granite City. Rangers had won honours, but they were not a good team, a point that some of their more perceptive supporters would acknowledge in a weak moment. Like Celtic, their record in European competitions was shameful and deplorable.

Those Rangers supporters who had been playing golf that Sunday morning or even been to church would have been pardoned for not believing the evidence of their TV screens, for after 15 minutes of the game, with Parkhead in an uproar, the score was Celtic 3 Rangers 0. Each of the three goals had been marvellously worked and had been the reward for a fine passage of play in which the Rangers defence had been totally overrun. Bobby Petta had rampaged down the left, Larsson and Sutton had run amok in the centre of the field pulling the Rangers defence all over the place, and the Celtic midfield in which McNamara, Lambert and Petrov had been outstanding kept up a constant supply of ammunition for the forwards. And only 15 minutes had gone!

Celtic were attacking the Lisbon Lions end of the ground that pleasant sunny Sunday lunchtime, and it did not take them long to get going. The theme of the first 15 minutes was of Petta making ground on the left, involving the playmaker Moravcik and Celtic scoring the goals. The first came after only one minute when after a corner on the left the ball broke to Larsson who didn't seem to get enough on the ball and it seemed to be going past until the ever-alert Chris SUTTON hooked the ball into the net. Eight minutes later Petta had once again forced a corner. Moravcik took it and the ball came to Stilian PETROV, curiously unmarked by the Rangers defence, and he scored with a powerful header. Another six minutes after that and it was Paul LAMBERT, in loads of space, with a crisp drive who thumped home another ball from the left.

It was all too much for Rangers manager Dick Advocaat who panicked and substituted Fernando Ricksen. Ricksen had barely had a kick of the ball since the start and the damage had to a large extent been caused by Bobby Petta on the left, Ricksen's direct opponent. Even so a substitution before half-time is more than a little humiliating, and the luckless Ricksen trudged off to the jeers of contempt from the Celtic fans. As Abba might have said, 'What's it all about, Fernando?' Tugay took his place. He cannot have relished the thought of it.

The first half-hour bordered on the unbelievable, and there had even been some half-chances squandered as well. One had to believe that Rangers would make some sort of a comeback however, and they did. It was Claudio REYNA who allowed them to go in at half-time with a modicum of self-respect and even the possibility that they might get something out of the game. There may have been a touch of offside about the goal, but then Rangers scored again, this time through Wallace himself, only to find it chalked off for offside. Thus it might have been 3-2 at half-time, but it might also have been 5-0 or even 6-0 if the Reyna goal had been disallowed and if Henrik Larsson and Bobby Petta had scored with the opportunities given to them.

The first half was almost too much for the average supporter to take in. Celtic supporters were all too aware that the game was anything but over, and that a Rangers fightback was a possibility. What was vital for Celtic was not to sit back and wait for this to happen. They must retain the initiative, and must dictate the way that the game was to be played. There must be no death wish – the single factor which had allowed Rangers to have their stranglehold over Celtic for all these years.

There was indeed to be none of that. Henrik LARSSON scored many goals for the club, but few were better than the one he scored after five minutes of the second half. He was just inside the Rangers half when Sutton chested a ball down to him in a good position. He then evaded the challenge of Tugay, slipped the ball between the legs of Konterman, nipped round the back of him and then as Stefan Klos came out, lobbed the ball over the German's head. Money simply cannot buy a goal like that! 'The mark of a world class player,' said Davie Provan succinctly on Sky TV.

But then immediately after that, Rangers pulled one back from a softish penalty when Stefan Mahe went up with Rod Wallace in the box. It was clumsy, but not a deliberate foul. Some referees might not have given it, but Stuart Dougal did, and Billy DODDS put Rangers back in the game for a spell at least with the score now at 4-2.

But Celtic were not to be denied. The next two goals were great ones as well, albeit mundane in the context of what had gone before. If they had been scored in any other game, they would have been raved about all season, but there was a danger in this game that they might even have been forgotten about! In the 63rd minute whatever chance there might have been of a Rangers comeback was killed when Celtic won a free kick on the right. It was taken by the ubiquitous Bobby Petta and found the unmarked head of LARSSON who scored a Jimmy McGrory-type header. Just as time was running out, Chris SUTTON scored from a cross by Stefan Mahe to complete the rout.

It was not Rangers' day, and their misery was completed when Barry Ferguson lost the plot and was sent off. To be fair to Barry, it was just frustration, but any sympathy for him evaporated when he carried on the feud after the game. Rangers were now plunged into the depths of despair, for they realised that they were now up against a talented Celtic team with an intelligent new manager. What this game gave Celtic was a new thing called belief. They now *believed* that they could beat Rangers and it was the first step to a glorious treble.

Life was good for Celtic supporters and very soon t-shirts appeared with 6-2 on them as the legend 'And the cry was No Defenders...' a conscious mockery of the sectarian song 'The cry was No Surrender'. Celtic Park now became a place that one looked forward to visiting. The wheel was very clearly turning.

v **Kilmarnock** 3-0

Scottish League Cup Final, Hampden
18 March 2001

CELTIC	KILMARNOCK	REFEREE
Gould	Marshall	Mr H. Dallas,
Mjallby	MacPherson	Motherwell
Valgaeren	McGowne	
Vega	Dindeleux*	
Petta*	Innes	
Healy	Hay	
Lennon	Holt	
Lambert	Durrant**	
Moravcik**	Mahood	
Larsson	Cocard***	
Sutton	Dargo	
Subs: **Crainey*** ***	Subs: Canero*	
Smith **	Durrant**	
Boyd ***	McLaren***	

MARTIN O'NEILL had had a mighty impressive first season as manager at Celtic Park. The team had lost one game in the league – admittedly a bad one at Ibrox – but unlike other teams in the past who had gone into freefall after a similar reverse, this one had fought back, going, for example, from 10 December until 25 February without conceding a league goal, and scoring loads at the other end. Although there had been the customary European exit before Christmas – an unlucky one this time – progress had been made in both domestic trophies, and optimistic talk was heard for the first time for many years of a treble.

O'Neill had bought wisely. Players who were less than household names when they arrived – Ramon Vega, Neil Lennon, Didier Agathe – fitted seamlessly into what was a really classy Celtic outfit, but the main cause of the success was the brilliance of Henrik Larsson. Chris Sutton was clearly a great foil for him, and Larsson produced so much of what the Celtic fans craved – namely goals! Now shorn of his dreadlocks, with his short hair, he suddenly looked so much more athletic, so super fit, with the ability to score goals of any description – headers, long range shots, deft flicks, simple tap-ins – and how the crowd responded to him, calling him Henrik Larsson: 'the King of Kings'!

There was of course more to Celtic than that. If there had only been one great player in a mediocre team, then the opposition could mark or foul the star man out of the game. There was little point in doing that with this Celtic team – although one or two brutal defenders tried – for there were so many other stars in that mighty Celtic team, such as Lubomir Moravcik, Chris Sutton, Didier Agathe, and Stilian Petrov.

But as they approached the League Cup Final on 18 March 2001, Celtic fans were well aware that they had won nothing yet. All the good play of the season would mean nothing if no silverware was won. After all, this had happened before with Celtic teams. They had frequently in the past promised a great deal, but had delivered nothing. The fans needed trophies.

There was particular cause for concern in the approach to the League Cup Final against Kilmarnock, which was the unavailability of players. Goalkeeper Rab Douglas and winger Didier Agathe were ineligible. They were cup-tied after already playing in the competition (which had of course started in the autumn) for Dundee and Hibs respectively; Jackie McNamara and Alan Thompson had picked up suspensions, and then a mere four days before the competition, Stilian Petrov had broken his ankle in an SPL game against St Johnstone at McDiarmid Park. All this was bad enough, but it was also no secret that Chris Sutton and Bobby Petta were carrying injuries and were doubtful for the final. Kilmarnock knew about these injuries as well, and this would affect their tactics.

Kilmarnock were a middle-of-the-table side. They were managed by Bobby Williamson who had played for Rangers in the mid 1980s and had a few other Rangers connections in Ian Durrant and Ally McCoist, both playing out their careers after distinguished success at Ibrox, but now perhaps no longer the major threat that they once were. On 2 January on a cold day at Celtic Park, Larsson had been on top form, scoring four goals as Celtic beat Kilmarnock 6-0, and the odds would for that reason appear to favour Celtic. In addition, Kilmarnock had suffered the dispiriting blow of having gone out of the Scottish Cup the week before to a goal scored literally with the last kick of the ball, by Hibs. Kilmarnock's only slim hope lay in the fact that Celtic would be putting out a weakened side.

The Scottish League Cup had not exactly been the favourite trophy of either side. Kilmarnock had never won it; in fact they had only appeared in three finals, the most recent being October 1962 round about the time that the world almost suffered nuclear war over the Cuban missile crisis. With 11 victories, Celtic lagged well behind Rangers, a legacy of the dreadful days of the late 1940s, 1980s and 1990s when incompetent management of the club off the field and, therefore, feckless performances on it, earned their due reward. On this occasion, however, Rangers had been well disposed of in the semi-final and Hearts in the quarter-final. Celtic, in spite of all their problems of player unavailability, were clear favourites.

Celtic supporters were a little annoyed to discover that their team had to wear yellow while Kilmarnock appeared in a black outfit. This was because of an alleged colour clash, but seemed to the cynics as a device to promote the change strips. It was a fine spring day, still slightly cold, but warm enough to melt the snow that had fallen in various parts of Scotland overnight.

It was a good day for football, although the crowd of 48,830 was a little disappointing, a thousand or two short of the Hampden capacity, and it was clear that Kilmarnock had failed to sell their allocation of tickets. It was particularly disappointing for the Celtic fans whose regular attendances of not far short of 60,000 indicated that they could have found a home for the tickets.

O'Neill appeared to have taken a risk by fielding both his injured men, Petta and Sutton, but possibly felt that with youngster Colin Healy in the starting XI and with

Stephen Crainey and Jamie Smith on the bench, he was short of experience. In any case, Petta did not last long, for Kilmarnock had cynically, knowing of his injury, decided to take him out. Twice in the opening stages he was tackled hard by two separate players (so that no yellow card would be issued) and Petta had to be taken off. This was, frankly, a disgrace, and reflected no credit at all on Bobby Williamson. It seemed however that O'Neill had had a premonition that this was to happen, for the introduction of Stephen Crainey had no ill effect on the Celtic team.

The first half produced little in the way of good football. The under-strength Celtic team were more than holding their own, but not enough service was as yet being supplied to the potent strike force of Chris Sutton and Henrik Larsson. In the midfield however, it was clear that young Colin Healy, who had played only nine games this season (and most of them as a substitute) had won his spurs. Celtic's defence had rarely been troubled.

Only three minutes had passed in the second half when Celtic struck. Now attacking the King's Park end of the ground where most of the green and white bedecked sat, Celtic won a corner on the left after some good work from Healy. Crainey took the set-piece which found the head of Sutton who headed the ball on in the direction of Henrik LARSSON. This ball might have been beyond most mortals, but with his fast reactions and agility, the Swede was able to swivel, meet the ball in mid-air and score a goal that was a lot more difficult than it looked. He then indulged in his own inimitable celebration with tongue out and arms spread aeroplane style!

Celtic were now one up, and looked to be on top. But there was one issue that was still not resolved. This was the persistent petty fouling of Chris Sutton by men who knew (as they had known of Petta) of a pre-existing injury and were trying to aggravate it. Possibly O'Neill might have realised this and replaced Sutton by the ever ready and ever likeable Tommy Johnson, but he didn't and Sutton eventually cracked. His charge on Gary Holt was certainly a foul, and some referees might have awarded a yellow card for a tackle that was high and late. But referee Hugh Dallas, a man who sometimes seemed to go out of his way to court controversy – and not only with Celtic – brandished the red card to the shock of the Celtic end, and even the press and the TV commentators. It was a decision which was harsh, and did nothing at all to dissuade Celtic supporters that Dallas was irreconcilably anti-Celtic.

In the event it mattered little. For the last half hour of the game, Celtic's 10 proved far better than Kilmarnock's 11, with the midfielders Lambert, Lennon and Healy all playing outstanding parts. The second goal came in the 75th minute. Again it was LARSSON who scored, this time with a little good fortune for the ball took a huge deflection off a defender before it deceived ex-Celtic goalkeeper Gordon Marshall.

But if that one was lucky, the third goal can only be described as pure genius, and is possibly the best of all the goals scored in the Parkhead career of Henrik LARSSON. It was in the 80th minute when he picked up a ball on the halfway line, and despite being fouled several times by a desperate defender, managed to run on as Dallas wisely played the advantage rule with half the Kilmarnock defence in hot pursuit. As Marshall came out to narrow the angle, Larsson rounded him, transferred the ball from one foot to another and prodded home. After such genius, the Celtic end simply stayed on its feet for the remaining ten minutes of the game.

Kilmarnock were now a beaten team. Any sympathy for them had to be balanced by the reflection that they had quite deliberately gone out of their way to put Petta and Sutton out of the game. Indeed, even after that had happened, Freddie Dindeleux picked up a yellow card for persistent fouling, and even after that, kept on fouling! He really should have had a red card, but Williamson substituted him in the nick of time. Celtic on the other hand had shown that they had the resilience and the ability to recover from setbacks and the youngsters Colin Healy, Stephen Crainey and Jamie Smith (who had come on as a late substitute for Lubo Moravcik) deserved great praise. It would be the highlight of all their careers.

There was only one hero, though. Grahame Ewing in the *Daily Record* the following day introduces a rare element of Cold War politics when he writes: 'In the case of Henrik Larsson, even Stalinists would have to concede that some individuals are more important than others.' More of course was to come from the lovable Swede, but that hat-trick put him in the same bracket as Billy McPhail, Bobby Lennox and Dixie Deans for having scored three in a League Cup Final. And yet it did not seem all that long ago that we had seen him on our television screens with his leg horrifically broken on that awful night in Lyon... In fact, it was only 18 months ago, but then again resilience and fighting back is a great Celtic tradition.

v Hibernian 3-0
Scottish Cup Final, Hampden
26 May 2001

CELTIC	HIBERNIAN	REFEREE
Douglas	Colgan	Mr K. Clark, Paisley
Mjallby	Fenwick	
Valgaeren	Smith	
Vega	Sauzee	
Thompson*	Jack	
Agathe	Laursen	
Lennon	Murray	
Lambert**	Brebner*	
Moravcik***	O'Neill	
Larsson	Paatelainen**	
Sutton	Libbra	
Subs: Johnson*	Subs: Arpinon * ***	
Boyd**	Zitelli***	
McNamara***		

CELTIC'S HISTORY had been short on Trebles. The winning of all the three Scottish domestic trophies (the League Cup had been introduced in 1946 to supplement the much older Scottish Cup and Scottish League) had been achieved on only two occasions by Celtic – in the glory year of 1967 and in 1969 – and everyone at Parkhead was aware that Rangers had done it more often. 2001 was felt an appropriate time to land another Treble.

Celtic had had a superb season. The League Cup had been won in March, and the Scottish League three weeks later in early April with games to spare. The result had been that Celtic had been playing 'friendlies' since 7 April, the day that they beat St Mirren 1-0 to win the SPL and 15 April when they beat Dundee United to reach the final of the Scottish Cup.

Some friendlies! They had included a 3-0 win over Rangers at Ibrox, and perhaps more significantly a 5-2 win over Hibs at Easter Road.

This result was significant because Hibs were to be the opponents in the Scottish Cup Final. Hibs, managed by Alex McLeish, had had a good season, finishing third in the SPL and, very importantly for their supporters, quite clearly getting the better of Hearts in the traditional 'battle of Edinburgh'. It was well known, however, that Hibs suffered a complex about the Scottish Cup. '99 years in a row,' sang the Hearts fans to indicate that 1902 was the last time that Hibs had won the Scottish Cup. Stories of curses and hexes, jinxes and hoodoos abounded, and the jokes that appeared every time that Hibs reached the final were current once again in Edinburgh.

Celtic approached the cup final in fine fettle. Tribute had been paid to one of their really great players – arguably the best of the Lisbon Lions – when Bobby

Murdoch passed away having suffered a stroke in mid May. It was pointed out of course that Murdoch had been a member of the two previous sides who had won Trebles, and how appropriate it would be if Celtic could land another. It would somehow be fitting for the memory of this great Celt.

There were very few chinks in the armour of this great side. There were the mighty defenders in Joos Valgaeren, Johan Mjallby and Ramon Vega, good attacking players in Alan Thompson and Didier Agathe, with the little genius Lubomir Moravcik now reaching his full potential under O'Neill, and of course up front Chris Sutton and Henrik Larsson, who had scored 35 league goals this campaign and whose whole season tally would put him in the same bracket as Jimmy McGrory in 1936. To a historically-minded support like Celtic had, being mentioned in the same breath as McGrory, simply said it all.

Some of his goals were astonishing. The hat-trick scored in the League Cup Final against Kilmarnock was still fresh in everyone's mind, but for many supporters the bullet header scored against Dundee United in the semi-final of the Scottish Cup would take some beating for his best goal of all. A superb athlete, a thorough professional in his training, keeping fit and maintaining strict diet (things that he approached with almost obsessive thoroughness), Henrik Larsson thoroughly deserved all the adulation bestowed on the 'King of Kings'.

> Give me joy in my heart, Henrik Larsson
> Give me joy in my heart, I pray
> Give me joy in my heart, Henrik Larsson
> Keep on scoring till the break of day!

In the run-up to the cup final, three issues dominated conversation: the pitch, strips and tickets. Hampden's pitch was in a lamentable condition, having been disgracefully leased out for pop concerts and American football. It was the latter that caused most of the problems, and apart from the damage done to the turf, there were lines on the park in the wrong places with words like 'Claymores' written behind one of the goals. Thankfully, the authorities yielded to pressure (apparently there was a threat to move the game to Ibrox) and re-laid the whole turf to prevent the Scottish Cup Final becoming a laughing stock.

They were less yielding in their insistence that both teams change colours – because there would be too much green, they said, particularly as the supporters would all wear green and the linesmen would find it difficult to give offside decisions! This was ludicrous and much ridiculed by press and media who pointed out that the previous 'all green' finals of 1972, for example, had indeed been just that. No-one had complained then!

There was, of course, the nagging suspicion in most people's minds that this had something to do with promoting the sales of the second strip of both teams – the yellow of Celtic and the white of Hibs – and, not for the first time, financial considerations taking precedence over supporters' wishes and historical considerations. Celtic however assuaged the hearts of those who felt cheated by announcing that if Celtic won the cup, the players would don the green and white hoops for the presentation.

This was a major propaganda blow as well, of course, for it assumed that Celtic would indeed win the cup! They would have to do so however in front of less than half of their normal home support. This year the home support had been close to 60,000. For the Scottish Cup Final, they and Hibs would each receive the same allocation of 25,000, and Celtic supporters were entitled to ask where Hibs were going to find 25,000 supporters from. The *Celtic View* printed a cartoon of some Hibs supporters going to the final in the bus which had collected them from the Leith Old Folks Home asking questions about whether Pat Stanton and Lawrie Reilly would be playing!

It was a fine day as the two teams in unfamiliar garb took the field, Celtic playing towards their own supporters at the King's Park end of the ground. As is always the case in cup finals, play was distinctly edgy in the early stages, but then Celtic seemed to suffer a severe blow when Lubo Moravcik signalled to the bench that he was out of the game with what looked like a hamstring problem but was apparently the re-opening of stitches in a leg wound. Lubo had of course been one of the stars of this marvellous Celtic season, but any fears that he would be missed were soon dispelled by his substitute Jackie McNamara.

It was he who broke the deadlock. The goal came from Didier Agathe, an amazingly talented winger – apart from his final ball which was usually a shocker. He had clearly been working on this one though, for in the 38th minute he beat his man on the wing and instead of firing across a long and useless cross, he cut inside and slipped the ball to the onrushing Jackie McNAMARA who hit the ball, not exactly sweetly, for he seemed to miskick, but certainly effectively from the edge of the penalty box into the Hibs net.

Celtic might well have scored again before half-time, but they did fairly soon after. Once again McNamara was involved, this time slipping the ball to Henrik LARSSON who swivelled, causing a Hibs defender to slip and Henrik crashed the ball high into the Hibs net, reducing to silence the Hibs fans behind that Mount Florida goal. Henrik had been unhappy with his first-half performance and had changed his boots at half-time. These new ones were made of kangaroo hide!

Celtic were thus 2-0 up, and although in the past Celtic teams have eased off and thrown away leads, this was a mature Celtic set-up which ensured that there would be no slip up. Hibs did mount some sort of a revival, for they were a side not without talent and certainly Alex McLeish was very active on the touchline, but their fast-vanishing cause was dealt a fatal blow in the 80th minute when Celtic were awarded a penalty after Larsson had been fouled in the penalty box. LARSSON took the kick himself, and made no mistake.

The rest of the game was spent with the Celtic end in quiet happiness (not delirium, for the opponents were Hibs whom one did not really hate as one did others!) and the historically-minded among the support urging Larsson to score again to give him the honour of being put alongside Jimmy Quinn in 1904 and Dixie Deans in 1972 who had scored Scottish Cup final hat-tricks. Alas, it was not to be, but that was only a minor disappointment on what was otherwise a glorious day. Hampden was sunny and bright and the Celtic players, with a sense of history, put on the green and white hoops (some still called them 'stripes') and collected the Scottish Cup for the 31st time. Veteran Tom Boyd, still technically the club captain, had been brought on for the last few minutes so that he and Paul Lambert could together lift the famous old Scottish Cup from the then Chancellor of the Exchequer (one day Prime Minister) Gordon Brown, rumoured to be a 'crypto-Tim' beneath his Raith Rovers facade. There was nothing 'crypto' however about Jack McConnell, Scotland's First Minister. He was one of ours!

The Hibs end gradually emptied, but quite a few remained, seemingly very happy now with Celtic's performances. These were the infiltrators, the fifth columnists who had bought tickets from Hibs, merged into the Hibs support, held their tongues admirably while the game was in progress, but now had shown their true colours – if that image is appropriate on a day when everyone wore green anyway!

It was of course possible to sympathise with the genuine Hibs fans who would probably all say that they would prefer Celtic to anyone else. A century would now pass before they could win the Scottish Cup, and they would be subject to the jeers of the Hearts fans (who in all truth did not have all that much to cheer about either!) who had even, to their intense self-hatred, one feels, supported Celtic for the day! But for Hibs, since their glory day of 1902, generations of fans had emerged from those grim Leith tenements to go to Glasgow to see Patsy Gallacher in 1914, Joe Cassidy in 1923, Dixie Deans in 1972 and now Henrik Larsson in 2001 put an end to their hopes of Scottish Cup glory. Even the hardest-hearted of Celtic fans could perhaps sympathise with that in the midst of all their own rapture and happiness.

Jim Traynor, never exactly Celtic's favourite journalist but a lover of good football nevertheless, mixes his metaphors brilliantly in the *Daily Record* on the Monday when he writes: 'In one season, Celtic's fans have been transported from the dank depths of despair to the realms of unbridled joy and they have soared in the slipstream of a shooting star called Larsson.' Indeed, there was a great deal to be happy about that summer day in 2001.

v **Liverpool** 2-0
UEFA Cup Quarter Final Second Leg, Anfield. 20 March 2003

CELTIC	LIVERPOOL	REFEREE
Douglas	Dudek	Herr M. Merk, Germany
Sylla*	Carragher	
Thompson	Riise	
Mjallby	Hamann	
Balde	Traore	
Valgaeren	Hyppia	
Lennon	Murphy	
Lambert**	Gerrard	
Hartson	Heskey	
Larsson	Owen	
Petrov	Smicer*	
Subs: Smith*	Sub: Baros*	
McNamara**		

LIVERPOOL AND Celtic have many affinities. It was noticeable, for example, that the first game that Liverpool played after the Hillsborough disaster in 1989 was against Celtic at Celtic Park, and Celtic were frequently invited to play testimonial games for Liverpool players and vice versa. They share the song 'You'll Never Walk Alone' which is sung at both grounds; sometimes poignant, sometimes maudlin, but always impressive. They had played each other twice before in European competition – in 1966 in the Cup Winners' Cup semi-final when Liverpool had edged past Celtic with the help of an officious linesman who could not believe the speed of Bobby Lennox, and then in 1997 when Liverpool had won on the away goals rule.

And then of course there had been Mr Dalglish! He had played for both clubs, breaking the hearts of Celtic fans and bringing indirectly an end to Jock Stein's managerial career at Celtic when he went to Anfield in August 1977 in one of Celtic's darker hours. His departure had ushered in a prolonged period of mediocrity in both Scotland and Europe, and Celtic fans were forced to watch the sustained success of the player that they once idolised – but who now played in an alien shirt. That hurt!

But a great deal of water had flowed under the bridges over the Clyde and the Mersey since then, and when Liverpool met Celtic in 2003, the men from Merseyside were not enjoying a vintage season. They had had a poor December and midwinter, and were clearly not going to win the English League. They had exited the FA Cup surprisingly to Crystal Palace in a fourth round replay, but they had redeemed themselves in the eyes of their supporters by beating Manchester United in the final of the League Cup on 2 March. Celtic on the other hand were still in everything at the time of the first leg, but between the two games against Liverpool had been unlucky enough to lose the Scottish League Cup Final to Rangers on a nightmarish day when a good goal by John Hartson had been disallowed for offside. To compound the misery, Hartson had then missed a penalty and Neil Lennon had been sent off.

This defeat had hurt (losing to Rangers is always likely to) and Celtic fans began to dread the trip to Liverpool. The first leg at Parkhead had worked to Liverpool's favour, for it had ended 1-1 – both goals coming early from Larsson and Heskey, and Liverpool looking, frankly, the better team, with their ball distribution and general footballing know-how. El-Hadji Diouf however had not exactly endeared himself to the Parkhead crowd by spitting into a section of them in the Main Stand. He would have to answer for that.

Thus it was that Celtic fans approached the game at Anfield with a little dread. It was not that Celtic were a bad team, they certainly were not, but they did not always produce their best when required to do so. Henrik Larsson had been out with a broken jaw and one wondered whether he was as fit as he could be, but of course with Henrik, a broken jaw was like the broken leg of 1999, a minor obstacle in the way of progress. Mental strength could be added to the list of other attributes, and the absolute determination not to let injury, even serious injury, stand in his way for very long. He was a superb player, generally reckoned as such, and much would depend on him at Anfield. He was all the more necessary because Chris Sutton had injured his wrist in the League Cup Final, and would miss the game.

By the time that the day of the game arrived, the cliché 'Battle of Britain' (always offensive and plain stupid) was even less appropriate than previously, for Great Britain was once again involved in a major war. On the very day of the game, US and British troops had invaded Iraq allegedly looking for 'weapons of mass destruction', which were never found, but in reality to allow the US to vent their spleen on the Islamic world for their part in the dreadful atrocities of 11 September 2001. To their eternal shame, the British Labour Government of Tony Blair went along with it.

Whether one agreed with the operation or not (and very few did), it was, however, major world news, and a football match (even a high profile one like Liverpool and Celtic) had to play second fiddle to this war. Within a month, Saddam Hussein had been toppled (superpowers usually do quite well against third world nations, in the same way as you would back Celtic to do well against Elgin City!) and quite a lot of lives had been lost in a conflict about which the world has not yet heard the last.

Celtic fans arrived in strength on Merseyside in spite of the pitiful allocation of tickets. This did not stop them however, for they were quite happy to go to local pubs instead to watch the game. They would see a remarkable game of football, one of the few times that a Scottish team had beaten an English side, and one which showed to the world that Celtic were back in a European as well as Scottish context. It was all the more sweet, for the media in both Scotland and England had confidently predicted the demise of Celtic, patronising Celtic after the first leg showing and their defeat in the League Cup Final, and had dismissed their chances by saying things like Liverpool would dismiss Celtic like how a 'gentleman swats a fly'. They had been similarly dismissive about Celtic's chances against Blackburn Rovers in a previous round and had clearly failed to learn a lesson.

Liverpool of course knew that a 0-0 draw would see them through, and they did not feel any great need to attack, at least in the early stages of the game. They dug in and held the line, paying particular attention to the ever dangerous Henrik Larsson who did indeed have a few shots on goal, but nothing to bother Jerzy Dudek in the Liverpool goal too much.

But towards half-time Celtic went ahead, and it was a most unusual goal. Celtic had won a free kick on the edge of the penalty box at the Kop end of the ground. Celtic, traditionally strong on set pieces, sent Alan Thompson to take it, while Liverpool formed a wall and Celtic's predators – Larsson, Hartson and a few others – took up positions. There are several objections to the building of a wall. One is that it obscures the view of the goalkeeper, another is that it takes players away from marking dangerous opponents and the third is that it does not always do its job.

This was what happened here. This particular wall could have been constructed by a cowboy builder for all the good that it did. Admittedly harassed by the presence of a Celtic player in amongst them, they must however take full responsibility for what happened. As THOMPSON shaped to take it, something in his body language must have suggested that he was going to fire a high one in on goal – and they all jumped! Thompson's shot (which was by no means unstoppable) actually went underneath them with Dudek deprived of a good view because of the wall, and Celtic thus went in at half-time one up!

It would have been interesting to hear what Gerard Houllier (Liverpool's manager) thought of that one! The poor man had been off ill with serious heart problems a year or two previously and this particular incident cannot have done him much good! It did however put Celtic in a strong position, stronger perhaps than merely being a goal in the lead, for it now meant that the away goals rule, so often the bane of Celtic and other Scottish teams in Europe, would actually now work in their favour. A goal against Celtic did not eliminate them. It merely took the game to extra time (during which period the away goals rule would mean that a further strike each would see Celtic through), whereas a goal for Celtic would leave Liverpool needing three to win.

Celtic were now composed as they faced the second half. The defensive trio of Valgaeren, Balde and Mjallby were outstanding, and they were well supported by Lennon, as the much vaunted Liverpool players like Gerrard and Heskey failed to get into the game. Celtic were riding the storm and the massive TV audience were watching the clock and counting the minutes as they ticked away.

There were 80 minutes gone when a probable Celtic victory was made a certain one. This was due to a brilliant goal from John HARTSON. John had a point to prove after his penalty miss in Sunday's League Cup Final, for many of the supporters had pointed the finger at him for his sometimes apparently lethargic approach to the game. He was never the fastest player on earth, but on this occasion he picked up a ball about 20 yards from goal, played a quick one-two with Larsson, charged across the field with no-one challenging him, and then from about the edge of the penalty box fired home a magnificent goal.

There was simply no answer to that, and Celtic were very comfortably into the semi-finals of the UEFA Cup to the delight of their fans, who began to sing:

There's only one John Hartson
There's only one John Hartson
He's got no hair, but we don't care
There's only one John Harston!

with some of this singing coming from the Main Stand and even the Kop end of the ground where some Celtic fans had managed to infiltrate! The media were stunned after all their pessimistic predictions, and Martin O'Neill had done it again! Even some Rangers supporters were glad to see this blow delivered to the status of the English Premiership about which one sometimes heard rather too much.

It was a great night for Celtic supporters, and it would be nice to report a happy ending to this story. Unfortunately, Celtic were actually in the middle of a poor run. The defeat to Rangers on the previous Sunday was matched by an even more distressing one on the following Sunday when a grossly underprepared Celtic team flew up to their old Scottish Cup foes at Inverness and lost again!

Without anyone being too aware of it, the domestic season was being sacrificed for European success. Celtic would of course lose in Seville in a typical quintessentially Scottish way by earning loads of credit for everything – good goals, respectable performance, great fans – but nevertheless losing the game and coming home with no UEFA Cup and then losing the SPL on the following Sunday. 2003 remains a little painful to recall, but there were loads of great performances, not least this wonderful night in Liverpool.

v Rangers 2-0 after extra time
Scottish League Cup Final, Hampden
15 March 2009

CELTIC	RANGERS	REFEREE
Boruc	McGregor	Mr D. McDonald,
Hinkel	Whittaker	Edinburgh
Loovens	Weir	
McManus	Broadfoot	
O'Dea*	Papac	
Caldwell	Davis	
Nakamura	McCulloch***	
Brown	Ferguson	
Hartley**	Mendes	
McGeady	Miller*	
McDonald	Lafferty**	
Subs: Wilson *	Subs: Novo*	
Samaras**	Boyd**	
Vennegoor of	Dailly***	
Hesselink** ***		

CELTIC SUPPORTERS didn't really know what to expect from this cup final. They were at the top of the SPL, but had last week, in the most distressing of circumstances, gone out of the Scottish Cup to St Mirren (whom they had beaten 7-0 in the SPL the week before!) and there was a certain unpredictability about the team. The question 'Which Celtic is going to turn up?' was frequently asked, and it was undeniably true that, with the exception of the St Mirren game a fortnight before, Celtic were quite simply not scoring enough goals.

For a team with a famous attacking tradition like Celtic, this went against the grain with many supporters. The front men, Vennegoor of Hesselink and Samaras, apart from the odd exceptional game, were simply not doing it. It was not that they lacked ability. Samaras, in particular on one day in the autumn at Kilmarnock, had produced some fantastic, individual goals. Sadly we were not seeing nearly enough of this. The game against Rangers on 15 February had ended 0-0 and was generally agreed to have been a dreadful spectacle, and Celtic had only reached the final of the League Cup thanks to a penalty shoot-out against a stuffy Dundee United side.

The defence on the other hand had been strengthened. Gary Caldwell was having a tremendous season, and with the help of Glenn Loovens, the sieve (as disparagers called it) had been mended – or had it? Aberdeen for example had managed to score four goals at Pittodrie against Celtic, and that sort of thing could not be allowed. Fingers began to be pointed at Stephen McManus.

The jury also remained out on Artur Boruc. Immensely popular with the fans who called him the 'Holy Goalie' for his religious observances in front of Rangers fans who simply couldn't handle religious diversity, Artur nevertheless did not always handle this cult hero status well. Those of the support who felt that the 'Holy Goalie' song did not really do him any favours had ammunition to back up their cases by his occasional high profile lapses, notably against Rangers at Parkhead at the beginning of the season, and a succession of horrors at Easter Road against Hibs on more than one occasion. A story of fisticuffs involving himself and Aiden McGeady had trickled out of the Lennoxtown training centre in early February, and whether true or not, did perhaps give the impression that, as with Tommy McInally and Charlie Tully of old, the personality cult of Artur Boruc among the fans did not always extend itself to his fellow players. He was however, on his game, a star performer, showing great agility, positional sense and commitment.

The midfield had seen some great performances from Scott Brown. Scott had now learned the virtue of keeping his mouth shut, and his game had improved immeasurably as a result. He was having a great season, but we were less impressed by Nakamura whom the game seemed to miss so often. Aiden McGeady could be the hero of the team on occasion. Sometimes he was less successful, but when he was on his game, no-one could match him, and he was rightly the subject of a song much enjoyed by the Celtic fans:

He goes to the left
He goes to the right
Aiden McGeady
He makes the Huns look s****

The support were divided about Gordon Strachan. His supporters pointed out that he had won the SPL in 2006, 2007 by some comfortable distance, and in 2008 in a breathtakingly exciting comeback when all had looked dead and buried. In addition he had won each of the Scottish domestic trophies once, and had on two occasions kept Celtic in Europe beyond Christmas in the Champions League.

Against that, there had been some unsatisfactory performances, with a particular inability to achieve much away from home in Europe. Boasting about reaching the last 16 sits ill with the supporters of a club which had once won it, and the continual bleating about the amount of money that English clubs received from television as distinct from the comparative pittances that Scottish teams received, did not really help. The opening and closing of the January transfer window in 2009 without any major players being bought was a matter of some angst, but it was not in itself necessarily fatal. Jock Stein had once proved that money is not everything in Europe; we were desperately looking for someone to do it again. Frankly, it was not happening.

But there was another problem about Strachan. He had, to his credit, overcome the hatred that Celtic fans had nurtured, not without cause, of him since his Aberdeen days, with his antics in the 1984 Scottish Cup Final, in particular, difficult to forget. He had won over most of the Celtic fans – yet he persisted in alienating his supporters by his perpetual desire to be flippant, even cheeky, to TV interviewers who'd asked perfectly fair and straightforward questions, under the mistaken idea that he was being funny. Celtic supporters would have been far more impressed with straight answers.

Opinion among the experts was divided about this cup final, with odds marginally favouring Celtic who probably had the better players. The question would be if they could all produce the goods when required... Rangers were, of course, still in a position where they could win the treble, something that Celtic had denied themselves by their insipid performance against St Mirren last week. Would this make Celtic all the more determined to prove a point to their fans, or would they be disheartened?

The first half with Celtic playing towards the Mount Florida end, took a little while to get going, although Celtic possibly finished the half stronger, with a drive from Scott Brown going just over the bar, but neither side had established any supremacy. The second half saw Celtic beginning to take command but never getting the breakthrough, although they came very close when Glenn Loovens's powerful header had to be cleared on the line by Mendes. Bookings were frequent in a feisty encounter, but full time came with Celtic possibly having the edge, but neither team able to make the breakthrough.

And so we moved on to the nerve-wracking extra-time period with exhausted players and the supporters of both sides well aware that you seldom get a second chance in these periods; usually one goal seals it, or, more frequently, there are no goals at all and we then move to the pain and agony of a penalty shoot-out. Celtic had already gone through that in the semi-final against Dundee United, and could appreciate what it meant. Where Celtic did have the advantage that day, however, was in their support, who outshouted their Rangers counterparts that day. Such things are important to tired players in the heat of the battle.

There would be no need for a penalty shoot-out this time. Early in the first period of extra time, Scott McDonald won a free kick on the left. It was taken by Nakamura, and up popped the unlikely head of Darren O'DEA to head home. This happened at the distant Mount Florida end of the ground, and there was a split second of silence before the Celtic fans erupted. It had been a good goal, but the opinion was expressed that it was a shame that this had not happened within the regulation 90 minutes, instead of compelling Celtic fans to sit through some gut-wrenching extra-time tension.

In fact, Celtic now took a grip of this game with Glenn Loovens in the centre of defence now in total command. The result could have been settled ten minutes later when Georgios Samaras was through on the goalkeeper, but he couldn't put it away. Poor Georgios! He had only come on as a substitute late in the second half of regulation time, and this was his chance to win over his doubters and grab some glory for himself, but sadly he could not avail himself of the opportunity.

Half-time in extra time came and went, but not before we had had the slightly laughable spectacle of Barry Ferguson and Celtic coach Neil Lennon having a little spat about getting the ball back for a throw-in! Celtic were still holding on quite comfortably, somehow seeming to receive some sort of a boost from the fact that they were now playing towards their own fans. Indeed they were far more in control of the game now than at any other stage – much though the fans behind the goal besought and begged the referee to bring things to a close.

As early as the 115th minute we began to notice the breaking of ranks at the other end as the trickle to the exits began, and then more or less on time, Aiden McGeady broke through and was fouled in the box by Craig Broadfoot and referee Dougie McDonald, who had had a good game in a difficult atmosphere, had little option other than to award a penalty kick. Broadfoot was also sent off, a decision justified only in the strict application of the letter of the law – 'denying a goalscoring oppor-tunity' – rather than by any feeling of outrage at a vicious tackle.

It was McGEADY's reaction that was significant. He got up and immediately called for the ball, for he was not in a mood to let anyone else take the spot-kick. Amidst growing anticipation in the massed ranks behind the goal, Aiden sank the penalty, and Rangers just had time to restart the game before referee McDonald blew for full time.

The trophy was presented to 'Mick' McManus and one of the angles of the presentation shows empty seats behind him. Those were where the Rangers supporters used to sit! They had deserted their men in their time of need, unable to contemplate the sight of Celtic lifting a trophy. Many Rangers supporters still consider themselves the 'establishment' team of Scotland and the sight of a trophy being presented to someone else sits ill with them. The Rangers players, to their credit, showed a little more generosity and magnanimity than their supporters did.

It was a great day for Celtic, and was much celebrated in Celtic areas of Scotland and the world that night. It was something tangible. There was a trophy bedecked in green and white ribbons – and that is always something that Celtic fans like! Sadly, it would turn out to be Celtic's only trophy for that season, and Gordon Strachan's last one as manager, but it was a good day. The memory of it beamed bright in that awful May of 2009 when goalscorers once again failed to do their job and Celtic lost the SPL after having been in a strong position.

Yet this game will retain a special position in the hearts and minds of Celtic supporters in that it embodied a great deal of what Celtic are all about. Celtic have a deserved reputation for playing good football with good players. Success in itself in terms of winning medals and trophies is of course important – other teams have done that. What is better is if the success can be achieved by players playing with flair and panache, and this is why the long list of great players like Quinn, Gallacher, McGrory, Delaney, Tully, Johnstone, Larsson and so many others is important, even in this very cynical age of football when money making sometimes seems to be more important than actually winning games with style, and entertaining spectators. Aiden McGeady did enough that day to deserve his position in the pantheon of great players.

BIBLIOGRAPHY

The Story of the Celtic – Willie Maley, Desert Island Publishing

Dan Doyle, The Life and Death of a Wild Rover – Marie Rowan, Black and White Publishing

The Celtic Story – James Handley, Stanley Paul Press

The Glory and the Dream – Tom Campbell and Pat Woods, Mainstream Publishing

Dreams, And Songs to Sing – Tom Campbell and Pat Woods, Mainstream Publishing

Willie Maley, The Man Who Made Celtic – David Potter, Tempus Publishing

Jock Stein, The Celtic Years – Tom Campbell and David Potter, Mainstream Publishing

Our Bhoys Have Won The Cup – David Potter, John Donald Publishing

Celtic In The League Cup – David Potter, Tempus Publishing

Bobby Murdoch, Different Class – David Potter, Empire Publishing

Celtic's Cult Heroes – David Potter, Know The Score Books

The Encyclopaedia of Scottish Football – David Potter and Phil. H. Jones, Know The Score Books

The Scottish Football Book (various years) – Hugh Taylor, Stanley Paul Press